Understanding Society through Popular Music amply demonstrates how music provides a powerful portal through which to understand the social worlds we inhabit. Varieties of popular music are revealed as master symbols through which identities are formed and performed, life passages negotiated, values handed down or contested in families, and communities and social institutions are exemplified. Kotarba's engaging examples and cases reveal the many ways in which music acts as both a resource for, and mirror of, peoples' lives. Everyone who has ever had a favorite song will enjoy *Understanding Society through Popular Music.*

Eugene Halton, University of Notre Dame.

This is a terrific primer for showing (and not just telling) students how sociology can inform their understanding of pop music, whether they experience it intimately through their earbuds, or in collective ecstasy among festival crowds.

David Grazian, University of Pennsylvania, author of Mix It Up: Popular Culture, Mass Media, and Society.

Kotarba's *Understanding Society Through Popular Music* provides an insightful, illustration-filled introduction to the many ways music shapes, and is shaped by, our everyday social experiences. In so doing, Kotarba's text represents a useful work for captivating students and helping them recognize the power and influence of music throughout our social world.

Jason E. Sumerau, University of Tampa.

Understanding Society through Popular Music

Written for Introductory Sociology and Sociology of Popular Music courses, this book uses popular music to illustrate fundamental social institutions, theories, sociological concepts, and processes. The authors use music, a social phenomenon of great interest, to draw students in and bring life to their study of social life.

Joseph A. Kotarba, Ph.D., is Professor of Sociology at Texas State University and a faculty member at the Institute for Translational Sciences at the University of Texas Medical Branch, Galveston. His major areas of scholarly interest are culture, science, health and illness, deviance, everyday life social theory, and qualitative methods.

Understanding Society through Popular Music

Third Edition

Edited by

Joseph A. Kotarba

Routledge
Taylor & Francis Group
NEW YORK AND LONDON

Please visit the book's companion website at
www.routledge.com/cw/kotarba

Third edition published 2018
by Routledge
711 Third Avenue, New York, NY 10017

and by Routledge
2 Park Square, Milton Park, Abingdon, Oxon, OX14 4RN

Routledge is an imprint of the Taylor & Francis Group, an informa business

First edition published by Routledge 2008
Second edition published by Routledge 2013

Library of Congress Cataloging in Publication Data

Names: Kotarba, Joseph A.
Title: Understanding society through popular music / Joseph A. Kotarba.
Description: Third edition. | New York, NY : Routledge, 2017. | Includes bibliographical references.
Identifiers: LCCN 2017000144| ISBN 9781138806511 (hardback : alk. paper) | ISBN 9781138806528 (pbk. : alk. paper) | ISBN 9781315751641 (e-book)
Subjects: LCSH: Popular music—Social aspects.
Classification: LCC ML3918.P67 K67 2017 | DDC 306.4/8424—dc23
LC record available at https://lccn.loc.gov/2017000144

ISBN: 978-1-138-80651-1 (hbk)
ISBN: 978-1-138-80652-8 (pbk)
ISBN: 978-1-315-75164-1 (ebk)

Typeset in Adobe Caslon and Copperplate
by RefineCatch Limited, Bungay, Suffolk
Printed and bound by CPI Group (UK) Ltd, Croydon, CR0 4YY

I dedicate this book to my favorite quintet:
Polly, Chris, Jessie, Andrew, and Stan.

CONTENTS

Preface

When I began thinking about assembling the third edition of my successful textbook, *Understanding Society through Popular Music*, I reminded myself of the main lesson I learned from the first edition: the materials and examples culled from the world of popular music became out-of-date very quickly. To some degree, this is an unavoidable problem. In contrast to the majority of textbooks in the field that take an historical perspective on popular music, I felt the classic sociological obligation to write about current trends and events. Well, my students—and the students of other instructors who assigned my book—were my greatest critics in this regard. I recall lecturing in class one day about gender issues in popular music when the topic of Avril Lavigne came up. I thought I was on top of things when I smugly questioned whether getting married would shatter Avril's in-your-face punk image, when a number of students in unison laughed and said that Avril was not only divorced, but on the verge of getting her own scent and designer clothing line. She has since moved into acting and set up the Avril Lavigne Foundation to fight Lyme Disease and to support the Special Olympics. Does this mean I must regularly consult *Entertainment Tonight* to stay on top of events in the world of popular music? At least, I need to continue reading my *Rolling Stone* magazine.

I guess the next logical question is: what has changed and what has remained the same in the world of popular music since our first edition was published in 2009? Well, as one would expect, many things are new in popular music, but sometimes it seems like little has changed. Digital music, ear buds, and Bluetooth headphones are pandemic, as we increasingly listen to recorded and radio music alone. Yet, concert attendance, especially performed by older established groups, continues to grow. Music Festivals, such as Austin City Limits and Lollapalooza, are huge. The varieties of dance and hip-hop styles continue to expand, if not dominate, populist music—and Jay-Z and Beyoncé remain the (conservative) first family of pop music. We now archive our personal music collections in the clouds, but the music per se does not seem all that different. We have Lady Gaga, Katy Perry, and Nicki Minaj—are they that much different from Madonna, Janet Jackson and Mary J. Blige? And, music styles increasingly intermingle and blend to make traditional categories obsolete, as witnessed by Taylor Swift's shuffle between Nashville country and New York pop.

What has and continues to change is the audience for all this music. There seems to always be a market for a Taylor Swift and a Justin Bieber; as we continue to replenish the population, we will have a constant influx of pre-adolescent kids who are anxious to learn about themselves, others, relationships, and feelings. So that, as is convenient for we sociologists, there is constant social change impacting the world of popular music. Baby boomers have not changed their tastes in music significantly from the 1960s and 1970s but their ability and desire to keep purchasing music in various formats, as well as experiencing music personally, have not slowed down much over the years.

Popular music is ubiquitous; it truly serves as the soundtrack of our everyday lives. Indeed, it seems as if a tune is always accompanying our daily rhythms: from the wake-up call through our alarm radio and our favorite morning tunes on the ride to work and school, to the beats of campus life or office cubicle culture, and from the gas pumps to the supermarket and health club. Not to mention music television, pervasive iPhones, movie scores, and the very sounds and melodies of the spaces that surround us: from the chirping of sparrows to the crashing of waves. Music is everywhere. There is a sonorous dimension for everything: for every purpose, every group of listeners, every mood, and every occasion. And everywhere we listen, music comes to us (or from us) as a product: the product of technological relations which resulted in its creation and distribution; the product of geographic dimensions which shape trends, availability, and connection to space and place; the product of historical periods which shape fashions, costs, expectations, and considerations on what is appropriate or not appropriate; the product of social classes, genders, age-groups, and ethnicities, each with their relation to preferred forms of musical styles; as well as the product of familial, religious, and biographic particulars which influence the tunes that strike a chord with our heart and our sense of self. Music is not just the product of harmony, melody, and rhythm relations, but perhaps more importantly a *social product*. Many people are involved with creation of our musical experiences, as well as our music per se.

As a social product, music is a prime object of sociological investigation. Sociology examines both the processes and outcomes through which diverse forms of sociality take place. In light of that, studying a song or musical preferences is no different from studying family structure or the particular shape that labor relations take in a country. If sociology is the study of what people do together, and if music is something that people do together, then the sociological study of music is as "natural" as the sociological study of class, gender, race, social organization, or identity. In spite of this the sociological study of popular music has not always been as common as the sociological examination of, say, the economy. Sociologists in the past have often felt that music and all forms of popular culture were too trivial for serious social scientific business. Thus, at best, music was treated as a derivative of basic social structures, pegged as an opiate of the masses, and scoffed at (under the guise of theory) for being less refined than it should have been. But, as we are going to discuss in our introduction, things have changed. After the advent of the so-called "cultural turn" in social sciences—itself a symptom of the great cultural shifts shaping most of Western society in the 1960s and early 1970s—sociologists and other cultural science scholars began to closely heed the advice of those like the critical theorists of the Frankfurt School and the urban ethnographers of the Chicago School, who were pushing for a wider definition of *culture* as a broad way of life. As those movements unfolded, popular music—and popular culture in general—began to occupy a more central role in sociological endeavors.

The study of popular music has now evolved into a substantial area of interest among many sociologists over the past 25 years. Sociologists in the United States and Canada—as well as in Europe, Africa, Asia and South America—have witnessed the growth of popular music as both a societal as well as cultural force. In doing so they have begun to reflect on the links between musical production, distribution, and consumption, and the behaviors, emotions, and thoughts of music fans, the intentions of producers and distributors, the consequences on local and global cultures and social organization and more. Thus, just as sociology in general is becoming quite specialized, we have scholars of popular music who focus on the economy of music, or on the social regulation and organization of music-making, on the technology and culture of sound, on the relation between identity, gender, politics and music, and so forth. In writing and revising this book we hope to survey the vast diversity of both popular music studies and sociological studies. Of course, we can only aim to skim, at best, this great body of knowledge, but in doing so we will try to introduce you to an exciting body of sociological knowledge which will hopefully be of interest to you.

In fact, the purpose of this textbook is to integrate growing interest in the sociological study of popular music with mainstream sociological instruction. This book has a take on popular music that reflects that growth, while taking advantage of the growing sophistication of the field. In writing it, my collaborators and I benefit from the work of several researchers of popular music who have laid the foundation before us. The seminal early textbook on the sociology of popular music, Simon Frith's famous *Sound Effects* (1981), has been a mainstay in numerous courses over the past 20 years. Frith focused on a range of topics central to the world of popular music itself: the history of rock'n'roll; the roots of rock'n'roll in country music and the blues; popular music and politics; the popular music industry; and so forth. More recent texts that have left a mark on this territory include Andy Bennett's *Cultures of Popular Music* (2001); Reebee Garofalo's *Rockin' Out* (2013); and Michael Campbell's *Rock and Roll: An Introduction* (2007). These fine texts illustrate two major themes in the ways the sociology of popular music is organized. The first, on the one hand, emphasizes the great varieties of styles of popular music as well as the lifestyles and subcultures that give life to these musical styles. In such texts we learn about the social and cultural particulars underlying surf, punk, heavy metal, and other genres of music. The second, on the other hand, emphasizes the chronology of historical events that have shaped popular music: the advent of mechanical reproduction of music; the end of World War I; early rockabilly; the Civil Rights movement and the war in Vietnam; the end of the Cold War; the corporatization of music; and the current era of the proliferation of pop and rap styles. Numerous other texts that you can access to advance your understanding of the social and cultural dynamics of popular music—as we ourselves have done—exist. *Popular Music Studies* by David Hesmondhalgh and Keith Negus (2002) outlines the history and development of popular music studies. Dan Laughey's (2006) *Music and Youth Culture* focuses especially on young listeners and their practices. Simon Frith's (2007) latest *Taking Popular Music Seriously* includes several of Frith's classic essays on popular music studies. Richard Peterson's comprehensive yet scholarly *Creating Country Music: Fabricating Authenticity* (1997), Tia DeNora's (2000) *Music in Everyday Life*, and Deena Weinstein's classic *Heavy Metal: A Cultural Sociology* (1991), Andy Bennett and Richard Peterson's *Music Scenes* (2004), Andrew Herman, John Sloop and Thomas Swiss's, *Mapping the Beat* (1997), and Sara Horsfall, Jan-Martijn Meij, and Meghan Probstfield's *Music Sociology* (2013) are very specific, in-depth analyses. All of these texts—and there are others—treat popular music as an important social product with deep consequences for social structure, selfhood, and culture. We intend to locate our work in this tradition.

Our purpose and approach mark an important difference between this book and other texts. This concise textbook is organized in terms of conventional sociological topics and is oriented to the needs of two precisely defined audiences. The first audience is made up of undergraduate students of introductory sociology, for which the textbook is meant as a supplemental text. Each chapter is tied to a traditional topic in introductory sociology. We use popular music to illustrate fundamental social institutions, theories, sociological concepts, and processes, and this is the first in doing so in the hope of drawing readers into the fascinating and ever-relevant world of sociology. We write with confidence that reading and thinking about popular music will open up class discussions, debate, and reflection on the power of sociological study and the importance of a sociological imagination. The second audience is made up of students of courses in the sociology or social science of popular music. The uniqueness of our book for that audience comes from our placing popular music within the complex and ever-changing context of everyday life. We help students *see* popular music through a distinctively sociological—yet with a taste of interdisciplinary insight—lens. We hope that both audiences benefit from our accessible language, our use of diverse and contemporary data and examples from the world of popular music and popular culture, and our personable tone.

Regardless of audience considerations, the essential principle of this textbook is that popular music is one of the most important sources of culture in our society. Popular music provides the soundtrack for everyday life while offering practical meanings for making sense of everyday life. Accordingly, the textbook is organized to accomplish two instructional objectives. First, we show how popular music relates to all major social institutions. Second, we show how popular music can be used to illustrate fundamental sociological theories and concepts. In other words, we are using a social phenomenon of great interest to students to draw them in, to bring life to their/your study of sociology.

In what follows we pay attention to the intersections between popular music and the family, religion, socialization, ideology, social and political organization, the economy, culture and subcultures, self and identity, race, class, gender, technology, deviance, community and globalization—only to mention some of the topics contained in the pages to come. Throughout, we hope to connect individual and group-based conduct, feelings, and thought with cultural rituals, values, norms, texts and performances, all within contexts shaped by historical, geographic, economic, political, and socio-linguistic relations. Aware that it is impossible for anyone to know everything about sociology, just like it is impossible for anyone to know everything about music, we hope that by bringing these two passions of ours together we can share a bit of our sociological and musical imagination with you.

This textbook is derived, not only from our personal interests in music, but also from my new collaborators' teaching and scholarly research on popular music. A major difference in the third edition is in authorship. I wrote the majority of the material in the third edition by myself, but I believe I was wise enough to invite six scholars to write chapters representing their state-of-the-art research on and scholarly insight into timely topics in popular music. They also add a distinctively interdisciplinary flavor to our text. Raphael Travis (Social Work) and Scott Bowman (Justice Studies) discuss their exciting research on hip-hop culture that shows the progressive input of rap music on addressing social problems. Christopher Schneider (Sociology and Justice Studies) writes on the social media's growing impact on the popular music experience. Rachel Skaggs and Jonathan Wynn (Sociology) discuss the business of music and music communities. And Katarzyna M. Wyrzykowska (Sociology) adds an exciting international flavor to our book by chronicling the evolution of popular music in Poland since the change to democracy and capitalism in the early 1990s, with an eye towards the place women have in this phenomenon.

I have taught undergraduate and graduate courses in the sociology of popular music at the University of Houston for 20 years, and currently at Texas State University-San Marcos. I conduct research in the fields of the sociology of everyday life and of popular culture, and am a founding member of the Sociology of Music Network, sponsored by the Culture Section of the American Sociological Association. I am a regular contributor to the music blog maintained by the Society for the Study of Symbolic Interaction. I have conducted research and published essays on popular music topics including the postmodernization of rock music, as exemplified by the ongoing popularity of Metallica; punk, heavy metal and Christian heavy metal club scenes; the rave movement; the evolution of Latino/a music scenes in America; popular music experiences across the lifespan; the use of popular music to create authenticity, and most recently, the relationship of popular music to science and the scientist's complex experience of self (Kotarba 2018). Perhaps most relevant to the style of the present text, I have taught my courses on popular music online for over 12 years.

The present text evolved from previous collaborations. In 2006, I co-edited a special issue of the sociological journal *Symbolic Interaction* with Phillip Vannini. The topic was popular music, and the contributions reflected both the enthusiasm and the sophistication of the study of popular music through an interactionist perspective. Papers included discussions of the jazz music scene; grotesque rock music, such as the Marilyn Manson phenomenon; and the work of the hip-hop DJ. This work produced the idea of expanding that work into a textbook, resulting in the publication of the first edition of this text in 2009. For the revised second edition of our text published in 2013, we decided to enlist the assistance of two scholars of everyday life, Patrick Williams and Bryce Merrill. They enriched and enlivened the text with cutting edge thinking on and current examples of music subcultures, politics, and technology. For the third edition of this text, I decided to bring six new scholars onboard to enrich the theoretical context of the text, and to address new and exciting trends in popular music. Although we work within our own particular theoretical perspectives, we are all students of what we call more generally *everyday life*. That means that we study, teach, and write about the ways people deal with practical problems in very practical ways. The "stuff" that we observe and use as data are *social meanings* (Kotarba and Johnson 2002; Vannini 2008), that is, the rules, values, rituals, customs, understandings, and experiences that people use on a daily basis to make sense of the world in which they live. Therefore, the topics we choose to examine in our work and to discuss in this text are issues that are important to the people for whom popular music is a key source of meaning for their lives. Sociologists of everyday life are often pegged as "micro-sociologists." Micro-sociologists, some believe, study small groups of people in precisely defined contexts while neglecting to take into consideration greater historical, political, or economic trends. Whereas we do focus on the study of cultural processes at the level of narrowly situated contexts, in actuality we pay close attention to "bigger" policy-relevant sociological issues. In fact, I explain in the introduction how we combine our "micro" interactionist approach with a critical theoretical sensitivity. Yet, in doing so, we continue to privilege the study of music from the perspective of those who listen to it and work in it, rather than from some kind of opinionated, dismissive, and critical standpoint. Being students of everyday life, we aim to explain, describe and understand the ways audiences, artists and everyone in between experience music.

One thread that runs through all our work and ties it together is our general use of qualitative methods to study music in everyday life. The concept *ethnographic tourism* (Kotarba 1984) pretty much summarizes the way we study popular music in everyday life. Our work is ethnographic to the degree that it attempts to describe popular music in terms of the natural situations in which it occurs, and in terms of the language, feelings and perceptions of the individuals who experience it. The metaphor of tourism applies in the following way. Most sociological research occurs in the researcher's own land. The researcher assumes that the phenomenon (or features of the phenomenon) in question are to be explored, since they are hidden by a background of an otherwise familiar, taken for granted, and immediately plausible world. The researcher identifies cases for analysis through strategic but systematic sampling. He or she then proceeds to venture into a territory to observe everything that goes on, while preparing oneself to describe these realities for later storytelling before academic audiences. This logic fits best when the phenomenon in question is relatively rare (e.g., deviant behavior or minority group behavior) or particularly curious due to its strangeness, uniqueness, and potential for revealing larger social issues.

When the researcher assumes that the phenomenon in question is everywhere, then he or she should act like—pretend to be—a stranger or tourist in a foreign land. Indeed the researcher should act like a foreigner in one's own land in order to *observe* the phenomenon that was previously ignored or taken for granted by both researchers and members of the culture at large. The world of everyday life and popular music fits this scenario well. Our primary research strategy involves observation of routine, everyday life activities of ordinary people, musical performances, personas, texts, rituals, and music-related objects. As we further discuss in the introduction, our ethnographic tourist strategy thus does not stop where a conventional tourist might (at the surfaces only), or where a conventional ethnographer of foreign culture might (at the depths only). Through the use of our own sociological imagination we engage in a continuous back and forth play between depths and surfaces, supplementing observation and description with interpretation, and interpretation with evidence. And we hope to have some fun while doing this too, not unlike a tourist would.

There is another group of collaborators in this project: our students in our undergraduate and graduate courses like the sociology of popular music, as well as courses in mass media and popular culture studies. These students not only help us learn about other people's musical experiences, share their rich musical experiences with us, and to further reflect on our tastes and ideas, but also help us stay abreast of changing styles, artists, music performance activities, and technology. We also make good use of data or information derived from observations and reflections on our musical experiences as well as those of our families—all pop music fans. I am particularly grateful to my online students who helped me develop instructional exercises that satisfy their distant needs and wants.

We have made some significant changes to *Understanding Society through Popular Music* in the third edition. In addition to updating the key chapters in our text, we have expanded the topics covered to include additional discussion of rap and hip-hop culture, country music, music as a core cultural and economic feature of community, the international pop music scene, and the great importance of mass and social media to the music experience. Perhaps most significantly, we have added discussion of women in popular music in all our chapters. The sociological interest in and understanding of gender issues in our society transcend the mere attention given to women and gender in a traditional single chapter. We have placed all concepts in *italics* with definitions, and we have listed all the sociological concepts in the index. We have expanded the details of our homepage for use by students and instructors alike. And, we have included two suggested student activities for each chapter. These activities are especially relevant to the growing number of on-line courses on popular music, so that students can profit by active involvement with course topics while at home.

We benefited from the gracious help of our editors at Routledge, Samantha Barbaro and Athena Bryan, who helped us to clarify our ideas, stay on task, clean up our writing and organize our thoughts with the quality of patience great editors have. Just like music, a book too is a collective social product.

Joseph A. Kotarba
San Marcos, Texas

Acknowledgments

I would like to acknowledge a few of the numerous individuals and organizations that have given me gracious support over the years for my teaching and research in popular music. The executives at the South by Southwest (SXSW) Music Conference and the Houston Livestock Show and Rodeo have provided me with access to their personnel, programs, and performers. Kent Finlay, the founder, owner and manager of the Cheatham Street Warehouse in San Marcos, welcomed my sociology of pop music students every semester for our "field trip." Mr. Finlay would greet us with a few of his own songs and remarkable stories about the history of the music scene at Cheatham Street (e.g., the home of young and emerging artists like George Strait and Stevie Ray Vaughan). Sadly, Mr. Finlay has recently passed, but I will continue this fruitful working relationship with the new management. Sharon and Walter Reece introduced me to the marvelous singer-songwriter, Hill Country music scene by encouraging me to volunteer for the monthly Susanna's Kitchen Coffee House in Wimberley that raises funds for numerous charitable causes. I got to mingle with artists ranging from Guy Forsyth and Butch Hancock to Ray Wiley Hubbard and Gretchen Peters. Drs. Vessela Misheva and Andrew Blasko helped me internationalize my teaching and research by inviting me to Uppsala, Sweden to collaborate with them on various music projects, and to get our graduate seminars involved through very productive class meetings via Skype. Finally, I want to thank my colleagues at Texas State University who have supported my teaching and research on popular music through their enthusiasm for programs such as my "Hill Country Music Symposium" in 2012 and the Couch-Stone Symposium, "Symbolic Interactionist Takes on Music" in 2014.

INTRODUCTION

THE SOCIOLOGY OF POPULAR MUSIC

JOSEPH A. KOTARBA

In March 2010, my daughter, Jessie, got married in New Orleans, Louisiana. It was a beautiful wedding on a beautiful day. The actual ceremony took place in Audubon Park in the historic Garden District. The reception was also in the park, hosted down the candlelit path in the elegant Tea Room.

Among all the neat things taking place that day, I can recall the important role music played in the festivities. Perhaps that is because I love music, or because I study music as a sociologist, or because everything about my only and favorite daughter's wedding was unforgettable. In any event, the memories are clear. The string quartet performed the instrumental "Hope on Board" by Tom Petty and the Heartbreakers as the guests were escorted to their seats. As the wedding party and family made their entrances the quartet performed the traditional Bach "Air on G String" and "Arioso." As I escorted Jessie down the aisle, the quartet played Schubert's classical version of the "Ave Maria." (I was in tears at this point.) The quartet performed "Hymne" by Vangelis during the flower exchange honoring the mothers. At the conclusion of the ceremony, the quartet played Taylor Swift's "Love Story" for the recessional as the bride and groom walked back down the aisle to the applause of the loving crowd. The quartet ended the ceremony with "Music for a Found Harmonium" for the postlude while guests made their way to the reception. During cocktails just before dinner, the peaceful air was permeated by my son Andrew's friend, Carla, playing classic standards on the harp. After dinner, the DJ played all sorts of requests, ranging from The Lettermen's "The Way You Look Tonight" as the soundtrack for the father–daughter dance, to "Hava Nagila" as requested and appreciated by the groom, Stan's, Jewish family. Other songs included the Black Eyed Peas' "I Gotta Feeling" to open the dance floor; Beyoncé's "Single Ladies" for the bouquet toss; Johnny Cash/Joaquin Phoenix's "Ring of Fire" for the cutting of the cake; "When the Saints Go Marching In" for the second line; and Israel Kamakawiwo'ole's "Somewhere Over the Rainbow/What a Wonderful World" for the last song.

Music is not just an important part of weddings; it is one of the most important aspects of our culture and thus the way we live our everyday lives. Music helps us order our life experiences and make sense of them. It helps us enjoy the good times as well as the bad, becoming the soundtrack for life. As Tia DeNora (2000: 16–17), one of the most insightful sociologists of music, put it so well:

> Music is not merely a 'meaningful' or 'communicative' medium. . . . At the level of daily life, music has power. It is implicated in every dimension of social agency. . . . Music may influence how people compose their bodies, how they conduct themselves, how they experience the passage of time, how they feel—in terms of energy and emotion—about themselves, about others, and about situations.

Music defines so many of the activities we engage in, especially those things that escape words or for which words are inadequate by themselves, to create the present and prepare for memories in the future. During the wedding, the string quartet itself provided a dimension of elegance through the application of a classical motif. The "Ave Maria" accomplished the same end, but also positioned Jessie's parents and guests into the scene, demonstrating respect for Jessie's parents by adding a Catholic theme to the otherwise fairly secular wedding. It also served to welcome Jessie's family and guests by painting the wedding as familiar, sacred, and comfortable. Taylor Swift's song reminded everyone that love is new; the string quartet established the moment to dissolve the wedding into the reception; while the aural harp music created a center of pleasant attention during cocktails. All the different kinds of music played after dinner—loud and soft, modern and old—reminded everyone of the inseparable link between music and dance. The Lettermen provided the soundtrack for a loving yet ominously terminal waltz between a proud dad and his princess daughter; the "Hava Nagila" provided the soundtrack for family pride and fun. When I jumped around playfully during "Hava Nagila," it marked the true melding of two great families.

How can we include all the different styles of music performed at such a wedding as popular music, as we do in this book? A traditional common-sense distinction in the study of music is that between popular music and classical music. Theodore Adorno (1976) argued that classical music has a liberating effect on its audiences insofar as it creates a healthy dialectic between a representation of the world as fact and a presentation of possible, perhaps even utopian, visions of society. Beethoven was his hero in this regard. Popular music, on the other hand, precluded open discourse between the objective and the subjective and instead presented a vision of reality that is whole, unchanging, unproblematic. Put simply, classical music supported democracy, whereas popular music supported the rigid worldview that ends up in fascism.

Adorno's insights are powerful, yet they unfortunately parallel oversimplified thinking that says that popular music is inferior because the audiences attracted to it are somehow inferior. The distinction between fine art/classical music and popular art/popular music ends up an elitist theory. As sociologists we must remain skeptical of all classifications. As sociologists of everyday life, we want to focus on the practices people use to make music an integral part of their lives.

In the present text, we argue that classical music is really a subcategory of popular music, for two reasons. First, if we agree that the word "popular" more or less means "of the people," then popular music is the music preferred by the people (that is, a good number of them). Following this argument, if many people today—and therefore not only, and not anymore, a hyper-privileged, "cultured," upper-class and aristocratic-like minority—enjoy classical music, is classical music not popular music as well? The answer would have to be an absolute "yes."

In fact, many more people across social classes enjoy classical music today than ever before. Attendance at the many productions around the world of *The Nutcracker* during the Christmas season increases every year (Kotarba 2013). Second, the industry that produces, records, promotes, and establishes performances of classical music is the same industry that creates popular music. For example, classical music has a "star" system that places celebrity performers on international tours as well as *The Tonight Show* and *Late Show* on TV as guests. Think of Joshua Bell, Yo-Yo Ma, Sarah Brightman, and Placido Domingo.

At this point some of you may feel a degree of satisfaction knowing that distinctions—like those between "high-status" musical styles like opera and "low-status" musical styles like rap or rock—are arbitrary, politically motivated social constructions. You might even be thinking about Facebooking that high-school classical music teacher who looked down on your mohawk to remind her or him of that. On the other hand, some of you may recognize that despite the arbitrariness of any objective or universal hierarchy of values between musical expressions, some differences amongst them do, indeed, exist. After all, you can't just show up for a night at the opera theater with a surfboard, for example. And your typical opera-goer, no matter how "local" he/she claims to be, wouldn't be allowed to surf your waves and share your surf rock on the beach in his/her sharply pressed tuxedo. In fact, while distinctions are always more or less ideological, in practice they do work. Another way of saying this is that reality may be a matter of conventions and ideas, but those conventions and ideas are really meaningful in their consequences. Such is one of the basic ideas behind the paradigm, or worldview, known as the Sociology of Everyday Life, the very starting point of our introduction to this book.

The Sociology of Everyday Life and the Sociology of Popular Music

Introduction to Sociology textbooks generally survey three bodies of sociological theory: functionalist, conflict and interactionist theories. *Functionalist Theory* was very important in the beginning of the sociology of popular music right after the end of World War II. Talcott Parsons (1949) and James Coleman (1961) were interested in understanding the way society would manage the great bulge in the American population today known as the baby boomer generation. Both saw the emerging "youth culture" as a mechanism society was establishing to do this. Parsons argued that the youth culture functioned as a *safety valve* to help manage and release all the energy—sexual and otherwise—and leisure time adolescence was producing. For example, rock'n'roll sock hops were controlled events, chaperoned by adults, at which kids could meet each other, dance, and have fun in a safe way. Coleman studied high-school culture and found that the varieties of popular music available to teenagers helped to organize them by social class and prepare them for adulthood. Working-class kids liked rockabilly, whereas middle-class kids like pop performers such as The Four Freshmen. Coleman was particularly interested in the rapid increase in the number of high schools that would not only accommodate—warehouse—all the teenagers but also would accommodate teenagers who found themselves the object of compulsory attendance rules that had become fashionable after the war. Functionalism is not the most popular approach in the sociology of music. Much of functionalist research examines the relationship between social class membership and the arts/music (e.g., DiMaggio 2010).

Conflict Theory sees society as an ongoing confrontation between social classes, genders, or races/ethnicities (Ritzer and Stepnisky 2014). One group tries to exert control over the other in order to profit materially, or to have one's beliefs or worldview be dominant over others. Conflict theorists thus see popular music—again, rock'n'roll in particular—as either a tool of the dominant group to keep others in economic or political submission (e.g., music as a way to divert the masses' attention away from significant issues), or as a tool for political resistance to the dominant group (e.g., anti-war and protest music). The focus on economic and political conflict tends to ignore certain topics near and dear to humanistic scholars who prefer to explore the sociological significance of music as a source of meaning for everyday life, for who we are, and as a mechanism for group solidarity.

Symbolic Interactionism is a theoretical perspective in sociology "that places meaning, interaction, and human agency at the center of understanding social life" (Sandstrom et al. 2013, p. 23). People interact or communicate with each other to achieve practical meanings for situations and objects in the world. The most important object we work hard to define is the *self*, the experience of individuality that makes humans distinctive among all forms of life. Symbolic interactionist work in popular music is among the most creative of all sociological takes. The annual series, *Studies in Symbolic Interactionism* has had two special issues dedicated to popular music, the most recent of which is edited by Chris Schneider and me (2016).

Now, symbolic interactionism is perhaps the most important yet only one branch of the more general theoretical perspective we call the *Sociology of Everyday Life* (EDL) that provides the intellectual context for this text. As Douglas (1976) notes, the sociolog(ies) of everyday life consist of those theories that see society as the product of people communicating, interacting and working hard to establish the semblance—if not at least the appearance—of social order and the meaningfulness of life. Everyday life refers to the actual situations in which people live, face problems, seek meaning for those problems, and apply practical solutions to those problems. Symbolic interactionist theory is the primary analytical framework in EDL, and the other theories all result from or are closely related to interactionism. Ethnomethodology, for example, sees talk or communication as the essence of social life, not simply a way of describing social life (Vom Lehn 2014). Dramaturgy sees everyday life as if it were a theater. People perform with and for each other by following scripts provided by their cultures (Jacobsen and Kristiansen 2015). Phenomenology locates the essence of social life in consciousness; social life is a reflection of the ways our minds construct the image of social life (Psathas 1973).

The two most recent varieties of EDL sociology are existential sociology and postmodernism. Existential sociology argues, like symbolic interactionism does, that the primary goal of social interaction is developing, nurturing, safeguarding and preserving the self: the sense of who you are. Existential sociology differs, however, in the emphasis it places on the contemporary social situation in which the self is constantly changing and adapting to a perpetually shifting social and cultural landscape. Existential sociology also sees the experience of individuality as value- and feeling-based as well as a cognitive or conscious experience. My recent (2013) book on baby boomer rock'n'roll fans discusses the many and varied experiences of self by and through which aging rockers continue to use music to make sense of themselves and the ever-changing world around them. I write about the *e-self* through which the boomer sees him or herself as someone who appreciates and is committed to technological innovations in music, for example, satellite radio. I also write about the *parental self* who utilizes music to communicate and shape relationships with his or her children. Postmodernism is perhaps the most radical of the sociologies of everyday life, and becoming a paradigm in its own right, in the way it argues society is not simply regulated by culture, as the functionalists maintain, but is culture per se. Our values, ideas and morals emanate increasingly from the mass media including the Internet, YouTube, social media, and of course television (Kotarba and Johnson 2002).

Everyday Life Sociology and Social Constructionism

A melding of EDL perspectives with the progressive features of conflict theory produces a style of EDL sociology that is very influential in understanding popular music: *Social Constructionism* (SC). SC prefers to study popular music as a meaningful set of practices, performances, and texts in the social world. In doing so it focuses on what people do together with music and with one another. In the case of music, constructionism explains, for example, how genres take shape; how people shape, follow, and abandon the musical fashions they have created; how people construct a sense of identity, individual and collective, around music; and so forth (Kotarba and Vannini 2006).

What makes constructivism unique and very useful for the study of cultural phenomena like music is the way it incorporates ideas from *Critical Theory*. Unlike conflict theory that is derived from Karl Marx's economic determinism, critical theory is instead more closely associated with the University of Birmingham's Contemporary Centre for Cultural Studies in England (henceforth, CCCS). The scholars at CCCS generated interdisciplinary interest in popular culture and popular music studies by blending critical theory's emphasis on the economic power exercised by groups that manipulate if not control the culture industries with everyday life ideas on agency, style, lifestyle, and meaningfulness. For example, Dick Hebdige (1979) examined the way politically disenfranchised youth in England co-opted upper-class *style* in clothing and entertainment as a form of symbolic resistance to the ruling class in Britain.

Now, a lot of theory consumed all at once can give anyone a head ache, so let us step back a bit for a second and return to popular music. Let us imagine a character, a guy or girl like many others. Let's give this character a name: Dana. Dana lives in Seattle. Not just any Seattle but the Seattle of the early 1990s. Yeah, the grungy one! Dana looks like many youths around town: jeans, a Mudhoney t-shirt and a hooded sweatshirt, disheveled look, mellow attitude yet politically aware and more or less involved in environmental issues and other social causes. Dana has a particular taste in music and is a huge music buff: grunge, indie-rock, anything heavy with the exception of glam, butt-rock-type guitar music. Dana is also growing up. Maybe wondering a bit about the future and worrying about paying bills and eventually having to settle down with a ballooning student loan debt. Dana works odd days at Kinko's (now FedEx), takes classes at Seattle Central Community College, drives his or her beat-up Nissan every other weekend to catch some good shows down in Olympia—and occasionally plays bass guitar with some Evergreen State College friends—and every now and then parties downtown at the Crocodile. A pretty normal life, right? So, why does Dana matter to us?

Dana matters to us as sociologists of popular music because his/her identity (among other things) cannot be understood without a comprehension of the role that music plays in his/her life. Only by focusing on the meanings that Dana attributes to music, by paying attention to how that music allows Dana to cement social ties with friends, to understand the politics of the world, to express emotionality and so forth can we hope to understand Dana a bit better. To do this we need to put ourselves in Dana's shoes. We need to understand how he/she makes his/her world, how he/she attributes meaning to it. In other words, we need to become ethnographic tourists in Dana's life. We need to hang out with Dana, listen to his/her stories, and see life from his/her perspective.

To put Dana's life in perspective we might need to understand his/her social position. As a grunge fan Dana has already engaged in a bit of social positioning of his/her own, whether he/she is aware of this or not. In its early stages, grunge emerged as a form of protest music: protest against the growing standardization of youth culture, against the superficiality of popular culture, against both the consumerism and excessive hedonism of the music of the 1980s, and against the idealistic and utopian values of the hippie generation that preceded it. Dana's musical identity might then very well be understood as a battle cry born out of social angst: angst toward his/her biographical particulars (such as growing up in a quickly expanding and increasingly wealthy city) and angst towards the general political marginalization of youth culture and youth issues by the political system. And this is what a critical approach to social/musical issues does: it attempts to understand the meanings of musical choices, discourses, and practices by critically reflecting on social positions and on the stratification of those social positions. It focuses on those particular historical and political discourses, musical (and other) texts, and practices through which social positions can be created and expressed, and through which hierarchies and inequalities can be highlighted and criticized. Put simply, social constructionism and critical orientation helps provide a broader societal context for understanding why music fans, artists, producers and distributors make decisions the way they do. We will see this critical approach in the chapters on rap music and popular music in Poland since the demise of communism in the early 1990s.

Music and Culture

Culture is a way of life. Despite the fact that some people refer to culture as an ensemble of artistic practices, folk customs, and educational background, sociologists and other social scientists view culture differently: as a system of symbolic meanings and a variety of processes of formation, exchange, and use of those meanings. When we understand culture as a way of life we become sensitized to seeing the presence of culture everywhere. This is why as sociologists of everyday life we feel particularly keen on attempting to understand and explain the most taken for granted and minute cultural expressions. Rather than explaining the concept of culture further by providing additional definitions, let us try to capture the uniqueness of the culture of our times by returning to our earlier example.

To anyone who has lived their life much earlier in the 20th century, Dana's life would seem full of choices. Dana didn't have to take a job at Kinko's, to choose to drive an old, beat-up Nissan, or to go to school at Seattle Central Community College. As a matter of fact, Dana—being from North Bend, outside of Seattle—didn't have to move to the city. Music, too, is a choice. And the choice for Dana is endless. Any shelves of any music store offer a vast choice of musical styles: country, heavy metal, R&B, rap, classical, industrial, etc. Dana's choice to abandon religion in his/her early teens is also a choice. Clothing style is also a choice. We could continue on and on but you get the point that we are making: if there is one distinguishing characteristic of the way of life of our times is that we have an unprecedented amount of choice. Ask your grandparents, if you can, about their choices when they were your age, like how many recordings they could choose from at the "music store." You'll get a different picture. And they'll get a good laugh out of your question. They'll laugh *with* you, of course.

Musical choices are cultural choices. After all, music is part of the way we choose to live our life. And if it is a culture of choice that we speak of, then perhaps we need to wonder what the deeper consequences of choosing are. Sociologist Anthony Giddens (1991) writes that never before has Western culture been so receptive to the power of choice. Indeed who we ourselves are, as individuals, is a matter of choice. Our self is a project of sorts. Dana, in fact, could very well decide to trade in his/her grunge rock CD collection for some rap music, sell back his/her clothes at Value Village and buy stretch pants and move to Los Angeles too. The following month, or year, Dana could start over, with another identity of choice. You could too. We could too. The reason why we don't change all the time is because change and the very possibility of change provoke some anxiety in all of us. Anxiety, doubt, and fearing the loss of any sort of grounding or safety net are the necessary counterparts of a culture rich in choices and in the power of choosing. Dana's angst comes in part from being a member of a generation that—perhaps more than any other generation before—has felt the freedom to choose. Angst, thus, comes in Dana's case from the absence of firm traditions: the traditions that your grandparents and especially great-grandparents will tell you about if you ask them about their choices.

Some sociologists have decided to assign a moniker that we have already discussed to the culture we have described: *postmodern*. By postmodern culture they mean a culture in which one's way of life is less grounded in traditions and more in choices, less grounded in certainties and more in doubts (Baudrillard 1994). A postmodern culture is marked by the seemingly endless availability of choice: fragmented musical styles, endless stimulation from multiple mass media of communication, the explosion of consumption and consumerism, the increased interconnectedness of the globe. Many more characteristics could be mentioned and many discussions could be opened. Yet, for the sake of brevity simply understand this: Dana's sense of self and identity, and Dana's way of life has the quality of an open project in a way that is more distinctly so than any other time in modern history. Sociologists who believe in the truth of this statement are known as postmodernists. Elements of postmodern theory, which have great impact on everyday life sociology, and references to postmodern culture, occasionally ooze all over our insights throughout this book, and hopefully now you will know what we mean by that ever contentious expression: postmodernism (see also Kotarba 1994a).

To conclude this section, let us reflect on an element of our example that we have so far neglected: the limitations and costs of choices. Let us return to our example. Although Dana's choice to become a grunge rock fan may seem arbitrary and inconsequential at first it is, in actuality, quite the opposite. Choices are hardly ever random. So if we spoke to Dana we might learn that he/she was never intending on becoming who he/she is. Yet, lack of educational opportunities in his/her hometown made it more or less necessary to move to Seattle. Some of his/her high-school friends were in the same position, so moving to a city was not only a necessity in relation to education but also represented the opportunity to maintain social networks. Dana might also tell us that the choice for a college was more or less forced by limited opportunities. Many of Dana's friends' parents were able to fund study at Evergreen State College for their children. Dana instead had to take a job at Kinko's to help pay for tuition. That took time away from playing in a rock band. It also made Dana resentful, politically motivated, and particularly sensitive to the appeal of lyrics like those of "Hunger Strike" by Temple of the Dog: "I don't mind stealing bread from the mouths of decadence."

Sociologists of everyday life, influenced by social constructionism and postmodernism, might then suggest that choice exists but it is *structured* or limited by several characteristics of the very social structures that enable ways of life and the amount of choice therein. Music, and musical cultures, are then a serious sociological business, business which allows us to understand a great deal about society and social theory in general: the very scope of this book. Even though by now it seems obvious to you that studying popular music is a very useful and smart way of understanding social relations, this was not always the case. In the next section we briefly review the recent history of the study of music within sociology and a little bit of the history of sociology itself.

A Very Brief History of the Study of Popular Music in Sociology

Since we have more or less erased the boundaries between popular music and classical music for the sake of subjecting both of those to sociological analysis, let us demarcate our territory—that is, the precise field that we explore in this book—by choosing an expression that captures the identity of the diverse types of music on which we focus here. Let us choose the expression *Popular Music*. Popular music is then intended to refer here to all types of music that are processed through, and that share, the logic of the mass media.

Please note: we use several terms or labels for musical styles that, hopefully, are not too confusing. *Popular music* is the most general category we will analyze. Popular or pop music refers to all styles of music that are mass produced, mass marketed, and in general, treated economically as a commodity in our North American societies. *Rock'n'roll* refers to that style of popular music that emerged after World War II as a distinct feature of youth culture. Rock'n'roll is loud, fast, guitar-driven, typically amplified, very danceable, and marketed towards young, teenage audiences (Kotarba 1987). We will argue that the rock'n'roll idiom has influenced virtually all other styles of popular music in terms of these characteristics, and especially in terms of marketing, instrument selection, and orientation to youthfulness. *Rock* refers to more contemporary versions of rock'n'roll. *Jazz, rap, dance, noise*, etc. are other styles of popular music. However, we will often use the term rock'n'roll to signify the spirit and energy that has led to more contemporary styles of popular music.

We ordinarily think of popular music as emerging during the early 20th century when music became an economic commodity in our society, to be produced and marketed like any other consumable goods. There were two technological events that fueled this phenomenon. First, the advent of radio in the 1920s brought music into the homes of millions of North Americans. Perhaps the major impact of radio on music was its ability to present new and different styles of music beyond the classical, family, church and community-based music to which people were previously accustomed. Second, the advent of recorded music, in a period that critical theorist Walter Benjamin (1969) referred to as the *age of mechanical reproduction*, turned music into a personal possession—with a price tag—that could be experienced and enjoyed at will, that could be distributed widely, and which could make music a lucrative business for producer, composer, and musician alike.

Much of the early scholarly work on popular music, including that of the Frankfurt School, was written from a critical if not elitist perspective. Theodore Adorno (1949), for example, frowned on jazz (his expression for what we call "pop music") as a low-status form of music that elicited non-rational, animalistic responses from its fans, in contrast to classical music that supposedly elevated one's mind and spirit. In addition, early critical thinkers like Adorno felt that capitalists marketed popular music to anesthetize the working class politically and to increasingly subjugate them economically.

In recent years, cultural scholars, including sociologists, have been much friendlier to popular music. These writers were largely baby boomers themselves who were raised not only on pop music, but on rock'n'roll music specifically. To them, popular music is a fundamental force in North American and—increasingly global—culture, to be appreciated as well as understood. Later generations of scholars who went through their youth in the late 1960s, 1970s, and 1980s felt very similar to their baby-boomer predecessors. The sociology of music then became overwhelmingly the sociology of rock'n'roll, and then the sociology of popular music. We argue that there have been four moments in the sociological analysis of modern popular music that closely parallel the historical development of pop itself in Western society over the past 50 years. We will briefly describe these four moments in order to understand the evolution of both social phenomena. The key theme that we emphasize in the next paragraphs is that the sociology of popular music has generally focused in its earlier years on rock'n'roll. With the growing diversification of rock and multiplication of styles that originate in but deviate from rock the sociology of pop music has become more diversified as well.

The first moment of the sociology of popular music occurred during the 1950s, when youth culture and rock'n'roll as we know them were born. We are acknowledging, of course, the fact the cultural and musicological roots of rock'n'roll can be traced back at least several decades (Friedlander 1996). It was during the 1950s, however, that rock'n'roll received its name and dramatically entered North American everyday life and parlance. Interestingly, early sociological views on youth culture in general, and rock'n'roll specifically, were quite positive and supportive of this cultural movement. As we mentioned earlier, James Coleman (1961) conceptualized rock'n'roll as *youth culture*. He observed, through his massive study of American high schools, that early rock'n'rollers like Elvis Presley and Buddy Holly provided a soundtrack for helping the community manage the burgeoning population of teenagers resulting from the success of the emerging middle-class family (1950s and 1960s). The growing varieties of popular music in the 1950s helped socialize young people into their "appropriate" social classes. Coleman saw rock'n'roll as the soundtrack for working class youth. In many ways, early scholarly writing on rock'n'roll discovered this music as it was already understood and experienced by its fans.

The second moment of the sociology of popular music occurred during the late 1960s and 1970s. Rock'n'roll music grew to become a cultural entity much greater than the beat for sock hops or the drive-in. It took on broader political implications through its links to the Civil Rights and Anti-War movements. In the second moment, sociologists like Simon Frith (1981) and George Lewis (1983) conceptualized rock'n'roll as *popular culture*. They focused on the transformation of rock'n'roll music to the more artistically and politically serious style of rock music, as the product of the popular culture industry in capitalistic society. They also acknowledged the fact that the rock audience was much more diverse than the notion of "youth" implies. Experientially, there were white, black, gay, men's and women's rock and, subsequently, markets.

The third moment in the sociology of popular music occurred in the 1970s and 1980s when rock lost some of its critical appeal and became increasingly entrenched in and controlled by the entertainment industry. The ensuing revolt against corporate rock, especially in terms of the new wave and punk movements in England, led British scholars such as Dick Hebdige and others writing from the Birmingham School to conceptualize rock as *subculture*. They examined the political nature of rock and other styles as subversive voices of working-class teenagers, especially in Great Britain. These scholars advanced the methodologies used to study rock from classic survey research to semiotics. This approach fit the objective of understanding how audiences define and integrate music into their already constituted realities (i.e., social class memberships). Thus, the working-class punk subculture appropriated elements of upper class culture, like dress, and used them to ridicule and criticize the life of the rich and powerful.

In the fourth moment of the sociology of popular music in the 1980s and 1990s, sociologists joined other scholarly observers to conceptualize rock as *culture*. They saw rock music as simply one feature of a post-industrial or postmodern culture undergoing radical transformation. The generational boundaries that so obviously delineated youth from their parents were cracking. Lawrence Grossberg (1992b), for example, proclaimed the death of rock'n'roll insofar as it no longer functions to empower teenagers by differentiating them from their parents and other adults, as it did in the 1950s and 1960s. By the time we entered the 1990s, cross-generational pop music that could be enjoyed by everyone had started to supplant rock as the dominant soundtrack in American culture. Rap music has taken over much of rock's political role. Yet, rock has not simply died. In the spirit of the postmodern era in which we live, rock has dissolved into the pastiche of popular music that results in white rappers like Eminem, rap rock groups Linkin Park and Rage Against the Machine, and pop acts ranging from Britney Spears and

Justin Bieber to Nicki Minaj and Adele. MTV and VH1 in the United States and Much Music and Much More Music in Canada have been major media forces in creating this cultural gumbo. As E. Ann Kaplan (1987) has noted, MTV is a reflection of the pervasiveness of the visual dimension of postmodern culture, as rock'n'roll has been absorbed by the overwhelming power of the television medium on which teenagers have been raised. Today, MTV has become less focused on pop music videos and more involved with dramatic programming. CMT (Country Music Television) is perhaps the channel most dedicated to music videos, a trend that reflects the growing importance of country music to the overall world of popular music.

Therefore, rock'n'roll and rock are no longer synonymous with popular music but should be seen as two facets of the increasingly complex musical and cultural phenomenon known as popular music. Popular music of all styles has taken on many of the attributes and values of the traditional world of rock'n'roll—volume, fast pace, sensuality, amplification, and so forth . . . just think of the ongoing controversy in country music. Are Keith Urban and Eric Church rock'n'roll or country? It's hard to say when the back-up bands appear to be rock bands with, on occasion, a pedal guitar or fiddle thrown in. Age is another factor in this growing complexity. Amid all these changes taking place in popular music and the entertainment industry's search for new audiences and ways to provide music to them, we witness numerous ways adults are increasingly present in and relevant to rock'n'roll and popular music. The Beatles CD compilations have been among the highest selling music at Christmas for many years. Middle-aged fans pay hundreds of dollars to sit in the "Gold Circle" seats at Eagles and The Who concerts, where they sip white wine instead of the Boone's Farm of their college days many years ago. The summer concert "shed" scene would be very thin without sold-out Aerosmith, Chicago, Kansas, Paul Simon, James Taylor, Crosby, Stills and Nash, Sting/Police and REO Speedwagon stops. Why have so many adults not outgrown rock'n'roll? Why do innumerable teenagers angrily shout to their parents to "turn that noise down" when mom and dad are grooving to an old Rolling Stones CD? Why do so many adults continue to operationalize "Popular Music" in terms of the rock'n'roll idiom with which they grew up?

In a very postmodern way, the continuing fourth moment of the sociology of popular music will try to understand the evolution of earlier patterns of performance, consumption, and style. Further, we can say that we may be in fact moving into a fifth moment of pop music and pop music studies within sociology. The fifth moment is a typically postmodern one: marked by extreme diversification of both musical offer and sociological offer, by increasing debates over the authenticity of pop music, by a nostalgic and pastiche-like recovery of the past, and by the increasing global fusion of styles matched by a blurring of differences among audiences, experiences, values and performances. Put simply, popular music and its attributes are getting increasingly difficult to classify, a primary analytical method in sociology. Sociologically, this translates in a coming together of theoretical perspectives on the study of popular music, and an explosion in the sociological interest in popular culture. Indeed, as culture industries try to appeal to consumers by listening to their needs for diversity, so do the "sociological industries." And, indeed, our book also attempts to answer to the introductory student's need for diversity in pedagogical scope!

I will close with the following illustrative observation from the AARP (American Association for Retired Persons) Bulletin, November 2016, p. 6:

> Perhaps the greatest collection of rock superstardom ever assembled—the Rolling Stones! The Who! Bob Dylan! A former Beatle!—staged one of the most successful music events ever. And that means shows like last month's Desert Trip will likely keep coming. Music festivals have been a growing business for a couple of decades, but they are mostly aimed at a youthful crowd, with cutting-edge bands, established alterna-rock acts and DJs performing to 20- and 30-somethings willing to camp out for a weekend. Desert Trip was different. This festival, near Palm Springs, Calif., proved that the 50-plus audience 'is a valuable, coveted market,' says Ray Waddell, senior editor for *Billboard*. 'There's a lot of discretionary income, there's a lot of passion about music.'
>
> *Billboard's* estimates put the Desert Trip take at $130 million. Pricey tickets (from $399 to $1599 for three days' admission sold

> out in five hours. It drew 150,000 fans of all ages, who shelled out even more for lobster rolls, vegan jackfruit tacos and wine, not to mention those $40 concert tees.
>
> The event offered two major acts each night, including Paul McCartney, Neil Young and Roger Waters; it was repeated on a second weekend. 'You can't top this for rock royalty,' says Waddell, who surmises that similar events will follow with 'the next era, more to the acts that were huge in the '70s: Springsteen, Petty, Seger, Stevie Wonder.' Get your credit cards ready.

Wow! Intergenerational rock music audiences, gourmet food trucks, luxury accommodation as well as blankets and tents . . . Our goal in this text is to help prepare the reader to understand the growing complexity of popular music and to appreciate the dynamics and change in the social world of popular music. We will approach the growing complexity of popular music as a challenge and not a puzzle.

Conclusion: Cultivating a Musical and Sociological Imagination

If we wish to understand the social meanings of popular music and be critical of those cultural practices and values which result in the formation or re-creation of cultural injustices, we need to follow an approach to the study of our subject matter which is interpretive and critical at the same time. In doing so, we privilege methods and data that allow us to take the role and perspective of the people we intend to understand, that allow us to focus on the construction of meaning through language and language use, and that allow us to interpret the significance of music-related practices in a precise historical, political, geographical, and economic context. In the preface I discussed our approach to the study of all this. We called it *ethnographic tourism*, and explained how it constitutes an example of the sociological study of everyday life. In this introduction, we have discussed the virtues of using the sociologies of everyday life to organize our critical analysis of popular music, explained how and why this perspective is best followed via the use of qualitative data, and how important it is to maintain a healthy skepticism towards all social facts.

Much of what we have done constitutes an example of *sociological imagination.* Critical and interpretive sociologist C. Wright Mills

(1959) coined the expression sociological imagination to refer to the ability to connect, by way of reflection, seemingly unconnected individual and social forces, and in particular biographical and historical issues. Sociology attempts to foster in all its publics—both students and stakeholders—a sociological imagination by getting them to reflect on the greater relevance of personal problems as social issues. Our focus on the study of pop music has precisely that objective in mind as well. Because few things matter to students as much as music does, we believe that by allowing students to reflect on the experience of music as a social accomplishment we can introduce students to sociological theory and research.

1

Social Interaction

Joseph A. Kotarba

Interaction is the essence of all varieties of interactionist sociology, and in fact of everyday life. One of the founders of symbolic interaction, Herbert Blumer (1969), stated unequivocally that society consists of people engaging in symbolic interaction. On a constant, everyday basis, we interact with each other, people in the past, people in the future, and ourselves. Through interaction, we become human, respond pragmatically to social situations, negotiate social meanings, shape our behavior, experience and manage emotions, and shape and refine culture (Sandstrom et al. 2013). Interaction can occur through any number of media: speech, visual symbols, written text, and—of course—music. Interaction is first and foremost the mechanism for generating and sharing meanings.

In terms of music, interaction occurs any number of ways. We talk over lunch with our friends about the *American Idol* contestants we saw last night on TV. We read about the latest music tours and artists' scandals in the *Rolling Stone* magazine. In fact, I am now pondering the black and white poster of the Rolling Stones perched over my desk as I write. (I don't care what the critics say, Keith Richards looks really cool smoking his unfiltered cigarette while wearing his sunglasses and funky hat.) We drag our dates to the Katy Perry concert tour documentary, *Part of Me*, to get a glimpse of the latest pink, purple and polka dot fashions. We turn our smartphones or laptops to YouTube to witness the Tupac Shakur holographic performance at Coachella everyone was talking about several years ago—now that's scary!

Symbolic interaction over music can range from the most personal and intimate to the most public and mass mediated. In order to illustrate the role interaction plays in our popular music experiences, we will provide two examples from the ends of the continuum. The first is personal interaction with one's self regarding what we will define as a distinctly sociological concept of the *pop song*. The second is the much more public interaction that takes place at *music scenes*.

The Pop Song: Stuck in Your Head

Commonsensically, we all know what a *pop song* is. Our general cultural and industry definitions include the following typical characteristics: formulaic; melody-driven; short (two minutes or so long); danceable; lyrics deal with love or fun; simple instrumentation; and happy—among other characteristics. Many of us say we hate the kinds of pop songs I am describing for the above reasons, but also because they sound childish or are marketed to (dumb) kids; are bad music; are wimpy and/or bubble-gummy; are unsophisticated; are "chic songs;" are commodified products marketed to us incessantly by the capitalistic music industry; are disposable; are mind-numbing, etc. You get the picture.

We all know this because these are commonsense definitions of pop songs. Music critics, professional and otherwise, generally share these definitions. Sociologically, we have a responsibility to look beyond commonsense to sculpt a definition of a pop song that unpacks—deconstructs—taken-for-granted definitions of, and assumptions about, pop songs. Put differently, sociologists of everyday life especially want to explore the actual experience of a pop song to see how meaning is attributed to or derived from a pop song. Furthermore, we are interested in the way people use pop songs to create a sense of self, definitions of situation, relationships, feelings, and other social objects (Mead 1934).

Case in point: Carly Rae Jepsen had the number one hit single, "Call Me Maybe," in the summer of 2012. Carly Rae is apparently a bit of a Justin Bieber protégé from Canada. Before her current hit, she was a singer-songwriter perhaps best known for her third-place finish on the 2007 season of *Canadian Idol*. Justin Bieber made her an international star when he tweeted "'Call Me Maybe' by Carly Rae Jepsen is probably the catchiest song I've ever heard" to his 22 million followers. Soon, celebrities ranging from Justin Bieber and Selena Gomez to Katy Perry and James Franco were uploading YouTube video clip versions they made of Carly Rae's hit (Green 2012).

Sociologically, the questions arise: Why was "Call Me Maybe" so popular? What do we mean when we say that a pop song is "catchy?" How do people experience a catchy song? Within the sociology of everyday life, the phenomenological perspective is a very useful tool for answering these questions. *Phenomenology* focuses on the way people perceive, organize, make practical sense of and define common, everyday events and social phenomena (Sokolowski 2000). I have conducted numerous exercises with students in my classroom and online courses in the Sociology of Popular Music at Texas State University. These students include both juniors and seniors from a wide range of majors. I set up a forum and ask students to discuss these questions. Their responses have been open, honest, well-written and sophisticated. (This is typically the case when students are asked to write about themselves and topics near and dear to them!) I derived a ten-point model of the "pop song" from the students' responses. I then applied the model to help understand the "catch-ability" of songs mentioned by the students (see Kotarba 2013 for a full discussion of the pop song model).

(1) *A pop song is catchy*. "Catchy" is the key experience in a pop song. My students talked about catchy in terms of the way a song occupies one's consciousness. The mind "plays" the song as if it was an iPod or radio in the mind. However, a song seems to be catchy only after the listener reflects on it to some degree, giving meaning to it. This meaning can be a reflection on the kind of situation the singer is creating with the song. An internal dialogue with the singer ensues that serves to enter the song into retrievable memory:

> 'Call Me Maybe' is a catchy song. When I heard it the first time all I heard was a girl singing, 'here's my number, call me maybe.' That sounds a little wishy washy to me. Almost like if the guy doesn't call her, oh well! But let's be honest, if a girl gives you her number, she wants you to call and if you don't she's going to internalize it and wonder what's wrong with her that you don't like! When I

> listened to the song a second time, really focusing on the lyrics, I heard a girl describe how this guy looks, how he makes her feel, etc. and her response is 'Call Me Maybe.' When I hear this song I do turn it up, it's got a great beat and is ok to listen to while sitting in five o'clock traffic. I don't sing along to this song, but when my girlfriend is in the car with me she does. Maybe this song is more relatable to girls?! This song sounds like it would be more for teenagers just trying to figure out relationships and the dynamics that go along with finding or being with someone else. While researching this song, I came across the YouTube video of the Harvard Baseball team dancing on the way to a game to this song. It's very funny!

The meaning can be the imagery of a social situation in which the song is initially experienced alone, but triggered or reinforced when experienced with another. Even so, a catchy song can be contagious if there is occasion to experience the song, such as an extra credit course assignment:

> When we were assigned this extra credit, I thought, 'Hmm. I guess I'll have to listen to it.' So I planned on looking on YouTube or something. Instead, one day I was driving home from work, flipped on a Top 40 station, and it was on (imagine that . . .). I heard it that day and literally all I could think was 'Wow . . . this is not a good song.' But it was danceable and catchy. By the second chorus, I found myself embarrassingly singing along.

Or, when driving around with a colleague from work:

> But, alas, I work at a news station and we all share cars. Got in the car with a reporter on the way to a shoot yesterday and—'HEY I JUST MET YOU . . .'—The reporter looked at me and said, 'Ugh. They play this too much.' But we both started singing it. And maybe dancing a little . . . a lot.

Or, even while writing up the course assignment:

> Then, all day (with very few hours of sleep, mind you) I was humming it, sometimes mumbling—'so call me maybeeee'—the lyrics to myself . . . I would catch myself, bobbing my head, tapping my fingers . . . and I would stop . . . for about two minutes . . . and there it was again. 'Hey I just met you, and this is crazy, but here's my number, so call me maybe.' . . . I would just like to add that I've also been singing it in my head the entire time I've been writing this post.

Yet, catchiness can be an unpleasant experience:

> As soon as the song went off, I changed the channel. Never wanting to hear it again. Maybe I would have liked it in my younger days . . . the Britney Spears days. I probably would have liked it in high school at some point, and that is who I think likes it the most: high-school girls (and boys if they'll admit it). I certainly don't like it . . . because it gets SO stuck in my head.

And it can be out of one's control:

> I believe that 'Call Me Maybe' has reached its status as the #1 single record in the country because of its catchiness. When I sat down and looked at the title the chorus began playing in my head. There also is no real way to get it out of my head no matter how hard I try. About all I have said so far is that I absolutely dislike this song. If just by mentioning it to me I start singing the chorus in my head I can't imagine for somebody that enjoys this song.

Several students, almost all men or middle-aged women, indicated that the song was not catchy for them, but they were generally able to explain, quite analytically, why they were able to maintain control:

> My issue is, I have a lot of other things on my mind. The younger students do not have kids or a husband to worry about. . . . Songs like that talk about things that are relevant to younger kids, like boyfriends, dates, falling in love, stuff like that. Besides that . . . it's the kind of song that goes up and down, emotionally or, well, in

terms of feelings. The older you get, the less you really want to vibrate, if you will, like that. I like my music to help mellow out.

(2) *A general, commonsensically belief is that pop songs are essentially "chick" songs.* We can define "chick" songs as those that are directed towards a specific female audience, often comprised of young women, and that contain simple if not naïve lyrics about love and romance:

When I heard this song for the first time I was at the pool with some friends and it was blaring over the radio and I could tell a lot of the girls there liked it because they all started singing or humming to it. I guess I was late hearing this song for the first time because everyone knew it except me. I thought it was catchy but not the type of song I would put on my iPod. Interestingly enough when I went home I YouTubed the song and realized how popular it was and that it even had its own dance. I think about the 5th or 6th time I heard 'Call Me Maybe' it started to grow on me and I can remember singing the lyrics in my head and saying the chorus out loud.

(3) *Listeners who do not like the pop song can generally surmise who might.* Phenomenologically, we can think of these explanations as members' theories. We all have explanations for events that take place in our worlds. In terms of "Call Me Maybe," the students who offered the most developed theories of why others like the song seemed to use their theories to create distance between themselves and song's fans:

Ok, so I admit the first time I heard this song was a couple days ago because of this assignment. I googled it and a YouTube video of the Miami Dolphins cheerleaders lip sync and dance routine to it came up, so I went with it. Later I did see the actual video for it, and it was surprisingly sexual for a song that seemed to have its target audience in its teens. I couldn't help but at least tap my toe to it, but maybe that was the cheerleaders. The fast beat made it easy to dance to, and it will appeal to a very wide demographic of young people, world-wide. It struck me as the same type of entry to pop music that Britney Spears had, with regard to age, sex, genre and sexuality in the video. Actually, it did remind me of the fact many mid-twenties and thirties women will totally rock out to this song even though they know that it is intended for a younger audience. Maybe because it takes them back to the times when they were in high school and rocking out to new pop songs. On the surface the song feels like something teenage girls are sure to listen to as an anthem for their early crushes in life. It's sure to make the middle school dances in the fall.

(4) *The pop song not only engages the listener, but draws the listener in.* There is a bit of a contagion factor with catchy pop songs:

> Well for sure this song is very catchy. I find it very annoying and I am unsure how it became popular. But every time I hear it on the radio, I somehow sing along and know the words. I don't know how or why I know it. The melody is so easy to hum along to it. It is one of those songs that just finds you and you know the song the second time you hear it. The first time I heard it I was confused and thought it was a parody of a real song, and then I heard it again and somehow was singing along. Yet I still find the song very annoying and I don't like it. I don't know who would like it and why, but I think that it's not that people like it, it's one of those songs that you can't get a rid of and plays on the radio every hour so you just deal with it. It's like that song that won't leave you alone.

The song seems to seep into one's consciousness when there is space for it, such as during episodes of boredom:

> When I'm at work, I get really bored sometimes. I could do my job blindfolded and asleep . . . You know, when your mind is not paying attention, you can get bad thoughts . . . boyfriend problems, something you forgot to do—lots of stuff like that. Now, that's when a song like that is fun. It fills your mind with good feelings, good things to enjoy.

(5) *The pop song's lyrics are either a non-factor in catchiness or sufficiently open-ended to allow for catchiness to the music per se.*

> The first time I heard this song was at work. I was writing up a marketing plan and found that I had begun humming and moving along to a song which in turn made me start to actually listen to the song and I had no problems catching on to the tune and by the end of the song I already knew most of the lyrics. . . . Listening to the actual words made me really dislike the 'song.' The beat is in fact catchy, thinking about it or even hearing someone mention the title and my head becomes filled with the tune and the most irritating part about it is I would have enjoyed the song as an adolescent.

And . . .

> This song is so simple, catchy, and almost meaningless. It fits perfectly the definition of a pop music song! . . . Now I will have this song in my head for the rest of the night. I don't think the song is great but it's not bad either. It's just your typical teen bubblegum pop trying to make it big. It seems like the lyrics are very easy to parody.

(6) *When the pop song is experienced alone, the effects of the song are personal and immediately pleasurable.*

> The first time I heard this song I thought it was absolutely ridiculous. I thought the lyrics were just plain stupid, and repeated over and over and over again. However dumb I think the song is, I do agree that it is catchy. It is upbeat and has a beat that you can easily tap your fingers or nod your head to. I cannot remember if I was doing this the first time I heard it but I just listened to it again and found myself shaking my head.

The song can even give the listener a sense of empowerment when pondering otherwise difficult situations, like meeting men in clubs:

> I have heard the song 'Call Me Maybe' multiples of times. After the first time hearing it I would catch myself singing along to the chorus and bobbing my head side to side while driving. It made me feel like I could get any guy in the club, no matter how attractive he was. It gave me confidence yet a little mystery in who I am. I would never truly find myself going up to just some hot guy and handing him a card—you can't do that, no matter what self esteem problems you may have. I have to say I love this song.

(7) *When the pop song is experienced in the presence of others, the shared experience is simple, pleasurable, and fun—play rather than intellectual or artistic meaning-making and sharing.*

> I first heard this song going to work at 5:30 in the morning. I'm a morning person to begin with, so when it got into the chorus, I found myself cranking it up and rolling down the windows for everyone to jam out to. I found the beat simple and catchy and I was beating on everything in the car I could find. My brother and sister were not that happy about it though, but when you're the driver you get to make the rules. My fellow co-workers like to put it on as we are doing our morning cleaning duties as life guards, because it puts us all in a good mood. We actually sing too loud sometimes and no one can actually hear the song playing, just three obnoxious boys singing at the top of our lungs at 6:30 in the morning. Life Guarding is a pretty dull job, so we have to keep ourselves entertained. I give many thanks to this song for making my mornings.

And at a different kind of work site:

> I first heard this song when I was at work about three months ago. My co-worker and I were unboxing projectors and testing them before we put them on the shelf. It was pretty typical for Bridget to play music while we were at work, but this one caught me off guard because she normally listens to country. At first, I was turned off because of the singer's high pitch voice. Also, since I am in a

> relationship I wasn't really into the whole 'call me, maybe' line. My co-worker kept replaying it though. So eventually it got stuck in our heads and we sang it the rest of the day. It doesn't surprise me that this is the number one song in the country right now. It is very catchy, it is playful, and it is about something universal—love!

(8) *The pop song is perceived as formulaic, as a replication, or merely as fashionable.* This can be true whether you like a song or not:

> First of all, are you kidding me? . . . secondly, really, are you kidding me? . . . this is the number one single in the country? . . . man, I am so fearful of what is to come of the music industry . . . this isn't even a song! . . . it's one long hook on repeat! . . . but it does stand to reason that she would be a Bieber protégé because his 'songs' are all constructed the same way . . . his mega hit 'Baby' was produced in the same track . . . unfortunately this is what the music industry is producing today and calling them hits . . . I think they need to add an 's' to 'hits' and then we'd have a more accurate description of this garbage that they're passing off as quality artistic expression . . . between these types of songs and the advent of autotune, anyone who has a cute face and can sing in at least one key effectively can be a pop star . . . but for real . . . #1 in the country? . . . you gotta be kiddin' me . . .

And . . .

> The first time I heard this song was about twenty minutes ago. It is most definitely not my kind of music. . . . The tune is kind of catchy I hate to say. It almost made me want to tap my feet, or sing along if I knew the words. The sound was interesting, but it sounded like tons of other pop songs I have heard before. . . . Overall, I would not listen to this song again unless it was what my fiancée was listening to. She really likes this style of music. I have to listen to this type of music sometimes in the interest of compromising. After all, in my truck she has to listen to my music the majority of the time.

(9) *The pop song provides good soundtrack music.* My students do not ordinarily listen to catchy pop songs with perfect attention. They are typically doing something else while the song is playing:

I first came across 'Call Me Maybe' early one Tuesday morning when I was searching iTunes for new music. The song had just been released that same day and I had listened to the 'Disney-Bop' sound. Later that week I was at a friend's apartment on a Saturday night getting dressed to go out and she had a playlist blaring from her iHome. As my friend and I were putting the finishing touches on our outfits and standing in the living room 'Call Me Maybe' started playing. Instantly my friend began singing and dancing around and I couldn't help but do the same; my dancing could've also stemmed from my intake of alcohol but either way I was enjoying the song and my irritation at the singer's high-pitched voice had subsided. While at first I was unsure about if 'Call Me Maybe' was my taste, throughout the night—getting dressed; driving to the bar; going back to my friend's apartment to raid the refrigerator—this song was always playing and I knew that my initial thoughts about it had dissipated and I thoroughly liked the song. Now I have 'Call Me Maybe' on numerous CDs and playlists and whenever I listen to the song, whether in the car or getting dressed, I always find myself moving my head even if the slightest amount. When I am driving, especially during a long drive, I play it as loud as I can manage without busting my car's speakers and always sing at the top of my lungs, especially if I am with a friend and we both know the song. I enjoy the song and it makes me happy and instantly picks up my mood when I listen to it and that makes me feel good knowing that if I am having a bad day all I have to do is go to a certain song and push play.

(10) *Repetitious play in the mass media reinforces the catch-ability of the pop song.*

Dumbest. Song. Ever. But it's so catchy! Annoyingly catchy. In fact, now that I've typed out the lyrics, I'm still singing the song in my

> head. I stopped listening to Top 40 radio stations a little over a month ago because of how often they play the same songs, so I was doing a very good job of never having heard this song until extremely recently. . . . I had seen the lyrics everywhere. People were posting them on Facebook as wall posts, photo album titles, comments, captions, etc. With as popular as the song was, I REALLY didn't want to hear it. . . . I would just like to add that I've also been singing it in my head the entire time I've been writing this post.

Jakubowski et al. (2016) conducted a formal psychological study of earworms, or what they called *involuntary musical imagery*. Through a survey of 300 respondents, they assembled a list of factors that lead to "the spontaneous recall and repeating of a tune in one's mind. . . . Songs that are up-tempo, with a familiar melody set apart by a catchy, unique interval pattern, are especially persistent."

Conclusion

My simple exercise, largely in accord with the more formal psychological study, illustrates several key sociological features of pop music. Perhaps the most interesting is the way popular music fits in with the other things we do and need to do in everyday life. Unlike classical music, which is a music experience that typically demands one's full attention (e.g., do not let your cell phone go off during a Chopin "Polonaise"—and no talking please!), pop music is very accommodating. This may be one of its strengths: it does not require us to change in any significant way.

In a related sense, the soundtrack function of pop music is valuable yet easily accessible. We all listen to music as we drive. We have our ear buds in place as we walk to the classroom building and take the elevator to the fourth floor. We listen to pop at work, at home, on dates, and just about everywhere else—do you listen to music during class?

Perhaps the most valuable feature of pop music to our everyday lives is the way it adds *motion* to our routines, activities, thoughts, feelings and sense of self. By motion we mean pop music can change the pace of everyday life, the relevance of time, acceleration of activities, and anticipation of future events. The value of Katy Perry's very popular song "Firework" to my everyday life is the case in point—the song is still stuck in my head even though it is several years old! The song is a fast-paced dance song, but you do not have to dance to it. Like "Call me Maybe," you can virtually dance in place to it: tapping your fingers, bobbing your head. "Firework" is very hummable, allowing talent-starved fans like me to take part in the performance, whether in the shower or while writing books. The song is complex, insofar as it contains a string element along with electronic accompaniment. The music, in addition to the story in the lyrics, provides spaces in the song to discover things, even after listening to the song many times. Like the best pop sings, "Firework" provides a great ringtone. It is a ringtone, however, that I can control with a bit of mystery and excitement, disclosing it only to people I want to hear it, never at a faculty meeting at the university, but among people I want to impress that I am a Katy Perry fan. During the 4th of July celebrations on TV since the song came out in 2011, "Firework" not only provided an appropriate title, but raised the level of excitement and pace for events that can be a bit long and, well, boring after a while. In a similar vein, Tia DeNora (2000: 16–17) writes about music in general as a *force*:

> Music is not merely a 'meaningful' or 'communicative' medium. It does more than convey signification through non-verbal means. At the level of daily life, music has power. It is implicated in every dimension of social agency. . . . Music may influence how people compose their bodies, how they conduct themselves, how they experience the passage of time, how they feel—in terms of energy and emotion—about themselves, about others, and about situations.

What about *your* favorite pop song? Recent examples of earworm songs include Bon Jovi's "Livin' on a Prayer," Lady Gaga's "Bad Romance," Rihanna's "Work" (featuring Drake), and Flo Rida's "My House."

The Music Scene: Tunes in the Community

We have just looked at some of the most personal, interactional features of the popular music experience. We will now move down the continuum to see how popular music is experienced at the level of community. Sociologically, we think of *community* in broader terms than commonly thought. A community is a group of people, real or imagined, who offer a sense of belonging to and a source of meaning for the individual (cf. Ferris and Stein 2011). People come together in a community, physically or virtually, on the basis of shared ideas, goals, and/or history. The particular kind of community we will explore is the *music scene*.

The Scene

The social scene is a useful concept for organizing thinking about culture in a community setting. John Irwin (1977) wrote about the scene as an inclusive concept that involves everyone related to a cultural phenomenon (e.g., artists, audiences, management, vendors, and critics); the ecological location of the phenomenon (e.g., districts, clubs, recording studios, and rehearsal rooms); and the products of this interaction (e.g., advertisements, concerts, recordings, and critical reviews). Scenes generally evolve around entertainment-oriented phenomena, such as music, theater, and dance. People typically enter or join a scene for its expressive and direct gratification, not future gratification. Participation is voluntary, and access is generally available to the public, occasionally for the simple price of admission. Irwin's original formulation of the scene used illustrations from 1960s and 1970s California lifestyles, but we will generalize his concept to include a wide range of music communities.

Barry Shank (1994) applied his notion of scene to the production of live music in Austin, Texas. He describes the "6th Street" phenomenon, near to and nurtured by the University of Texas, in terms of its history, cultural roots, and economic context. His focus is on the effects the production of music scenes has on the identities of their participants, an area of interest in this study as well. Pete Peterson and Andy Bennett (2004) extended these ideas in formulating the following definition of a music scene as the geosocial location that provides a stage on which all of the aesthetic, political, social, and cultural features of local music are played out. Of particular relevance to our research is Peterson and Bennett's focus on the way participants use local music scenes to differentiate themselves from others.

It should be clear, on the basis of these general definitions, that there can be many different kinds of music scenes. Peterson and Bennett

(2004) discuss the following music scenes in their book: jazz, blues, rave, karaoke, Britney Spears, salsa, riot grrrls, goth, skatepunk, anarcho-punk, alternative country, and others. We will now discuss a study of a group of Latino music scenes in Houston, Texas. I conducted this study with the help of a group of graduate students at the University of Houston (Kotarba et al. 2009; Nowotny et al. 2010). Each student was responsible for a particular Latino music scene. These scenes included: rock en Español, salsa, Tejano, Norteño, gay Latino dance, mariachi, and professional soccer supporters. We designed the study to be an *ethnography* that involved spending considerable time in the field examining the everyday activities of participants in the scene. We will now describe one of the more recent and most exciting of these scenes: rock en Español. This will give us a chance to illustrate some of the most important sociological features of music scenes in general.

Rock en Español

We can define rock en Español as an international movement to create and perform original rock music in Spanish that incorporates themes relevant to the everyday lives of Latino artists and their audiences (Kotarba 1998: 1). Rock en Español is especially important sociologically to study because it is related to other social processes, such as immigration; it illustrates how third-generation Latinos acquire an identity that integrates their Latino heritage, love for the Spanish language, and awareness and concern for current Latino political issues; and it illustrates the postmodern process of globalization that affects culture in general and Latino culture specifically.

Rock en Español is clearly international, with important production and performance centers in Mexico, Central America, South America, Spain and the United States. The songs are not merely English rock songs translated to Spanish, as was the case not too long ago when many rock en Español bands made a living covering popular rock songs for customers in Latin clubs. Furthermore, the music is not merely the marketing of novelty rock songs sung in Spanish, as was clearly the case with Ritchie Valens' "La Bamba" in the 1950s. And, unlike Valens, who felt it strategic—if not necessary—to shorten his surname from "Valenzuela," *rockeros* feel no need either to disguise their ethnicity or to demean it to make it acceptable to hegemonic Anglo audiences. Instead, *rockeros* celebrate their ethnicity (Kotarba 1998).

Participants in the scene refer to rock en Español as "*el movimiento*," or the movement. This term denotes the scene as a growing, fashionable trend that is gaining momentum and popularity. This term does not denote a political movement, although politics in the United States and in Mexico are relevant themes in the music. The scene can be found in coffee houses, mainstream rock venues, and even restaurants.

Rock en Español in Houston includes many different styles of rock. Whether indie, alternative, progressive, heavy metal, ska, or others, each particular venue tends to integrate several different styles of Latino music. Politics is pervasive in rock en Español. For instance, the music performed by Molotov from Mexico City, Los Prisioneros from Chile, and Libido from Peru consists almost entirely of songs of liberation, and most rock en Español bands include at least a few political songs in their repertoire. The political themes found in rock en Español represent the social class, ethnic self-definitions, and evolving political orientations of the artists and audience members. There is little if any lyrical discourse on personal disadvantage or discrimination. Put simply, the artists and their audiences, who are largely third-generation Americans, feel they are part of American society. With a sense of confidence in their individual and collective welfare as Americans, they focus their attention on political issues in the lives of *other* Latinos. For instance, it is very fashionable for rock en Español bands to perform songs decrying the plight of undocumented Latino/as in the United States.

Perhaps the most eclectic feature of this scene is the DJ's role. Before the bands begin at the Backroom, for example, DJ Raul performs. He operates the expected mixers, turntables, and tape players. This 25-year-old Houston native uses his equipment and DJ skills to display the global context of rock en Español, a globe united more by a common language than perhaps any other feature.

Rock en Español reveals an increasingly fragmented rock and roll audience (Barnes 1988). The audience in the Houston scene is interesting because it is not a traditional rock'n'roll audience. Rock en Español fans are generally young adults (in their twenties), either attending college or working at productive jobs. They are overwhelmingly third-generation Mexican Americans who are competently and proudly bilingual. They are upwardly mobile in their careers. There are two visible types of first-generation Americans in the audience. The first group is young, monolingual, working-class men (late teens and early twenties) who are recent arrivals to the United States. They can be seen at venues on the west side of Houston that ordinarily present Tejano or modern Spanish dance music. They attend the occasional rock en Español concert to meet women. The second group is composed of middle-class men and women from Central and South American countries, who attend rock en Español concerts featuring internationally famous artists.

When attending a rock en Español performance, an observer is immediately struck by the importance of the Spanish language. The performers speak fluent and elegant Spanish, at a time in American history when one would expect young, upwardly mobile Latinos to feel great pressure to become predominantly speakers of English.

Overall, rock en Español fans are much like any other rock'n'roll fans. They have even developed ways to type each other. These types allow members to locate others similar to them in musical tastes, interactional styles, and so forth. *Fresa* ("strawberries") are sophisticated fans, largely female, who prefer the lighter/pop versions of rock en Español. They like large crowds and lots of dancing. They can be seen, for example, at the concerts promoted by Edmundo Perez and Vibraciones Alteradas, which attract the widest range of rock en Español audiences. *Greñudos* ("nappy hairs") are working-class fans, largely male, who prefer loud, hard rock versions of rock en Español.

Scene participants use the scene as a cultural tool in various ways. For instance, although it may appear that rock en Español blocks assimilation through an insistence on Spanish-language use, it in fact functions as an efficient resource for upwardly mobile, third-generation Latinos to become American in the 21st century by creating a music that conforms to the sensibilities of both cultures. Additionally, participation in the rock en Español scene illustrates the current status of Latinos for whom Houston is home, and those for whom Houston is becoming home. Rock en Español functions primarily as a way to become American.

The rediscovery of one's heritage through language, culture, politics, and—perhaps most importantly—one's ethnic links with others is a preferred style of people of the third generation coming to grips with the world of their parents and grandparents. Third-generation Jews and Eastern Europeans are now experiencing the same longing for Israel, shtetl, klezmer, and Poland, Chopin, and Catholicism, respectively. Paradoxically, the *rockeros'* rejection of their parents' Tejano and Norteño music in favor of rock'n'roll is not a rejection of their parents but an effort to share their parents' world on terms that fit with being an American.

Analysis: Sense of Place

Sense of place refers to the ways we engage in a reflexive relationship with the places we occupy. We make places as places make us, our selves, and our identities (Gruenewald 2003). The concept of *sense of place* is important for understanding music scenes two ways. First, the people involved in producing the music try to create a certain sense of place for the audience, musicians, critics and others. The coffee houses that offer rock en Español try to meld the intellectual ambiance of the coffee house with the particularly bright and colorful aura of Latino culture. Second, Latino music, like other ethnically oriented music styles, has a magical way of creating realities. For rock en Español these realities can include the country or origin, America, or *La Raza*. Rock en Español is marked by a contrast between places. Artists and fans alike locate rock en Español on a continuum between cities that are musical and production and marketing centers—Monterey, Mexico, to Houston is a common link. The Latino experience is marked by movement and a clear sense of distance. The global dimension of rock en Español is reflected in the way DJs commonly sample music from Central American folk musicians as well as South American pop bands.

Analysis: Rock en Español as Idioculture

The second concept we will discuss is *idioculture*. Gary Fine (1979: 733) developed the interactionist concept of idioculture in order to stress the importance of studying culture of any kind—including music—in terms of the small groups in which it is lived. For rock en Español, the small groups include the bands, promoters, producers, publicists, fans and performance venues. Within these groups, fundamental features of rock en Español are worked out—for example, the integration of English and Spanish in composing and performing music favored by all possible audiences. One of the most important and common ways that people use the scene and the idioculture that pervades it is the experience of the *becoming of self*. As I note from an existentialist perspective (Kotarba 1984), the self is continuously evolving, changing, and adapting in a continually changing, contemporary social life. The resources for assessing and shaping a sense of self ultimately come from cultural experiences. The becoming of self is analytically noteworthy in our study of Latino music scenes, where many of our respondents are faced with rapidly changing social, political, and cultural environments in which they experience the self. These changes include high mobility (which leaves them with a problematic sense of place), navigation of multiple language communities, and unusual sets of life circumstances that include an ongoing quest for survival among the working class and the development of multiple identities. In light of this, the scene—and the music central to it—becomes an important medium for the "becoming of self" because music is an important cultural resource in Latino communities in general. We examine the ways respondents gravitate toward or even choose styles of Latino music that may vary from the styles with which they grew up or shared with others, as they gravitate toward musical genres that may better fit their many participants.

Conclusion

The argument presented here very likely appears to be self-evident: of course, music takes place in the presence of others. Music is designed to be shared. Nevertheless, sociology goes one step further. The actual experience, feelings and meaning of music is determined and shaped by the social worlds within which it exists. These worlds can be small, such as the inner world of our bodies and our minds within which we privately enjoy music, not alone, but *with ourselves*. Or, these worlds can be large, elaborate, complex, political, cultural, and busily interactive—like a music scene. Isn't music great!?

Activities

(1) Think of your most recent earworm song. When did you first hear it? Did you like it? If so, why? If not, why? When does it pop into your mind . . . under what circumstances? Do you hum or sing along with the song? Do you share the experience of the song with anyone? How do you get it out of your mind?

(2) Briefly describe the idioculture of the group with whom you hang around, listen to music, go to musical performances, etc. What are the group's tastes in music? What music does the group forbid or denounce among its members?

2

The Family

Joseph A. Kotarba

The family is one of the most important institutions in society and one of the most important topics in sociology. The family is what sociologists call a *primary group*, as it is among the groups that are most closely involved in the process of socialization of children to the adult world. We all live in families—whether by birth or by choice, or both—and our family lives are critical determinants of who we are, how we live, how we respond to situations in everyday life, and what our life chances (e.g., careers, health, and incomes) will turn out to be (Williams 1998). Families have cultures of their own, and increasingly borrow from the various cultures available in our contemporary social life to manage their everyday life affairs.

An early yet simple sociological definition of *family* is a "unity of interacting persons" (Burgess 1926: 5). Such a definition escapes, purposefully, criteria of legal or blood ties, and historical and cultural prescriptions. Defining family as a unity of interacting persons also allows us to focus on how families emerge as such unities, as well as on the roles associated with all the persons involved. When we focus on interacting individuals we also coincidentally zero in on the main focus of this type of interaction: socialization. Formally defined, *socialization* is the "continuous process of negotiated interactions out of which selves are created and re-created" (Gecas 1981: 165). Just like families, socialization never stops as we are constantly socialized—though at times more than others—into our society by virtue of sheer exposure to norms, values, roles, ideals beliefs, practices, etc. Families are, however, more central than most other groups to the socialization process because, by virtue of interacting with parental figures, a child acquires early on, and throughout a lifetime, key symbolic resources for the development of a sense of self. More on the self and the life course will be said later.

Not only do family interactions lead to the development of a self-concept, identities, values, beliefs, etc., but family interactions also contribute to nurturance and protection. Yet, even within a family household a child is not immune from external *socialization agents*, like the mass media, and music. Indeed, lay and professional critics have long cast a wary eye to children's culture that has evolved in capitalistic society, largely as a result of the decreasing influence of parental figures, and the growing influence of media as a primary group. We can call these critics *moral entrepreneurs*: individuals who work toward the definition and enforcement of moral values, especially to their liking (Becker 1963). Recently, some of these moral entrepreneurs have been especially critical of materials emanating from the electronic media. These materials include television violence (which allegedly leads to violent behavior among young viewers); music videos (some of which contain sexist or sexually promiscuous messages); and rap music (which is criticized for many reasons, including the promotion of criminal lifestyles and rampant materialism) (cf. Wilson 1989). Popular music has been critiqued most often and most harshly, being designated as a "social problem" ever since its inception over 50 years ago. The purpose of this chapter is to qualify, update, and balance this argument by illustrating the positive as well as potentially negative features of popular music within family settings (Kotarba 1993b, 1994b, and 2013).

Music as a Social Problem?

Everyday life sociologists do not view social problems as objective conditions. *Social problems* are instead seen as outcomes of negotiations over the meaning and moral value of an event, a state of being, or a situation. Thus, stealing from an early definition by Fuller and Myers (1940: 320) we can say "social problems are what people think they are and if conditions are not defined as social problems by the people involved in them, they are not problems to those people." To have a social problem, therefore, one needs first to work in concert with others—and perhaps in spite of those with opposing views—toward defining a subject matter as problematic and worthy of concern. That kind of work is known as *social problem work.* Social problem work is the work of moral entrepreneurs. Let us examine the kind of social problem work done by moral entrepreneurs in relation to family and popular music.

Popular music, as we know it today, has been heavily influenced by the rock'n'roll idiom in terms of styles, the star system, media distribution, criticism, volume, danceability, youthful excitement, power, and energy (Kotarba 2013). This popular music is now fully integrated in North American and European culture. For three generations, popular music has functioned as a primary source of meaning and leisure time activity for young people. Since its inception in the 1950s as rock'n'roll, popular music has been associated with adolescents, and has thus become a medium for both understanding and critiquing the adolescent generation. Some of the earliest sociological observers of modern popular music, namely rock'n'roll, focused on its positive functions for adolescent development.

Another key study, that was mentioned earlier, gives us food for thought on the social problem status of popular music. James Coleman (1961) conducted a now classic survey of adolescent attitudes and behaviors in various northern Illinois communities in 1955. Coleman was interested in studying both the secondary school experience and adolescent status systems. Coleman found that rock'n'roll was the most popular form of music among both boys and girls. Girls liked to listen to records or the radio more than boys, a phenomenon Coleman explains with the observation that boys had a wider variety of activities available to them. Nevertheless, both boys and girls used rock'n'roll to learn prevailing values for gender roles. Girls used romantic ballads and fan club memberships to learn about boys, dating, and so forth. Boys used "less conventional" stars like Elvis Presley to learn about adventure and masculinity. Overall, Coleman (1961: 236) viewed rock'n'roll positively, since "music and dancing provide a context within which (teenagers) may more easily meet and enjoy the company of the opposite sex." Many teenagers were "passionately devoted" to rock'n'roll (Coleman 1961: 315).

These early sociological observations have, however, been lost in a sea of criticism of the impact of popular music on adolescents (Martin and

Seagrave 1992). This criticism began in the 1950s with dramatic efforts to eliminate rock'n'roll. Organized burnings of Elvis Presley records because of their alleged association with sinfulness and sexuality were common in fundamentalist communities. In the 1960s, another coalition of moral entrepreneurs argued that rock'n'roll music was unpatriotic, communistic and the cause of drug abuse. In the 1970s and 1980s, the criticism became organized and sophisticated. Middle-class activist organizations, like the Parents Music Resource Center (PMRC) led by Tipper Gore, opposed much popular music for its alleged deleterious effects on the health of young people. In the 1990s, we find several court cases in which the prosecution and the defense have attempted to legally link popular music, especially heavy metal, goth, and grunge, with suicide and criminal behavior (Hill 1992). Most notably, the infamous Columbine shooting massacre has been linked with the culture of Marilyn Manson fans.

Allan Bloom was among the most influential moral entrepreneurs (1987). He wrote one of the most elegant intellectual attacks on popular music. Bloom, a professor of social thought at the University of Chicago, argued that American universities are in a state of crisis because of their lack of commitment to traditional intellectual standards. Bloom further argued that young people live in a state of intellectual poverty: "Those students do not have books, they most emphatically do have music" (Bloom 1987: 68). Plato, Socrates, and Aristotle all viewed music as a natural mechanism for expressing the passions and preparing the soul for reason. According to Bloom, university students' overwhelming choice in music today, rock music, instead:

> . . . has one appeal only, a barbaric appeal, to sexual desire—not love, not *eros*, but sexual desire undeveloped and untutored . . . young people know that rock has the beat of sexual intercourse . . . Rock music provides premature ecstasy and, is like the drug with which it is allied . . . But, as long as they have the Walkman on, they cannot hear what the great tradition has to say. And, after its prolonged use, when they take it off, they find they are deaf.
>
> (Bloom 1987: 68–81)

Needless to say, criticism of popular music skyrocketed since the inception of hip-hop and rap in the 1980s (see Chapter 7 in this text). In general, many moral entrepreneurs have viewed the varieties of popular music as either a social problem or a major cause of other social problems.

I will propose a contrasting argument. I am not arguing that popular music does not have its shortcomings and undesired effects. My purpose is to show, however, that listening to rock and pop music has multiple consequences, many of which are positive in light of the role they play in the socialization process and solidifying family relationships. The specific positive consequence to be discussed in this chapter is the many different ways music integrates families and serves as a bridge across generations. This generational bridge allows children, adolescents, and adults to share communication, affect, morality, ethics, and meanings. Later, I will refer to this generation bridge as a kind of *role-making*.

One major reason critics focus on the dysfunctions of popular music is because they ignore the increasingly obvious fact that it is pervasive in Western culture (Kotarba 2002b). We now have three generations who have grown up with rock-influenced popular music and for whom pop music is the preeminent form of music. It serves as the soundtrack for everyday life, providing the context for phenomena such as commercials, patriotic events, high-school graduations, political conventions, and so forth. The positive experiences of pop music simply do not attract the attention of observers, such as journalists and social scientists, whose work is structured around the concept of "the problem." In order to understand the pervasiveness of pop music and its positive as well as negative functions, we propose to somewhat ironically reconceptualize it as a feature of children's culture.

Pop Music as a Feature of Children's Culture

One of the central foci of interactionist research in relation to the family has to do with the role that family members play in socializing one another, not only to culture but also to subcultures, like youth culture. And yes, you read correctly: I did say socializing one another. As interactionists, we may view socialization as reciprocal and multi-directional. In other words, we do not believe that the only kind of socialization is done by parents and guardians unto their children, but also by children unto their parents. Think, for example, of the volume of music listening. How many times have your parents hollered at you to turn the volume down? Well, guess what? The minute you become a parent and you catch your kids listening to music one decibel higher than you're willing to tolerate, you will catch yourself telling them exactly what your parents have told you for years: "Turn it down!!!" Then, chances are, as soon as that sentence escapes your lips you will catch yourself thinking: "Goodness, I sound like my mom or dad!" In this particular case your children will socialize you to your role and related responsibilities by way of *altercasting* you, that is, by casting you in a role you are supposed to observe. Just like parents socialize children to adult roles, children socialize parents to adult roles! Altercasting is one of the many ways people make roles in everyday life.

Role is a key sociological concept. A role can be defined as a part an individual plays within a social setting. A part has rights and duties associated with it, as well as a social status. You can think of a role in a play, for example. Within a play a role is performed by an actor, who plays a script regardless of his/her personality, idiosyncrasies, etc. This happens in everyday social settings as well—as you remember from our loud music example. Also within a play we have minor and starring roles, like we do in society. However, there are some differences between theatrical roles and more mundane ones. A director, for example, strictly enforces roles in most theatrical productions, whereas individuals in mundane settings have more power to manipulate their roles and those of others. Within a family we have multiple roles, ranging from parent and relative to child. Roles are also age-graded. A parent is not always just a parent, but the parent of a teenager, or a pre-teen, or a college child, and so forth. Now, with this said, let us return to the music and to how family members socialize one another into specific roles and music-centered age-cultures.

My thinking posits pop music, especially rock'n'roll styles, as a key element of youth culture. The concept *youth culture*, which can be traced at least as far back as the works of Talcott Parsons (1949), is commonly used to denote those everyday practices conducted by adolescents which serve: (1) to identify them as a specific generational cohort, separate from children and adults; (2) as common apparatus for the clarification and resolution of conflict with adults; and (3) to facilitate the process of socialization or transformation into adulthood. Before I go much farther with my argument, let us reflect on the link between music and youth culture.

Conventional thinking isolates certain socio-economic-cultural developments since World War II to construct an explanation for the historically integrated, co-evolution of teenagers and rock and pop (Frith 1981). This theory argues that teenagers were a product of the post-war family. The general cultural portrait of this family is one of middle-class aspiration, if not achievement, suburban orientation, affluence, and consumption. Teenagers in the 1950s comprised not only a demographic bulge in the American population, but also an economic force. Teenagers are viewed as a product of the following formula: allowances + leisure time + energy + parental indulgence. Rock and pop music became an available and useful commodity to sell to teenagers. The music could be readily duplicated, the themes could directly address the angst and adventure of adolescence, and the 45 rpm record could be disposable through the process of the Top 40. As the post-war generation grew into adulthood in the 1960s, they took the previously fun-filled rock'n'roll and turned it into a medium for political dissent and moral/cultural opposition to the generation of their parents. But, as the baby boomers reached full adulthood, they traded in their passion for rock'n'roll for country music and Muzak, leaving succeeding generations of teenagers to consume the hegemonic cultural pablum of formulaic pop and MTV (Grossberg 1992b).

Yet, a powerful cultural experience like growing up with rock'n'roll cannot be simply be left behind by movement through the lifecycle, that is, by adults' socialization into their new, adult roles. One would reasonably expect to find at least some residual effects of rock'n'roll on adult baby boomers. So, my argument is that if rock'n'roll affected the way they dated, mated, and resisted, then one would reasonably expect rock'n'roll music to shape the way they make their roles, that is, the way they work, parent, construct and service relationships, and in other ways accomplish adulthood. Through my findings and focus, I reveal that paradoxically the presence of rock'n'roll in the lives of adults as well as adolescents can be discovered by locating it in the lives and culture of children. How is this possible?

Postmodern theory that I discussed earlier is a useful analytical framework for guiding the search for pop music in the nooks and crannies of everyday life. Postmodern theory reminds us that contemporary social life is mass mediated. Culture is less a reflection of some underlying, formal, firm, structural reality than it is an entity in its own right (Baudrillard 1983). Postmodernism allows the observer to see things not previously visible. For example, postmodernism recently has let us see gender as a critical factor in the process of writing history. Instead of gazing directly at the alleged facts of the past, postmodernism allows historians to focus on the process by which history itself is written. Similarly, postmodern theory lets the sociologist analyze cultural forms like rock'n'roll as free-floating texts with their own styles of production, dissemination, interpretation, and application to everyday life situations. Therefore, at least hypothetically, rock'n'roll is no longer (if it ever was) simply a reflection of the structural positions of adolescents in Western societies, no longer a possession of youth. Rather, cultural items in the postmodern world become available to anyone in society for their individual and subcultural interpretation, modification, and socialization. Rock'n'roll can permeate culture and heavily influence other styles of music and everyday life culture. Another way of saying this is that social roles are less rigid in a postmodern world. We now witness white, middle-class kids listening to and enjoying gangsta rap music. We see Bill Clinton belting out a bluesy-groove on his tenor sax, first at his appearance on Arsenio Hall's television program during the presidential campaign in June 1992 and, later, at one of his inaugural parties. To see popular music as a feature of children's culture and a resource for socialization and for role-making within the contemporary postmodern culture helps us to see its presence in all generations in the family, regardless of birth cohort. The concept *children's culture* denotes those everyday practices (1) used by children to interpret and master everyday life; (2) created, acquired, disseminated, and used by adults to construct and define parental relationships with children; and (3) ordinarily associated with children and childhood yet used by adolescents and adults to interpret, master, or enjoy certain everyday life situations.

What I wish to show and argue in the remainder of this chapter is that pop music serves as a symbolic tool for family members to cross boundaries generally associated with their roles as family members. In other words, music serves as a tool for *role-making* and thus for reciprocal socialization into generational cultures. Thus, for example, children socialize their parents to children's culture through music; parents socialize their children to their own age-specific generational culture. Furthermore, children experience popular music not only as children, but also as a way of learning about their parents' culture, and thus as resource for taking their roles. Similarly, adolescents experience popular music to extend childhood, and adults experience rock'n'roll to relive childhood. I will now provide an inventory specifically of rock'n'roll music as a tool for reciprocal socialization, and for blending experiences across generations. I have chosen rock'n'roll specifically here because it illustrates the historical changes that have taken place in the role that popular music has played in family relations over the past 50 years. I will emphasize those rock'n'roll experiences most taken for granted by professional and lay observers alike, because those experiences function positively as elements of children's culture. I will conclude with a brief discussion of the contribution of this style of analysis to the social scientific literature on rock'n'roll and a reflection on the status of popular music as a social problem.

Adolescents as Children

As mentioned above, standard wisdom on rock'n'roll argues that it has functioned largely to establish adolescence as a distinct stage in the lifecycle. Furthermore, rock'n'roll is seen as a weapon in conflicts between adults and adolescents. The mass media contribute to this overstated, over-romanticized view of rock'n'roll and adolescence. The film *Footloose*, for example, portrays the plausible scenario in which fundamentally conservative, small-town adults view rock'n'roll as an evil influence on their teenagers. Rock'n'roll is portrayed in the film as the gauntlet which forces teenagers to choose between good and evil by choosing their parents or dancing. The rebellious imagery of Elvis Presley portrays a prevailing cultural myth that allies rock'n'roll with youthful rebellion, unbridled sexuality, cross-ethnic intimacy, and a wide range of delinquent activities. The punk and heavy metal imagery has also done this in recent years. These cultural images support an ideological vision of youth culture that overemphasizes the independence, rebellion, and integration of teenagers.

A revisionist or postmodernist reading of this history finds much more diversity within youth culture. For every Elvis Presley fan in the 1950s and 1960s, there was an *American Bandstand* fan. *American Bandstand*, especially in its early days when it was broadcast live after school from Philadelphia, portrayed rock'n'roll as a form of pop music, in much milder and more acceptable (to adults as well as teenagers) ways. The kids on *American Bandstand* were "All-American" kids. They dressed modestly and neatly. They all chewed Beechnut gum, provided by the sponsor of the program. And, above all, they were extremely well-behaved. The boys and girls, especially the "regulars," tended to match up as boyfriends and girlfriends, not as potentially promiscuous dates and mates. *American Bandstand* probably represented most teenagers in American society at that time. And, teenagers could not participate in activities like *American Bandstand* without the approval, if not support, of their parents. After all, someone had to drive the kids to the studio or at least give them permission and money to take the bus there, just as someone had to provide the television and permit watching *American Bandstand* at home.

Parents were and continue to be cautious supporters of their children's popular music activities. There is more of a tendency among parents to manage popular music as though their teenagers are children who need to be nurtured and protected, rather than adolescents who must be controlled, sanctioned, and feared. For example, my research on heavy metal and rap music has found the continuation of three generations of ambiguous parental feelings of cautious support toward these styles of pop music. At a recent Metallica concert in Houston, numerous teenagers indicated that their parents did not approve of heavy metal music for various reasons (e.g., volume, distortion, immorality, and potential affiliation with evil like Satanism). Yet, these same parents carpooled their teenagers and friends to the Astrodome on a school day and, in most cases, bought or provided the money for tickets. One plausible explanation is that, although the parents did not approve of their children's tastes in music, they wanted to do all they could to minimize the risk of anything going wrong that afternoon and to pander, if you will, to their kids. A similar situation exists among African-American and Hispanic parents in terms of the popularity of rap music among their teenagers (Kotarba 1994b). Mass-media-generated images of obstinate if not rebellious youth generally ignore the reflexive relationship between teenagers and their parents. As long as teenagers live at home as legal, financial, and moral dependents—that is, as children—their parents provide the resources for creating musical identities (e.g., allowances, free time, and fashionable hip-hop clothing). Parents then respond to the identities they helped create by controlling, criticizing, sanctioning, and punishing their teenagers for living out their popular music-inspired identities—responding to them as if they were autonomous, responsible adults.

From the teenagers' perspective, popular music is commonly experienced as an extension of childhood experiences. The Summer of Love in 1967 is an historical case in point. Mass-media accounts treat the Monterey Music Festival and Haight-Ashbury as benchmarks in the emergence of the youth counter-culture. The Summer of Love marked the fulfillment of rock'n'roll as an instrument of adolescent rebellion, within a context of heavy drug use, free love, and political liberation—a clash between young people's values and those of their parents. The media argue that the political events of the late 1960s institutionalized and radicalized the unbridled, individualistic and existentially youthful rebellion of the 1950s and early 1960s.

A revisionist, postmodernist re-examination of these events suggests that the innocence of middle-class, postwar, baby-boom childhood served as the primary metaphor for these young people. High status was attributed to the "flower child," whom the counter-culture posited as the innocents who simply rejected the oppression of the adult establishment. Women in the movement with high status were known as "earth mothers," who nurtured themselves and their peers through natural foods, folk arts, and the ability to roll good joints for the group. Whereas the mass media stress the centrality of Jimi Hendrix and Jim Morrison to the music of this period, more child-like songs like Peter, Paul and Mary's "Puff, the Magic Dragon" and Jefferson Airplane's "White

Rabbit" (inspired by *Alice in Wonderland*) were at least as significant. The 1960s generation popularized the use of animation as a format for rock'n'roll (e.g., the Beatles' "Yellow Submarine"). Perhaps the most interesting support for my argument is the way the 1960s generation drifted away from the adult world of commercialized and confined concert halls to the park-like atmosphere of the open-air concert festival, where the audience could play with Frisbees and other toys.

Adolescents have continued to experience rock'n'roll-inspired popular music *qua* children at play. In 1984, Van Halen's "Jump" was a very popular rock song. Many lay and professional critics of hard rock chose to interpret the song as an invitation to youthful suicide. It appeared that the kids did not. At the Van Halen concert held in the Summit in Houston that year, the fans—who appeared to range mostly from 14 to 17 years of age—let out a collective scream when Eddie Van Halen began the song with the now famous keyboard riff. At the chorus, when David Lee Roth shouted "Jump," 18,000 teenagers did just that: they all jumped up together like a bunch of little kids in the playground during recess. Justin Bieber and the various boy bands still in operation elicit similar behavior. At what kind of concert do you jump and scream like a kid?

Even the darker moments of rock'n'roll have their child-like attributes. Some teenage fans experience heavy metal music as a mechanism for managing lingering, childhood anxieties. Metallica's "Enter Sandman" was a popular video on MTV during 1991–1992. As part of an ethnographic study of homeless teenagers, I asked these kids to talk about their music. This particular video was very popular with them. I asked them specifically to interpret a very old, scary looking man in the video. The street kids tended to see the man as a reflection of their own real nightmares, such as physically abusive parents and drug-infested neighborhoods. In a contrasting set of interviews with middle-class kids, I commonly heard them say that the man represented nightmares, but only the inconsequential nightmares children have and ultimately outgrow (Kotarba 1994a).

Children as Children

The pervasive mass media increasingly expose young children to popular music. The Teenage Mutant Ninja Turtle rock concert tour and movie,

Saturday morning cartoon television and, of course, Sesame Street, all focus on pre-adolescent audiences. Nor does it stop there. Several school supply companies are now marketing math and reading enhancement programs based upon popular music icons and idioms, such as the "Reading, Writing, and Rock'n'roll" curriculum.

But beyond simple marketing, popular music informs our general cultural views of children. *Honey, I Blew Up the Kid* was a popular film comedy in 1992. The story line had a bumbling, scientist father mistakenly turning his infant into a colossus. As the child innocently marched down a boulevard in Las Vegas, he grabbed the large, neon-lit guitar from a music club and proceeded to pretend to play a rock'n'roll song (a generic, rockabilly song was actually playing in the film's background). The guitar served as a toy for the baby. The imagery suggested the baby as adolescent, an absurdity that helped establish the overall absurdity of the story.

Young children can grasp rock and pop even when it is not intentionally produced for or marketed to them. When the pop band Los Lobos covered the 1950s hit "La Bamba," it became a hit among elementary school-aged children. Like many rock and pop songs, young kids find its simple lyrics silly and its beat fun to dance around to. As country music broadens its appeal by "crossing over" to rock and pop music audiences, it also creates an audience of children. Hannah Montana's (Miley Cyrus) father, country singer Billy Ray Cyrus, had a hit with "Achy Breaky Heart" in the early 1990s that has remained a fun song for many children over the years.

An interesting development in children-oriented pop music has been the Gorillaz phenomenon. Gorillaz is an animated rock band that is like a cartoon, except that it is appreciated by adolescents and children alike. Its award winning videos are animations, and several of its songs have been radio, iTunes and MTV hits. Fans also have access to play figure toys for all the Gorillaz characters. Gorillaz have remained popular from 2001 to the present. Several mainstream pop or rock music groups have produced and performed music for children, in addition to their work for adult or teenaged audiences. Wilco created the theme song, "Just a Kid," for the soundtrack of the 2004 Spongebob Squarepants movie. Let's not forget the Carpenters' classic "The Rainbow Connection" originally performed by Kermit the Frog.

As is the case with much media programming, children's programming involving rock'n'roll material is increasingly posted on the Internet. One of the more popular programs is "Chu Chu TV Rock'n'roll" on YouTube.

Adults as Children

Adults who grew up on rock'n'roll may want to relive the fun, excitement or meaningfulness of their earlier music experiences. This can happen in two ways. First, adults may simply retrieve the past through nostalgia. In many cities, oldies or "classic rock" music stations remain very popular, catering largely to baby boomer audiences. Rock'n'roll nostalgia also appears in the guise of circa 1950s and 1960s clubs. These clubs are often decorated in a post-war diner motif, offering period food such as meat-loaf sandwiches and malted milk shakes. Parents—and grandparents—and their children dine to piped-in oldies, within an atmosphere resembling that of the *Happy Days* television program.

The baby boomer generation's attempts to maintain the feeling of childhood through rock'n'roll extend into their encounter with adulthood. From the 1980s on, the baby boomer generation has been the strongest supporter of contemporary versions of the rock'n'roll festival. Every large and most medium-sized cities now have what are referred to as "shed venues." These outdoor concert sites—such as Ravinia in Chicago, Wolf Trap in Washington D.C., and the Mitchell Pavilion in Houston—serve as the setting for baby boomers to bring their blankets and their picnic baskets—and often their children and grandchildren—to hear mellow music concerts ranging from Heart and the Dixie Chicks to Josh Groban, Chicago and Earth, Wind and Fire. New Age artists, such as Enya and Enigma, are very popular on the summer shed circuit. New Age, by the way, fits our broad definition of rock'n'roll-inspired popular music, if not as a genre at least as a concept. It is simply mellow, electronically amplified music appreciated by adults who want to extend their rock'n'roll experiences, but who, for physical or status/cultural reasons, choose to give up the volume and anxiety of pure rock'n'roll.

Rock'n'roll nostalgia is interesting because of the types of music chosen by programmers to attract and please their audiences. The music is typically 1950s and early 1960s style rockabilly (e.g., numerous cover bands), 1960s pop rock (e.g., the Beach Boys and Crosby, Stills and Nash), and 1970s and 1980s arena rock (e.g., Aerosmith and Foreigner). The primary audience for oldies programming, however, grew up with the somewhat harsher and harder music of the later 1960s (e.g., psychedelia and anti-war music). Most choose to forsake their own music for the easygoing, fun music of their older siblings who grew up in the 1950s. In the language of postmodernism, the oldies culture is a *simulacrum* (cf. Baudrillard 1983). It never existed in its original state as it is now presented to consumers. Again, adults commonly choose to relive the child-like side of their reconstructed adolescence, not the adult side.

Second, adults may engage in continuous rock'n'roll experiences that are constructed in the present. Many adults, especially males, maintain their original interest in rock'n'roll. They are visible at live concerts of 1970s and 1980s performers who are still "on the road" (e.g., the Rolling Stones, Led Zeppelin, The Who, The Moody Blues, and Bruce Springsteen). They continue to buy recorded music, probably more than teenagers do. An intriguing bonding and gift-giving ritual among middle-class and middle-aged adult males is the exchange of CDs. One fan will purchase a new recording (preferably on compact disc) and proceed to burn high-quality CDs for distribution to neighbors, co-workers, business associates, and others with similar tastes. Van Morrison fans are a good example of this trend.

Yet, adults are supported in their pursuit of rock'n'roll by advances in technology and marketing. Adults can listen to their very specific styles of rock'n'roll, without the commercials intended for young people, through satellite radio. They can also purchase their music of choice from the comfort of their home office via amazon.com and iTunes (Kotarba 2002b).

Adults may also use rock'n'roll as a medium for rebellion. Practical and proven strategies developed during adolescence to enrage parents and other adults are retrieved to use against current opponents, such as wives. I know men who turn up their stereos at home simply to aggravate their wives. In contrast, I have also heard of wives who banish their husbands to the basement or the garage to play their loud music, similar to the shaming banishment of a cigarette-smoking spouse to the backyard (Kotarba 2002b).

Adults as Parents

As we have seen, members of all generations use some version of rock'n'roll music in everyday life. The major argument here, however, is that popular music also serves as a bridge across the generations. Popular music is shared by children, adolescents and adults. As one would easily guess, much of this sharing takes place within the family. Yet, contrary to common wisdom, we will argue that much of this sharing is functional and positive: rock and pop help integrate families.

From the early days of Elvis Presley to current issues surrounding rap music, our mass culture has portrayed rock and pop as a source of tension within families (Martin and Segrave 1993). Whether this conflict is over lyrics or volume, or whatever, the fact is that children could not experience music without the implicit if not explicit support of their parents (as we have seen in the case of *American Bandstand* and Metallica). The cultural pervasiveness of pop music lets it function in many different ways in the family, much like religion or television have. We will now present an inventory of these—largely taken for granted—positive features of pop and rock music.

Mother and Daughter Bonding

Rock and pop have always served as a special commonality between mothers and daughters. They shared Elvis Presley in the 1950s, Frankie Avalon and the Beatles in the 1960s, and Neil Diamond in the 1970s. In the feminist era of the 1980s and 1990s, however, the object of sharing shifted to other women. Madonna is the case in point.

Madonna represented a popular phenomenon that is attractive to both baby boomer mothers and their daughters. Madonna is a multifaceted star whose appeal rests upon lifestyle, clothing style, and attitude as well as musical performance. During the Houston stop on the "Like a Virgin" tour, I interviewed a number of mother–daughter pairs who attended. The pairs typically were dressed alike, in outfits such as black bustiers and short black skirts, with matching jewelry. During the interviews, they talked about Madonna in similar ways and appeared more like friends than family. In virtually all cases, they noted a distinct lack of true appreciation of Madonna by the men in their lives (e.g., fathers, husbands, brothers and boyfriends who may look at Madonna and only see a sex object). And in most cases, the mothers indicated that Madonna served to bring them closer to their daughters.

Gwen Stefani is a pop music phenomenon that is attractive to both mothers and daughters. She is an intriguing singer who makes a fashion statement with an attitude. She is one young, but not too young, performer to whom mothers can relate—unlike marginal artists such as Miley Cyrus (to the super young side) or Amy Winehouse (to the edge). Molly is a 45-year-old account executive who accompanied her 17-year-old daughter to a recent Gwen Stefani concert: "I like Gwen Stefani because she reminds me a lot of a younger Madonna. She sings with style and dresses with style—although I would never wear some of her outfits."

A currently fashionable style of music shared by mothers and daughters are hip-hop performers like Jason Timberlake and Kanye West. Other female pop performers who fit this category include the recent winners of the *American Idol* television competition, Kelly Clarkson and Carrie Underwood. Which mother–daughter duo does not like Katy Perry?

Father and Son Bonding

Fathers and sons also use rock and pop music to bond, but in different ways than one might expect. Fathers who learned to play guitar in the 1960s or 1970s teach their sons how to play. Sharing music is difficult, as the younger generation today continues the traditional ideological belief that their music is better than that of their parents. Fathers and sons are considerably more vehement than women in their allegiance to their generation's music. In recent years, musical bonding has been relatively easy in light of the resurgence of 1970s and 1980s reunion bands on tour. In 2017 alone, the Rolling Stones, U2, the Eagles, Led Zepplin, Bruce Springsteen and the E Street Band, Van Halen, and Tom Petty and the Heartbreakers all played the type of loud, guitar-driven rock'n'roll that many dads and sons can share. Also think of how music-centered video games like Guitar Hero bring together kids and parents to rock out over classic and more recent rock anthems.

During my study of the evolving rave phenomenon in Houston (Kotarba 1993b), I heard one 16-year-old boy exclaim: "I hate my dad's music. He listens to that old shit, like Led Zeppelin." On the other hand, recent trends like rave (i.e., dance parties held in clandestine locations, to the beat of loud synthesized music) display a renaissance in the 1960s counter-culture. Psychedelia is "in," for example, with LSD as the drug of choice and lighting provided by mood lamps. Teenagers see rave as a way of retrieving the romance and simplicity of the 1960s. In a way, these kids accept their parents' claim that growing up in the 1960s was special. Other examples include Deadhead fathers sharing the Grateful Dead experience with their sons, or old school fathers sharing the magic of Tupac Shakur with their hip hop sons.

In my own family, I have had three very special rock'n'roll experiences with my oldest son. When he was five years old, we were driving out to a fishing hole in our old pick-up truck, when the local hard rock radio station began playing songs from the Van Halen album *1984*. This is one of my all-time favorite albums and, in a sociological sense, definitive of the state of rock music in the mid–1980s. When the pounding, driving anthem "Panama" came on the radio, it began with the loud rumble of a motorcycle taking off. Chris proceeded to jump around in his seat to the excitement of what he knew as the "motorcycle song." Like any proud baby boomer father, a tear left my eye when I realized that my son was OK . . . he liked rock'n'roll! When Chris grew up, he eventually attended law school and has been practicing international tax law in California. He has been able to apply his talent for tenor saxophone as a key member of the Law Rocks group his firm sponsors to raise money for charity. At a recent battle of the bands that his firm won, Chris's proud dad ran around the audience cheering on Chris and his band and taking tons of pictures. And, at a recent family reunion in Oregon, I was virtually overcome with pride watching Chris jam with his younger brother, Andrew (on clarinet), for the first time ever. All those years of music lessons paid off.

Family Leisure Activities

Rock'n'roll fits well with the burgeoning family leisure and vacation industry. Family theme parks typically have some attraction related to rock'n'roll, such as the complete mock-up of a 1950s small-town main street in the Six Flags Fiesta Texas theme park in San Antonio. The artists performing at the amphitheaters in the Six Flags parks include REO Speedwagon, the Eagles reunion band, and the latest version of The Who.

Whereas the concept "family entertainment" in the 1950s, 1960s, and 1970s referred to phenomena such as wholesome television programming, Walt Disney films and home games, it increasingly refers to pop today. The rock and pop presented usually addresses a common denominator acceptable to both parents and children, such as rockabilly or pop groups like Cheap Trick, The Cars, and Aerosmith.

Religious Socialization

Rock'n'roll functions as a mechanism for teaching religious beliefs and values in families, whether or not rock'n'roll is compatible with the particular family's religious orientation. For mainstream Protestant denominations, rock'n'roll increasingly fits the liturgy. For example, when Amy Grant played a concert in Houston several years back as part of her *Angels* album tour, her music was loud and fast (e.g., a seven-piece band with double drummers and double lead guitars). Parents accompanying their children to the concert peppered the audience. One father, in his thirties, brought his wife and 10-year-old daughter to the concert (which he learned about at his Lutheran church). When I asked him about the compatibility of Christian rock music with Christianity, he stated:

> We love Amy Grant. She is married and tours with her husband, which is not the case with regular rock stars. Her songs are full of Christian messages. Any way you can get the message of Christ to your kids is OK with us.

The variety of Christian rock styles is growing. A particularly intriguing version is Christian heavy metal (Kotarba 1991). One rock club in Houston routinely books Christian heavy metal bands on Sunday evenings. One evening, they booked a Christian speed metal band, White Cross, that played extremely loud and fast music about Christ. I talked to several parents who accompanied their children to the concert. The parents were very polite, clean-cut, middle-class, Southern Baptists surrounded by a sea of punk rockers and head bangers. They very much seemed like the parents of the *American Bandstand* generation discussed above. They created the opportunity for their teenagers to attend the concert by carpooling them and their friends in from the suburbs. They hoped that the message emanating from the long-haired rockers was indeed Christian, but they wanted to see for themselves to make sure that Satan was not infiltrating the event.

Certain Christian denominations view rock'n'roll of any kind as evil, whether under the guise of Christian rock or not. Parents in this faith focus their attention on rock'n'roll as a way of establishing moral boundaries for their children. For example, a very popular video among conservative youth ministers is called *Rock'n'roll: A Search for God*. The producer, Eric Holmberg, displays numerous rock album covers to illustrate his argument that rockers, especially heavy metal rockers, advertently or inadvertently proclaim satanic messages. For fundamentalist parents, rock'n'roll functions as a convenient and accessible way of teaching their children clearly and directly that Satan and evil are present in today's world and can take various attractive forms.

Moral Socialization

Rock'n'roll, in particular, functions as a mechanism for articulating general moral rules and values for particular groups. Although the Parents Music Resource Center was broadly based politically in the 1980s, it supports the religious right's concern for the threat rock'n'roll poses to the moral, physical and psychological health of their children (Weinstein 1991). For middle-class and upwardly mobile African-American parents, rap music clarifies the issue of gender abuse within their community (cf. Jay-Z 2011). In a more institutionalized sense, rap music is becoming the medium of choice among inner-city teachers for transmitting emerging moral messages. For example, rap music is now allowed in the Houston public schools for student talent shows. The local news regularly highlights school programs in which students use rap idioms to convey anti-smoking and anti-drug messages.

Historical Socialization

Families use rock'n'roll to relay a sense of history to their children. For example, every year on Memorial Day in Houston, various veterans' organizations sponsor a concert and rally at the Miller Outdoor Theater. Most of the veterans present fought in Vietnam, the first war for which rock'n'roll served as the musical soundtrack. Most of the veterans bring their children to the event. Among all the messages and information available to the kids is the type of music popular during the war. A popular band regularly invited to perform is The Guess Who, whose "American Woman" was a major anthem among soldiers. I have observed fathers explaining the song to their teenaged and pre-teenaged children, who would otherwise view it as just another of dad's old songs. The fathers explain that the song had different meanings for different men. For some, it reminded them of girlfriends back home who broke up with them during the war. For others, the title was enough to remind them of their faithful girlfriends back home. For still others, the song reminded them of the occasions when they were sitting around camp, smoking pot and listening to any American rock'n'roll songs available as a way of bridging the many miles between them and home. Today, with a distinct absence of Vietnam-era anti-war bands performing, certain country bands—for example, the Zac Brown Band—carry the patriotic torch. In Houston, Juneteenth and Cinco de Mayo activities function much the same way for African-American and Latino families, respectively.

The current "green" environmental movement is a contemporary illustration of moral socialization. The audiences for Live Earth in 2007 to Lightening in a Bottle in 2017 were—and are—very intergenerational and, ironically, created a situation in which children may have sent environmental messages to parents.

The Social Construction of Evil in Popular Music

As I mentioned above, sociologists of everyday life focus on the social mechanisms by which agents of social control construct or define what is evil and what is not. There are two noteworthy examples of the social construction of evil in popular music in general, and rock'n'roll in particular.

The first example is a telephone call made from a group of concerned parents to the editor of the *Houston Chronicle* back in 1993. The leader of the group was concerned about the way rave parties were allowing under-aged teenagers to attend and obtain dance drugs (e.g., Ketamine, LSD, and Ecstasy). The youngsters would either be able to purchase the drugs on the dance floor or simply be given drugs by older predators in the crowd. The editor called the Texas Commission on Alcohol and Alcohol Abuse for help, and TCADA called me, who they knew as a sociologist who studied music and youth subcultures. I enlisted the help of a group of graduate students to conduct a study of the emerging rave phenomenon (Kotarba 1993a). I soon learned that the parents' "group" that first voiced concerns over rave consisted of one parent, a father from Kingwood, Texas.

The second example occurred in 2010. The producers of *Sesame Street* on PBS broadcast a music video in which Katy Perry and Elmo chased each other around. They were clearly playing a game like tag or Gotcha! Katy Perry was dressed like, well, Katy Perry: Crayola colored dress, perhaps a bit too short on top and on the bottom, but not otherwise revealing. PBS pulled the video in reaction to objections raised by parents that Katy Perry was not a good role model for their very young children. In a conversation with PBS staff in Austin, Texas, I was told that there were perhaps two or at most three parents who complained about the KP video.

Discussion and Conclusion

What do we make of the two examples above of social/music control? Were the parents wrong in demonstrating concern for their children's welfare? Probably not—that's what parents are for! Did the parents overreact? In the case of the rave parties, maybe not. Recreational drugs and underage kids are not a healthy mix. We can commonsensically ask the following rhetorical, if conservative, question: do the parents have the primary responsibility to make sure their 14-year-old daughters are at home that late in the evening? That moral or even legal judgment is really not within the purview of a sociological analysis. The one, clear sociological observation is that the nature of the "agent of social/music" control in our society has changed. Parents, like the rest of us, have powerful access to the mass media. Parents can communicate their concerns publicly through Facebook, Twitter, and regular email, in addition to the traditional letter to the editor or mayor. Thus, the extent or pervasiveness of a parental concern over popular music is less clear than would be the case, again, with a traditional medium such as a signed petition.

We have only touched upon the many ways popular music in general and rock'n'roll specifically works positively for people, as a medium of culture and means to family integration. There are obvious limitations to this analysis. The illustrations certainly do not represent all popular music experiences in a systematically sampled way. The generalizations presented here are clearly based primarily upon the experiences of white, middle-class rock'n'roll fans and their families, yet the principles of family culture use discussed here apply across subpopulations in Western societies.

While our empirical focus has been on the family, we have also touched on another important domain of sociological investigation: the study of social problems. The intellectual field of social problems study is predicated on the assumption that social phenomena can be denoted as "problems" because they somehow differ from the norm, the reasonably expected, or simply other phenomena. But when a phenomenon is pervasive throughout or endemic to a group, it is difficult to call it a problem. Rock and pop music are a social problem only if one assumes that it is limited to a portion of the population (teenagers) who use it to harm themselves or others. However, rock and pop "belong" to all portions of the population.

These findings are evidence for the argument that the true "cause" of social problems associated with children and adolescents lie beyond the music they choose to listen to. On the one hand, music simply serves too many positive, integrative functions at the family and individual level for its audiences to be considered a "problem" in its own right. On the other hand, these findings strongly suggest that we look deeper for the roots of children's and adolescents' problems, such as the structure of the family itself. Rock'n'roll is all too often merely a convenient scapegoat for these problems.

Activities

(1) What was the earliest experience you had with rock'n'roll/pop music? Did you know the song title, the lyrics, and/or the

performer? Describe the situation in detail. For example, with whom did you listen or share the song? What role did your parent(s) or other adults play in this experience? Did you dance to the song?

(2) In what part of your family life did or does music play? Gifts? Family activities? Church? Did you argue with your parents and/or siblings over music?

3

THE SELF, IDENTITY, AND THE LIFE COURSE

JOSEPH A. KOTARBA

The notion of *life course* is important to a particularly sociological perspective on people and their behavior. In general, sociologists believe that people are only partially shaped by their biological and genetic capacities. Instead, our self and how we approach social life are constantly shaped by events and experiences that happen all the way through life. We change constantly, if not occasionally dramatically. The concept of *life course* holds that socialization is a lifelong process (Furstenberg 1991). Accordingly, our appreciation for and use of popular music is a dynamic process that does not end when we become adults.

Social scientists have traditionally focused on popular music experiences among young audiences. The focus has been on pop music specifically as a feature of adolescent culture and, therefore, of teenagers' everyday life experiences. As Simon Frith (1981) noted in his famous sociological text, *Sound Effects*, rock music has been fundamental to the experience of growing up ever since the end of World War II. Similarly, sociologists have demonstrated increasing interest over the years in rock and pop music as an indicator of dramatic changes occurring in the social and cultural worlds of teenagers. We can trace this interest at least as far back as David Riesman's (1950) classic examination of the emergence of the *other-directed* personality in post-WWII American society. The new middle class was marked by a weakening of parental control, a preoccupation with consumption, and a shift in the meaning of leisure resulting in the masses—the lonely crowd—desperately trying to have fun. The time was ripe for the emergence of a youth culture defined by what have come to be known as pop and rock music.

The popular music industry that drives rock and pop continues to expand dramatically—beyond multi-billion dollar annual sales, globalization, CDs, smartphones, Beats, Spotify, iTunes, YouTube, bluetooth and wifi speakers, and other technological advances, and even the resurgence of vinyl! Yet, lay and scholarly observers have generally ignored or underplayed an important element of social and cultural change: rock'n'roll and rock and pop are no longer limited to, nor solely the possession of, teenagers. The original generation of rock fans—the baby boomers—are now parents and, in some cases, grandparents. The music and musical culture they grew up with has stayed with them, becoming the soundtrack of global cultures.

The purpose of this chapter is to survey the many ways rock and pop pervades the everyday lives of adults in North American society. In commonsense terms, we examine what happened to the first, complete generation of rock fans: the baby boomer generation now in late middle age. We argue that rock-oriented pop music continues to serve as a critical meaning resource for its adult fans as they continuously experience the becoming of self throughout life. To better understand how music works throughout the life course we begin by discussing in some depth the concepts of self, identity, and the life course itself.

Self, Identity, and the Life Course

The *self* is probably the most important concept for sociologists of everyday life. Yet, it is often used improperly or confused with the concept of identity. Before we proceed to examine the empirical material unique to this chapter, let us discuss in some detail these important ideas. And let us begin with the self. The self, as the word itself suggests, is a reflexive object. Think, for example, of its common use in expressions like: "I hurt myself." When you hurt yourself you direct attention (the realization that you are in pain) to you as an object. In doing so you are both a subject (knower and feeler, in this case) of your action, and an object (known and felt). You are a subject in the sense that you are the one who is mustering attention and directing focus, and you are an object in the sense that such attention is focused on you. In doing so, George Herbert Mead (1934) tells us, you are *minding* yourself. It is by minding that indeed we create a sense of self. We mind our self into being by, for example, engaging in internal conversations (e.g., thinking about oneself), monitoring our sensations, experiencing feelings about the self, and so forth. The "doing" of all these things is the "doing" of the self. The self, in other words, is a constant process, a way of "self-ing" ourselves into being as a result of our actions as a subject (the "*I*"), and as an object of our actions (the "*me*").

Song lyrics are great for illustrating the components of the self as identified by Mead. Consider the following made-up (and totally mind-blowing) pop song lyrics:

> I love you girl.
> You mean the world to me.
> You make me feel like a squirrel.
> That's weird and so is me.

In these odd lyrics, the subject part of the self (the "I") is obvious. The subject is the person writing the lyrics and singing to his fictitious "girl." Think of the "I" part of the self as the lyricist. The second part of the self, the object, is the "me." The lyricist is writing about his self as if it were a thing, something separate from him. In the English language, sometimes we refer to ourselves as "me" and other times as "I." In the lyric above, the use of "me" is grammatically incorrect, but it rhymes and, more importantly, that "me" is the "me" part of the self as an object. Of course, the lyrics are crazy, but not the work of a schizophrenic. The sociological view of self is that it is simultaneously a "subject" and an "object," or the lyricist and the lyric. The final part of the self, the one that *minds* the self, is what Mead referred to as the *generalized other*. This term refers to how we think of ourselves from the perspectives of others or, more appropriately, how we imagine others see us. Perhaps these lyrics are weird because the lyricist's generalized other is strange—it has been shaped by life in the deep South—but they are not entirely unusual in the realm of popular music. Singing about love and girls and even being lyrically silly are generally approved-of ways to write pop songs.

The generalized other is the most social part of the self, telling the "I" how to think about the "me" based on how the self imagines the point of views of others. Popular music heavily influences many people's generalized other, and in this way it exerts a sizable influence over our selves.

Identity refers to something different from self. An identity is a typification of self, either imposed upon an individual by others (*social identity*) or adopted by self (*personal identity*). For example, if others view me as a punk rocker and treat me as such my social identity is that, indeed, of a punk rocker. Others could treat me as a punk rocker in spite of the fact that I carefully distinguish my identity amongst available punk styles (and identities) and identify myself as a hardcore punk rocker (my personal identity). An identity can be more or less stable across social settings. For example, my youth friends may have always identified me as punk rocker for all my life, but if one evening I were to attend a grindcore concert and enjoy it I may very well, at least for that evening, identify myself as (and be identified by other concert attendants as) a grindcore fan. We can refer to these momentary identities that we take up and shed on a regular daily basis as *situational iden-tities.* So for example, despite our more enduring social and personal identities, on any given day we can have situational identities such as bus-rider, grocery-shopper, pedestrian, etc.

The discussion above highlights the processual nature of self and identity. Think of the self as a molecule of water. A molecule of water is made by two components: hydrogen and oxygen. A self is similarly the result of the combination of two components: the "I" and the "me." A molecule of water is always in flux throughout its life. When suspended amidst clouds and then falling from the sky it assumes the identity of a raindrop; when frozen up high in the mountains it has the identity of an ice crystal; when melting and flowing down the mountain it has the identity of river water; and when merging with the ocean it assumes the identity of sea water. Now, of course a molecule of water has no reflexivity (and no personal identity), but from this example you can at least see that its life is a never-ending process and that throughout this process it assumes different identities in light of the settings it inhabits. The same can be said of the self: throughout the life course an individual assumes different social, situational (and also personal) identities as a result of the fluidity of life and the social "pools" with which we come into contact. We now turn to the concept of life course.

A *life course* is a patterned temporal trajectory of individual experiences. Some scholars, notably social psychologists and psychologists, like to identify objective and universal stages typical for all individuals. Interactionists and constructionists are instead less interested in determining fixed stages and more in examining how individuals assign meanings to their progression through life. In the words of Clair, Karp, and Yoels (1993: vii), their focus is more precisely on "how persons occupying different locations in social space interpret and respond to repeated social messages about the meanings of age." Reflecting on the contribution of these authors, in an influential overview of the concept and research on the life course, sociologists Holstein and Gubrium (2003: 836) write that:

> (1) age and life stages, like any temporal categories, can carry multiple meanings; (2) those meanings emerge from social interaction; and (3) the meanings of age and the course of life are refined and reinterpreted in light of the prevailing social definitions of situations that bear on experience through time.

As you can obviously see, the life course is therefore about the becoming of self: the fluid process through which we acquire new and diverse roles, social identities, and personal identities. Music, we argue, provides a set of symbolic resources for the definition and reinterpretation of these identities: through music we continuously "self" ourselves into being. But, how, precisely, do we do so?

The Becoming of Self

The existential sociological concept of *the becoming of self* is a useful guide in seeking the sociological answers to this question. Existential social thought is heavily derived from, and very close in nature to, symbolic interactionism. A difference is that existential sociology views the self: "as a unique experience of being within the context of contemporary social conditions, an experience most notably marked by an incessant sense of becoming and an active participation in social change" (Kotarba 1984: 223). The incessant sense of becoming is a reflection of the contemporary need for the individual to be prepared to reshape meanings of self in response to the dictates of a rapidly changing social world. The well-integrated self accepts the reality of change and welcomes new ideas, new experiences, and reformulations of old ideas and experiences that help one adapt to change (Kotarba 1987).

The idea of *becoming* is one of the most important ideas in existentialist thought across disciplines because it places responsibility for fashioning a self on the individual. Whereas Jean-Paul Sartre (1945) argued dramatically that we are condemned to be free and to choose who we are to become, Maurice Merleau-Ponty (1962) insisted more moderately and sociologically that we must ground our becoming-of-self in the real world in order to cope effectively with it. Thus, an effective strategy for becoming begins with a foundation of personal experience and the constraints of social structure, while evolving in terms of the resources presented by culture. We argue that middle-aged North Americans work with a self, built to some degree on the meanings provided by the rock'n'roll idiom, and they continue to nurture the self within the ever-present cultural context of rock'n'roll.

Jack Douglas (1984) notes that there are, in fact, two analytically distinct stages of becoming-of-self with which the modern actor contends. The first is *the need to eliminate or control threats to the basic security of self* (e.g., meaninglessness, isolation from others, shame, death). Although existential psychotherapists like Irvin Yalom (1978) argue that chronic insecurity—or neurosis—is pervasive in our society, Douglas argues sociologically that it is more common for the sense of security to vary biographically, situationally, and developmentally. In general, adults try to shape everyday life experiences in order to avoid basic threats to the self. Basic threats to the adult self in our society would include divorce, the loss of a job, the loss of children (e.g., the empty nest syndrome), illness, disability, and poverty. The second stage of becoming-of-self involves *growth of the sense of self*. Growth occurs when the individual seeks new experiences as media for innovative and potentially rewarding meanings for self (Kotarba 1987). It is through growth, or self-actualization as it is often referred to today, that life becomes rich, rewarding, full, and manageable.

Adults who maintain interest in and commitment to the rock'n'roll idiom do so for two reasons. On the one hand, keeping up with the music and the culture that were so important to them when growing up helps them maintain *continuity* with the past and thus solidifies the sense of self security. On the other hand, working hard to keep rock'n'roll current and relevant to their lives helps adults grow as parents, as spiritual beings, and as friends. Joanna Davis (2006), however, presents a different view of aging and rock'n'roll in her research on "growing up punk." Davis's research reveals how certain members of the punk scene age gracefully, but in other cases, an "old punk" is an oxymoron. A critical point about the self is illustrated by her documentation of how the punk "scene" rejects or accepts aging, which is that the self is inherently social. We all require, to a greater or lesser extent, validation and input from others to determine who we are and are allowed to be.

The concept of the *existential self* tells us that the experience of individuality is never complete; the answer to the question "who am I?" is always tentative. In the postmodern world, the mass media—including popular music— serve as increasingly important audiences to the self. The self is situational and mutable (Zurcher 1977). One can be various selves as the fast-paced, ever-changing, uncertain postmodern society requires. In the remainder of this chapter, I will provide a working inventory of the various ways adults self themselves into being. These are experiences of self that are common in everyday life, closely related to roles and social and personal identities, and predicated by or embedded in rock'n'roll culture.

The E-Self

As the rock'n'roll fan ages, many of the attractive aspects of the earlier self become increasingly difficult to maintain. There is a tendency for youthfulness, energy, risk-taking, appearance, sensuality, and other aspects of the adolescent or young-adult self to become either less available or less desirable. Our culture does, however, provide the resource of an image of social identity that resonates with the affluence of middle age, as well as with the continuing need to establish status/self-esteem. The *e-self* (or electronic self) refers to an experience of individuality in which the affective and philosophical self-resources of rock'n'roll media are displaced or at least supplemented by the increasingly technological and commodified aspects of the media. For the middle-aged fan, what you play your music on can be at least as, if not more, important than what you play.

Middle age results in less concert attendance and more music experience in the comfort of home, automobile and, for the energetic, on the jogging trail. A quick reading of *Wired* magazine (2016 issue), which is geared toward the affluent and technologically-interested middle-aged person, discloses the strategy of marketing rock'n'roll to its audience. There are advertisements for sophisticated cell phones that allow the consumer to "keep rockin' with your favorite iTunes." The promotion for "THEWIREDAUCTION," on eBay that benefits a children's foundation, includes a "limited edition series precision bass guitar signed by Sting" among other high-end music items. The advertisement for the Bose Music intelligent playback system highlights "its unique ability to listen to the music you play and learn your preferences based on your likes, dislikes, or even your mood at the moment." In fact, elaborate automobile sound systems are very fashionable albeit expensive today. There are numerous advertisements for satellite radio systems and the luxury SUVs that include them as standard equipment.

Such marketing sometimes resonates with the adults it targets. George is a 51-year-old, Anglo electrical engineer who has just purchased a Lexus with satellite radio. He sees two benefits of his musical purchase: "I don't have to mess with CDs or radio anymore. I get to play only the music I like to hear . . . There are channels dedicated just to '80s heavy metal. Cool." George has effectively eliminated the hassles of concert crowds and debates over musical tastes with peers. High technology puts his e-self in control of his musical environment. George can experience his music with the aura of cultural independence that affluent adults seek.

The Self as Lover

A significant aspect of the continued popularity of rock-inspired pop music is its use in helping make sense of others, especially in intimate relationships. Numerous observers have correctly identified the sexist messages present in rock (e.g., McRobbie 1978). A postmodern existentialist view, however, highlights the fact that rock'n'roll music displays an open-ended horizon of meaning for its audiences. What a pop music performance means is largely a function of the situation in which it is experienced and the particular self-needs of the audience member (Kotarba, 2013). As time passes, the audience matures, biographies evolve, men's and women's relationships change, popular music commodities come and go, cultural themes available through the media advance, and we would expect the actual lived experience of popular music to change.

A particular self-need of the adult pop music fan is to interpret romantic phenomena. This can happen two ways. First, fans can (re)interpret music to fit romantic needs. In my autobiographical writing as a rock'n'roll fan (Kotarba 1997), I described the way I used Dion's 1961 classic song "Runaround Sue" to account for the way a girl back in eighth grade rejected my very timid show of affection in favor of a more aggressive, older teen-aged boy. Like the Sue in the song, my Sue was a *bad* girl and I was merely a victim of her wiles. Twenty-five years later, at a class reunion, I used the same song as the basis for a conversation with the same Sue. We laughed about the silliness of those elementary school days, but my heartbeat jumped a bit when she admitted that she really did like me back then but was too shy to tell me!

Second, fans can gravitate towards music that can be perceived as romantic. Autobiographically, "Smokey" Robinson and the Miracles' "Tracks of My Tears" was a constant play on my 45 rpm record player in 1965, when it put comforting words to yet another heartbreak in my life. I would not have been drawn as much to this new record if I did not have a personal need for its plaintive prose. In general, fans gravitate towards music that fits their everyday life concerns.

Baby boomers use pop music materials for a range of romantic purposes. They use music (e.g., CDs and DVDs) as birthday and Christmas gifts. They use music to help them appreciate other media such as films and television. One of the more interesting romantic uses of rock'n'roll music is the *our-song* phenomenon, in which a musical performance serves to define a relationship. Our-songs are clearly not limited to baby boomers. Pre-adolescents, for example, commonly choose songs that remind them of a boy or a girl, but are often too shy to disclose this fact to the other, as we have seen!

For mature fans, the our-song can function at least two ways. First, it provides meaning for benchmark events in the relationship. Shirley is a 52-year-old, Latina sales person who is a big Los Lobos fan. She builds anniversary activities around one particular song she and her husband both enjoy:

> We fell in love with 'Nadie Quiere Sufrir' at a Los Lobos concert when we were still just dating. It is a very pretty waltz that actually comes from an Edith Piaf song . . . I make sure the CD (with the song) is in the car when we drive to (our anniversary) dinner. He bought me the CD for our anniversary a few years ago . . . Oh, I guess it just makes us feel young again.

Second, the our-song can help the person feel like a lover. As couples age and perhaps find themselves feeling and acting less romantically over time, the our-song can function as a quick emotional fix. Rob is a 58-year-old, Anglo executive who has maintained a serious relationship with Tommy, a 47-year-old artist, for about 15 years. Their song is Queen's "Bohemian Rhapsody":

> There will never be another Freddie Mercury. It was really special to have our own gay rock icon . . . I surprise Tommy by playing 'Bohemian Rhapsody' now and again. Tommy is still thrilled that I remember it . . . Why? Well, it's one of those songs that make you feel good, to feel that you can be gay and a rocker at the same time . . . I like doing things for Tommy. We are just so busy with our careers, 'makes us feel like an old married couple!

Needless to say, the popular music industry is aware of the market for rock'n'roll goods and services. One of the more recent examples is the advent and growing popularity of rock'n'roll cruises. Carnival Cruise Lines offers the following "Rock'n'Roll Cruise Vacation" in an on-line advertisement:

> What could be cooler than a seven-day Caribbean cruise with legendary big-hair 1970s/80s rockers Journey, Styx and REO

> Speedwagon? Well . . . we'll reserve comment. But, if your idea of a totally awesome vacation is a seven-day cruise with legendary big-hair 1970s/80s rockers Journey, Styx and REO Speedwagon, you're in luck.

Interactionist sociologists—as you can glean from the above—are not only interested in what individuals experience throughout life course, but also in "how the life course is interpretively constructed and used by persons to make sense of experience" (Holstein and Gubrium 2003: 841). In order to construct meaning, Holstein and Gubrium (2003) tell us, we utilize *narrative resources*: tools for building, shaping and re-shaping, and making sense of the becoming of self. Music is a narrative resource. By employing narrative resources and constructing a sense of self endowed with a feeling of continuity and growth we engage *in biographical work* (Holstein and Gubrium 2003).

The Self as Parent and Grandparent

As we have shown in Chapter 1, the impact of popular music on one's self as parent is possibly the most pervasive aspect of the personal rock'n'roll biography. Baby boomers grew up experiencing music as a major medium for communicating with parents. Managing music illustrates one's skill at parenting, as well as one's style of parenting.

There is a greater tendency among parents—apparently across ethnic groups and social classes—to manage pop music as though their teenagers are children who need to be nurtured and protected rather than as adolescents who must be controlled, sanctioned, and feared. Mass-media-generated images of obstinate if not rebellious youth generally ignore the reflexive relationship between teenagers and their parents. Parents then respond to the identities they helped create by controlling, criticizing, sanctioning, and punishing their teenagers for living out their rock'n'roll-inspired identities—responding to them as if they were autonomous, responsible adults.

This *congenial* style of being a parent appears to extend into the next cycle of life: that of grandparent. As Mogelonsky (1996) and other family researchers have noted, grandparents have a tendency to interact with their grandchildren in ways very similar to the ways they interacted with their own children. If pop music was an important feature to them as parents, it will be the same as grandparents. What changes, of course, are styles of music, music technology and the moral context of pop music. Frank is a 61-year-old retired public school teacher who has two grandchildren: 17-year-old Bobby and 11-year-old Denise. Bobby has been easy to please with musical gifts and experiences. Just as he did with his own son 30 years ago or so, Frank has given Bobby birthday and Christmas gifts of music, but according to current styles: iTune gift cards and tickets to a Radiohead concert. However, Frank will not share musical experiences with Bobby because: "Bobby listens to a lot of rap, and I just cannot stand that stuff."

Denise presented other kinds of difficulties. In addition to a Carrie Underwood CD she wanted for Christmas, she begged Frank for tickets to see Miley Cyrus in concert at NRG Stadium in Houston. Her father told her that the family could not afford tickets, so she strategically asked her doting grandpa. Frank's response was "how can I tell my little girl no," but the task of actually getting tickets was monumental:

> I heard that all tickets sold out in about ten minutes. I went on-line and couldn't get in for almost a half-hour. I actually drove down to the NRG box office later that morning, and it was the same story. I then went on-line to eBay and paid $400 for two (nose) bleeds. . . . You're old enough to remember when concert tickets were ten bucks at the door. Man, how things have changed, but I promised her.

The Self as Believer

As we have seen, baby boomers' early experiences of music were complex. They learned to love, play, and dissent through the idiom. They also experienced spirituality (Seay and Neely, 1986). In adulthood, the spiritual dimension of rock'n'roll continues to impact the self as believer. The lyrics and mood created by such performers as Van Morrison (*Astral Weeks*) and U2 (*The Joshua Tree*) provide baby boomers with non-sectarian yet religion-friendly soundtracks. New Age Music, such as that produced by Windham Hill, functions the same way.

Rock and pop music has also had direct influence on spirituality by helping shape organized religious ceremonies and rituals to fit the tastes of the adult member. For example, Catholic baby boomers grew up at a time when the Church, largely as a result of the Vatican II Council, encouraged parishes to make use of local musical styles and talent. Witness the emergence of the rock'n'roll mass in the 1970s. Today, the very popular Protestant style of praise and worship music, with its electronic keyboard and modern melodies, is infiltrating Catholic liturgy.

An integral segment of the self-as-parent is moral, if not religious or spiritual, socialization. Rock and pop function as mechanisms for teaching religious beliefs and values in many families, whether or not rock is compatible with the particular family's religious orientation. For mainstream Protestant denominations, rock'n'roll increasingly fits with the faith. Take for example the success of Jars of Clay—a soft rock Christian band—or Sufjan Stevens, a more "indie" but equally spiritual musical act. In these cases too we can see how music functions as a resource selected by fans and made meaningful in their building of a sense of identity.

The Self as Political Actor

Rock'n'roll music has specifically served as a soundtrack for the situations in which baby boomers perceive themselves as political actors. Rock'n'roll can add both atmosphere and meaning to political events. For example, New York punk poet and singer Patti Smith performed a concert in Houston on March 28, 2003—right at the beginning of the war in Iraq. The concert was originally scheduled simply to support an exhibit of her art displayed at the Museum of Contemporary Arts. The audience was overwhelmingly middle-aged people, dressed up in their jeans and long (hippie) skirts. Through conversations with numerous fans after the concert, it was clear that they *enjoyed* the concert. Patti Smith's poetry and songs (e.g., "People Have the Power") gave them a relevant and identifiable venue for sharing their overwhelmingly negative *feelings* about the war.

Young people today have not responded dramatically to, nor made sense of, war through popular music. Although the United States has been at war constantly over the past ten years or so, there has been relatively little anti-war music produced. During the Iraqi War mentioned above, there were relatively few songs against the war focused on young people's concerns and styles. These songs were in fact buried in albums and not performed for mass audiences, in contrast to anti-war songs during the Vietnam war that were routinely performed for large audiences such as Woodstock. Two examples are "Bagdad," by The Offspring, and "March of Death," by Zack de la Rocha (San Roman 2013). There are no memorable songs related to current wars in Afghanistan, Syria, Iraq, Yemen, etc.

Numerous political observers have noted that individuals are most likely to engage in political activities, cultural or otherwise, when the issue at hand impacts them directly. In addition, the anti-war activities of the 1960s are very difficult to replicate, given the commercialization of collective events, especially those including popular music acts (Patch 2013). Yet, there is a bit of resurgence in the performance and production of political critical popular music. The recent hotly contested presidential campaign in the U.S. evoked a strong political response by young people, as reflected in the political involvement of artists. It seemed like most popular performers and bands either spoke out against Donald Trump (e.g., Green Day), or spoke in favor of Hillary Clinton (e.g., Katy Perry). A number of artists reacted negatively to Donald Trump's inclusion of their music into his campaign. Most bands invited to perform at President Trump's inauguration refused, and the list of actual performers was short and led by country singer Toby Keith. Music again became a soundtrack framework for voicing one's sense of self in terms of personal concerns—not war since it has become drone and volunteer army driven—but immigration, and civil rights.

In summary, rock'n'roll and popular music is vital to maintaining a sense of the political self because many baby boomers learned their politics—and how to be and feel political—from Country Joe McDonald (and the Fish), Jimi Hendrix, and the Grateful Dead. Younger audiences obtain political meanings for self from rappers (e.g., Kendrick Lamar and Kanye West) and indie rock/punk groups (e.g., Green Day).

Conclusion

I have described several contemporary experiences and manifestations of self to illustrate the ways the rock idiom has remained a major cultural force in the life course of mature fans. There are obviously other experiences. Furthermore, these experiences are not limited to fans. Rock music is also a preeminent aspect of the musician's self who performed rock music many years ago, and who continues to perform. These musicians redirect their careers in directions more comfortable if not more profitable. Kinky Friedman comes to mind. He was a Texas-based bandleader in the 1970s (of the infamous Texas Jew Boys). He now performs acoustically in small clubs, while managing a very successful line of men's clothing and authoring popular mystery novels. As time passes (Kotarba 2002b), rock'n'roll provides narrative resources for the aging self's biographical work. In my interviews, I routinely hear respondents note how the recent deaths of aging rock'n'roll artists, such as Leon Russell, David Bowie, Keith Emerson, and Leonard Cohen, are disturbing because these afflictions may be more the result of aging than the excessive lifestyles associated with the premature deaths of artists such as Janis Joplin, Jimi Hendrix, Jim Morrison and more recently, Amy Winehouse. It will be interesting, then, to see the various ways in which baby boomers draw upon the rock idiom as they move beyond middle age. For example, what new meanings will aging boomers attach to the rock idiom? What place will rock have in the grandparent–grandchild relationship? Attending to such questions will highlight the role that music plays in the ongoing becoming-of-self.

Activities

(1) I want you to post a list of the five songs you would want to have played or performed at your memorial service, funeral, etc. Indicate the reasons why you chose each song, for whom in the crowd you are playing the song, and what memory of you the song will hopefully elicit. They can be any songs.

This is a sociological exercise because music helps form, define and maintain our relationships, even after we are "gone." Here are five of my songs, and for whom . . . .

"Ave Maria"	Andrea Bocelli	For the Catholics in the crowd
"Childish Things"	James McMurtry	The elegance of Texas music for the Yankees in the crowd
"Watch Her Drive"	Wade Bowen	For my wife, great Texas "red dirt" guitar rock
"Deus Tuus"	Henryk Gorecki	Choir of New College, Oxford—The Spirit of Life
"Firework"	Katy Perry	For my kids . . . Go live your lives!

(2) Think of one of the (important) *our-songs* in your life. What was it? How did it enter your consciousness, your life? How did you share it with the other person? Did he or she even know that you had an our-song? Is the song still part of your life, and if so, how?

4

Youth, Deviance, and Subcultures

Joseph A. Kotarba

Deviance has been a topic of interest in sociology ever since the discipline's inception during the industrial revolution. The study of deviance is crucial to the overall goal of sociology for one simple reason: social life is based in large part upon social rules. Consensus theorists (e.g., structuralists and functionalists) usually focus their attention on how social rules such as customs, culture, or laws determine or otherwise shape people's behavior. Sociologists of everyday life, on the other hand, emphasize how people actively create, negotiate, reshape, and use social rules to make sense of people's behaviors within situations. But, regardless of theoretical orientation, understanding deviance is the key to a better understanding of social rules, order, and individual and collective behavior.

Deviance seems like an obvious thing . . . you know it when you see it, right? But it's really not so straightforward. A superficial understanding of deviance conceptualizes persons, acts or events as deviations from some norm. For example, listening to the band Psycroptic, a technical death metal band from Tasmania, Australia, might easily lead you to define the music, or the band, as deviant, using words like "terrible" or "senseless noise" or "sick." Or, you might like it and silently thank me for tipping you off to some new tunes. Either way, simply defining something like death metal music, its musicians, or fans as deviant explains little and instead raises important questions such as "who decides which forms of music are normal or deviant?" By asking questions like this, the sociological significance of deviance becomes more apparent—focusing on deviance helps make clearer how normal or non-deviant behavior is accomplished. This everyday life approach seems to us much better equipped for understanding deviance and normality than simply assuming that each exists. It is objectively real because it emphasizes the meanings shaped by social actors and associated with a sense of order. Again, we are arguing that understanding social rules and order is best accomplished by observing situations in which norms are challenged. Observing challenges, though, means that we understand at least something about norms already. After all, we don't all walk around with rulebooks explaining what we can and cannot say or do. Nor are we born preconditioned to speak a certain language, be attracted to a certain kind of person, or appreciate a certain music genre. Rather, such "normal" things are learned and internalized through participation in everyday life.

This is where the concept of *culture* becomes very useful. Culture has been an important conceptual tool for scholars studying both the macro- and micro-levels of society for decades to describe how social rules work. Symbolic interactionists see culture as having to do with how people think, feel and act in concert with others with whom they share understanding. Within social groups, such thoughts, feelings, and actions become patterned and thus shape future thoughts, feelings and actions. They were around before you were born, but they are also shaped through interaction with your fellows (Becker 1986). Those patterns may change from situation to situation, as would the meanings we attach to them. For example, drinking a beer and feeling giddy while thinking about kissing that cute person across the room may be fine when out with friends on a Friday night, but none of these—the act of drinking alcohol for pleasure, the feeling of giddiness, or sexual thoughts—are acceptable while in a worship service on Sunday morning.

In Chapter 2, we heard questionable claims about whether certain styles of popular music "cause" deviance (e.g., delinquency, suicide) among young people. I explained that as an instance of social problem work. This chapter will broaden the discussion to make sense of the relations among music, patterns of behavior, and deviance. It is not that any one of these factors cause any other. Instead, the focus will be on the cultures of people who prefer music that may be quite normal to them, but have been labeled more or less as deviant within the context of the larger group culture in which they live. The discussion is not just talking about culture, but specifically about *subculture*—a culture that differs from the "mainstream" through marginality or opposition (Williams 2011). A subculture emerges around a "bounded (but not closed) network of people who come to share the meaning of specific ideas, material objects, and practices through interaction. Over time, members' interactions develop into a discourse that structures the generation, activation, and diffusion of these ideas, objects, and practices" (Williams and Copes 2005: 70). Whether marginal (labeled as deviant by the mainstream) or oppositional (choosing not to conform to mainstream culture), or some combination of the two, there are many subcultures that have emerged around the consumption of music that provide rich and complex patterns of thinking, feeling, and acting through which members share musical experiences.

The following is an historical take on music subcultures that have emerged in the U.S. and U.K. as we build up an interactionist understanding of deviance, inspired by constructivist political sensitivities. Concepts from two theories—Howard Becker's (1963) "labeling theory" and Stanley Cohen's (2002) theory of "moral panic"—are key to this discussion, as we trace the significance of a number of (un)popular music genres, from blues, jazz, and swing in the early 20th century, to hippie, heavy metal, and rap in the latter half of the century. The chapter concludes with some consideration of the role that social media plays in subcultural music experience and deviant labels.

What Makes Music (Un)Popular?: The Role of Labeling

Some popular music scholars argue that the relationship between music and alternative youth cultures is a product of changes that occurred in the post-World War II political economies of the West, which gave young people more free time and more spending power than they had ever had before (e.g., Bennett 2001; Clarke et al. 1976). From this perspective, "youth" as a cultural category is a primary driver in the emergence of music cultures. There is certainly good reason to believe such a claim, not the least of which are the "deviant" music cultures that we will describe in this chapter, which emerged since 1950. However, to argue that there were no cultures of popular music is a bit of an oversimplification. There have always been local styles of music we now refer to as folk or indigenous music, not quite at the scale of popular music. Some of these popular music cultures emerged because musicians and fans created scenes that supported that musical genre. In other cases, people who were not fans of a particular style of music used political and economic resources to label groups of musicians and fans as different or unacceptable. This is not to say that all musicians and their fans are subcultural. Nevertheless, one way to understand this social phenomenon is by referring to how deviant cultures are constructed by both insiders and by outsiders of music scenes.

Take, for instance, blues music. Blues music is one of the earliest styles of distinctively American popular music. Blues emerged in the rural U.S. South and river towns in the 1910s and 1920s as a form of folk music (Jones 1963). Referring to the depressed moods (as in, "feeling blue") that could characterize everyday life at the very bottom of the social ladder, blues originally signified the experience of working, rural, black poor in the Deep South and developed from a mix of spirituals, work chants, and the reflexive narratives of performers. The distinction between performers and audience members was often blurred, as everyone might take turns singing, playing, and listening to stories relevant to the everyday lives of all present. Before the technological advances that would enable electrified music decades later—and which would also open up the genre to more white listeners—the lack of financial resources in the blues scenes precluded any attempt at developing an organized popular music form per se. Mainstream "WASP" (White Anglo-Saxon Protestant) culture, with its racist tones, as well as the economic problems experienced in the South for decades after the Civil War, resulted in a situation in which blues musicians and their audiences were satisfied to keep their music to themselves. Much of the meaning of the blues was encoded in the lyrics via metaphors and innuendos, and blues remained a subcultural form that few outsiders understood or appreciated.

Jazz music emerged at more or less the same time as the blues, but in different locations (e.g., New Orleans and New York) and developed different scenes (i.e., middle-class urban blacks and whites). Jazz was a popular music genre during the "roaring twenties," brought into the limelight via electricity, radio and motion pictures, and the immense popularity of dance clubs. While blues was marginal, jazz represented the interaction of (predominantly) black musicians with European musical traditions (Berendt 1982). Jazz itself had many varieties and it became possible to earn a living as a jazz musician in major cities. Rather than the music being part of the everyday culture of the poor, jazz musicians were an amateur and professional lot who chose the lifestyle. Sociologist Howard Becker, who developed "labeling theory," was himself a jazz musician, and several of his published works detail the subcultural lifestyle surrounding jazz. In urban areas, jazz became associated with racial tolerance and women's and gay rights, and recognizable subcultures emerged, such as flappers. Part of the lifestyle involved the use of drugs such as marijuana and heroin, and scene members developed unique "argot"—subcultural slang—to mask the meaning of subcultural communication from straight society:

> Much of the 'hip talk' comes directly from the addict's jargon as well as from the musician's. The 'secret' bopper's and (later) hipster's language was the essential part of a cult of redefinition, in terms closest to the initiated.
>
> (Jones 1963: 202)

As jazz became a widely recorded style of music, marketed in entertainment centers like New York City, it produced its own cultural media, where jazz music criticism helped convey the jazz vernacular to a wide and appreciative audience via newspapers and magazines dedicated to the genre, further assisting its spread into popular culture.

As this comparison of 20th-century blues and jazz suggests, "popular" music is a relative term. Blues was popular among marginal black populations of the rural Deep South, but not in WASP society. Meanwhile jazz, which shared musical roots and similarities with the blues, was popular among a much wider cross-section of the U.S. public, as well as in the U.K. and Europe. And yet, as we will see in the next section, what is popular to one group of people in one time and place may not be to others in another time or place. This is how deviance itself operates in society; it is a consequence of imbalances among people's definitions of "popular."

Becker viewed the work of moral entrepreneurs as a crusade of sorts: "The crusader is not only interested in seeing to it that other people do what he thinks right. He believes that if they do what is right it will be good for them" (1963: 148). Sociologically speaking, if a crusade is successful it will result not only in the construction of a social norm, but also in the labeling of those people, events or objects that stand contrarily. Labeling is thus a very important concept. When we label someone or something as deviant, we exercise moral force. As Becker put it, by labeling people we make outsiders of them. Deviance, for Becker and other interactionists, is thus a "consequence of the application by others of rules and sanctions to an 'offender.' The deviant is one to whom the label has been successfully applied" (1963: 9). In his influential study of outsiders, Becker focused on both the construction and application of social norms, and the consequences of labeling in terms of the identities and social status of those who are labeled. At the time of its publication, and still to this day, Becker's study is insightful. Instead of focusing on the structural consequences of objectively defined deviant acts, or instead of treating deviants as psychologically abnormal, Becker posited deviance as an outcome of social interaction.

Social norms are one of many symbolic and material resources that individuals take into consideration more or less consciously when acting in concert with others. For most of us, most of the time, our knowledge of social norms is rather unconscious and implicit. We see difference and label it as problematic.

Music, Subcultures, and Moral Panics

Along with Becker's work on labeling, Stanley Cohen's (2002) theory of *moral panic* is important because it explains the process through which deviance becomes a problem for an entire society. According to Cohen, simply labeling persons, actions or events as deviant is not enough; society needs to be shown the danger that deviance represents in order to legitimate intervention. Going back once more to the pre-World War II period, let us consider the case of swing music in Nazi Germany in the 1930s. Swing music was a form of American big-band jazz that spread across the U.K. and Europe in the 1920s. In Germany, swing was popular among educated, affluent German youths, who were most likely to appreciate music from abroad. Many swing fans were the children of Nazi Party members and, thus, were expected to be upstanding citizens. In what way could the sons and daughters of the respectable German upper classes pose a threat to the State? According to Wallace and Alt (2001), the threat came from the music they loved. Swing's biggest names were African-American and Jewish and the music came from the English-speaking world. German swing kids bought imported records, listened to the latest big-band hits on BBC radio, dressed in English clothing, and engaged the English language through reading and speaking. From the youths' perspective, listening to swing was not intended to be antagonistic toward the dominant cultural order of the day. They were not organized in terms of resistance to the State, yet were labeled as a threat to German society's core value structure, which promoted the racial and cultural superiority of Germany. Nevertheless, swing music was seen as a direct provocation to the National Socialist's ideology of superiority. By 1938, Nazi officials, operating as moral entrepreneurs, had created an exhibition on "Degenerate Music" to inform the German populace about the unacceptability of jazz music, and its consumption was informally banned. From 1939 (when the war started) onwards, listening to the BBC or to Jewish or "Negro" music became illegal activities. The Gestapo and members of the Hitler Youth were tasked with surveiling dance parties and other swing activities, such as listening to the BBC or playing records. Being identified as a repeat offender further increased the likelihood of being labeled as deviant versus a person caught once, who might be warned to be more careful about how she or he chose to spend their leisure time.

Over time, a nationwide moral panic associated with swing music emerged and reactions became increasingly severe as the war went on. In 1940, swing parties were officially banned, and editorials and cartoons began appearing in newspapers that ridiculed the subculture. Parties were raided and attendees arrested and interrogated. Minors could be expelled from high school, thus ruining any chance of a university career, while those who were old enough were sent to the front lines as soldiers, or to penal camps for rehabilitation. Arno Klönne's (1995) archival research demonstrates just how drastic social reaction against swing kids became during the war, when a letter was written to S.S. leader Himmler, stating:

> Since the activities of these 'Swing Youth' in the home country damages [*sic*] the strength of the German people, I would recommend that they are brought immediately into a work camp. [. . .] I would be very grateful if you could give instructions to the . . . authorities to act against these 'Swing Youth' with the harshest possible measures.
>
> (Cited in Wallace and Alt 2001: 284)

A symbolic interactionist approach to deviance highlights that labeling and reacting are not uniformly managed. In the case of swing, the nature of social reaction depended on the meaning attributed to the individuals involved. Some were sent for rehabilitation; those with Jewish or communist connections were sent to concentration camps; and at least one with "good connections" was released. Nevertheless, to think that listening to popular music could get you thrown into a concentration camp seems drastic. But "drastic" is relative and we must keep in mind that one's definition of "popular" music is not always shared with others.

The Post-War Era: Youth Culture and Deviance on Wholesale

Reactionary ideologies are not limited to Nazi Germany. In fact, all societies have moral entrepreneurs who actively work to solidify control of the hearts and minds of fellow citizens. It is against the backdrop of conservativism that oppositional youth subcultures are often discussed—think of hippie, punk, metal, and hip-hop to name but a few. These subcultures represent the oppositional (rather than the marginalized) version of deviance. They are the "others" who choose to build their own rules as they break mainstream social norms and orient to a subculture instead. Each of these cultures is known for a number of things, but they all share two common features—music and resistance (Williams

2009). While it would be problematic to conceptualize music as *the* source of inspiration for oppositional subcultures, it also cannot be denied that music is important. But let us not simply romanticize these subcultures, viewing them as heroic stands against culture industries or agents of social control, nor reduce them to the nihilistic actions of disaffected youths. Looking at a series of subcultures in turn, we can instead consider the roles that music and related behaviors have played in communicating resistance to mainstream culture on the one hand, while not ignoring the role of "the system" in creating deviant labels as part of its efforts to control people's behaviors.

To do this seriously, we need a concept that allows us to link music and resistance together in some meaningful way. As I said earlier, there is a correspondence between a particular culture of deviance and its internal rules. The concept perhaps best used to interpret the internal structure of a culture is *homology*, which "refers to the relationships among ideology, image, and practice" within a subculture (Williams 2011: 76). Popular music scholar Richard Middleton (1990: 9) further describes homology as "a structural resonance . . . between the different elements making up a socio-cultural whole." Are there certain types of music that go best with specific behaviors? Would the hippie subculture have been the same if its music and drugs had been angrier, or would punk be the same if it had been wrapped only in hope and love? Further, in what ways might music be resistant? These are the kinds of questions that homological studies seek to answer.

Let us jump to the mid–1960s, where the presence of recreational drugs such as marijuana, alcohol, and LSD became widespread among adolescents alongside the mixture of politicized rock and folk music that together characterized what we know today as the hippie counter-culture. Besides drugs and music, the hippie counter-culture was also known for its collective movements against the war in Vietnam, as well as against social inequalities such as racism and sexism. According to some sociologists, hippies typically came from middle-class backgrounds and could afford to react against the straight-laced culture of the 1950s in which they had grown up (Clarke et al. 1976; Willis 1978). Yet, the hippies were not all white, not all middle-class, and not all interested in radical political change. Instead, many were just youths looking for something fresh and fun, and popular music and drugs were readily available leisure pursuits.

There was a lot of politically oriented popular music during the late 1960s, which was instrumental in disseminating counter-cultural ideologies among youths across North America and beyond. Hippies' drugs of choice, especially marijuana and LSD, were also significant to hippie music scenes because they enhanced introspective and communal feelings—hallmarks of the counter-culture—for musicians and fans alike. Consider Timothy Leary's famous exhortation for American youths to "turn on, tune in, drop out."

> *Turn on* meant go within to activate your neural and genetic equipment. Become sensitive to the many and various levels of consciousness and the specific triggers that engage them . . . *Tune in* meant interact harmoniously with the world around you—externalize, materialize, express your new internal perspectives. *Drop out* suggested an elective, selective, graceful process of detachment from involuntary or unconscious commitments. *Drop out* meant self-reliance, a discovery of one's singularity, a commitment to mobility, choice, and change . . . Unhappily my explanations of this sequence of personal development were often misinterpreted to mean: 'Get stoned and abandon all constructive activity.'
>
> (Leary 1983: 253)

The implications of Leary's words resonated with counter-cultural youths who sought alternatives to what was happening in the larger world (they were the first generation to be able to "consume" the meanings of foreign wars through near-instant television coverage and with the Civil Rights movement still unfolding) and who sought ways to detached themselves from "involuntary or unconscious commitments," refusing to follow rules just because they were there to be followed. According to Hall (1968, p. 24), the meaning of Leary's words brought drug use and resistance together.

> 'turn on' . . . invites the hippy to switch to the use of mind expanding drugs and to turn on as many members of straight society as he

> [*sic*] can reach. But, again, metaphorically, it also means to switch to a more authentic mode of experience, to leave the routes of middle class society. . . . 'Drop out' . . . means, literally, that the hippy should reject work, power, status, and consumption . . . .

Together with "tune in," which may be interpreted as a call to use available media channels, including music, to stay up-to-date with what was going on in the world, the counter-culture of the late 1960s drew together rather clearly the connections among music, drug use, and counter-cultural ideologies. "It is only through an appreciation of such cultural values, acquired via a total absorption in the hippie lifestyle, that the 'correct' use of drugs and music can be learned and practiced" (Bennett 2001: 32).

The 1970s witnessed a decline in the counter-cultural power of politicized rock music within the context of an increasingly conservative, post-Vietnam era, but the popularization of music-based hedonism continued to grow. Popularly known as "disco" in the 1970s, the phenomenon confronted the conservative, WASP America that had seemingly prevailed against the hippies with newly liberated homo- and heterosexualities as well as equally avid, lifestyle-based drug use (Braunstein 1999). Disco became a dominant form of popular music via what was by then a well-oiled machine of modern music production. Discotheques could be found in almost any city, while the music and style could be heard on the radio, spotlighted in television shows, and film. Disco was both "good" and "bad," with the proliferation of cocaine and heroin use coinciding with the popularity of all-night dance parties. Whereas the mellowing drugs among hippies fit homologically with the cultural imperatives of introspection and community-building, disco culture was tied to the use of "uppers" to fuel frenetic music consumption.

At the same time, rock'n'roll was developing into the heavier and more aggressive forms of punk and heavy metal. Yet heavy metal, with its less overt opposition to the mainstream and superior musicianship versus punk, held more appeal for popular music consumers. Heavy metals acts in the 1970s such as Led Zeppelin, Black Sabbath, and Ted Nugent played shows to tens of thousands in stadiums, and sold millions of records, while many punk bands struggled to feed themselves and maintain their equipment at the same time. By the 1980s, metal had developed a new type of relation with mainstream culture. On the one hand, metal contained elements of social disaffection and a critique of mainstream cultural values. On the other hand, many bands signed to multinational record labels and earned a considerable profit off their fan's consumptive habits. Consider the following statement by a conservative journalist, Jon Pareles (1988, pp. 26–7) that describes the band Metallica in a way few readers today could imagine:

> The heavy metal rock band Metallica plays loud, high-speed music with lyrics that dwell on dark subjects such as death, madness, nuclear war, and drug abuse. While adhering to heavy metal's basic tenets, the members of Metallica rebel against many of the conventions associated with hard rock music and refuse to package themselves for mass consumption. The band has never made a video for MTV, and, until the advent of all-hard-rock radio formats, Metallica albums were never played on commercial rock radio stations. Nonetheless, the group has attracted an avid following, mainly through tours, heavy metal fan publications, some college radio exposure, and word of mouth.

The "dark subjects" of heavy metal music—visible in album art, attributable to the heavy tones and speed of the music, and audible in the lyrics—became a concern for neo-conservative politicians, religious leaders, and other public interest groups who fueled the fires of moral panic surrounding youth popular music genres. The 1980s in particular witnessed a sustained moral panic around the links between heavy metal music and dangerous activities (drug use, truancy, atheism or occultism), with the Parents' Music Resource Center (PMRC) playing an institutionalized role as moral entrepreneur. Working under the auspices of concerned parenting and "neutral fact-finding," the PMRC was able to create the image of heavy metal fans as subcultural and "to mobilize parental hysteria while avoiding the adult word censorship." The PMRC made it clear that heavy metal was "a threat because it celebrate[d] and legitimate[d] sources of identity and community that [did] not derive from parental models" (Walser 1993: 138). Artists and bands such as Ozzy Osbourne, Judas Priest, and Twisted Sister were vilified as wicked and debase, bent on the entrapment and subjugation of young people's minds. It was claimed that heavy metal records contained hidden messages through "back-masking," instructing listeners in acts of violence and destruction. The PMRC's tactics to control media content and distribution were predicated on making artists appear as deviant and dangerous as possible, framing young fans more as victims than as willfully disobedient kids.

To help the labels stick, social control agencies such as the American Medical Association published warnings about some lyrics being dangerous to its fans:

> The American Medical Association (AMA) and the American Academy of Pediatrics have voiced concerns about certain lyrics used in heavy metal and rap music. The AMA says that messages in these genres may pose a threat to the physical health and emotional well being of particularly vulnerable children and adolescents. The AMA has identified six potentially dangerous music themes: drug and alcohol abuse, suicide, violence, satanic worship, sexual exploitation, and racism. Both the AMA and the Academy of Pediatrics support voluntary regulation and increased social responsibility in the music industry.
>
> (Levine 1991: 16)

Law enforcement officials also performed key roles as moral entrepreneurs in identifying and shaping society's informal definitions of normalcy and its reaction to deviation. In Orange County, California, the local government established a program called "Back In Control" (BIC), which provided parenting workshops for families, especially those with "problem" children. One explicit dimension of the program was to help parents regain control of subcultural minors. In the BIC publication, *The Punk and Heavy Metal Handbook*, parents were told that

> . . . punk and heavy metal music oppose the traditional values of those in authority and encourage rebellious and aggressive attitudes and behavior toward parents, educators, law enforcement,

> and religious leaders. Further . . . punk and metal generally support behaviors that are violent, immoral, illegal, frequently bizarre and that generally promote drug and alcohol abuse.
>
> (Quoted in Rosenbaum and Prinsky 1991: 529)

Police not only gave special talks to high-school student bodies (usually with mandatory attendance policies), but also offered seminars for neighborhood and community groups in which they would outline "warning signs" for parents. These warning signs were stylistic in nature, including T-shirts advertising punk or metal bands, clothing that was black or that had spikes/studs, so called "punk" jewelry, having more than one piercing in an ear, or wearing dyed or spiked hair. Police talks with parents also focused on heavy metal and punk song lyrics, album artwork, and the lifestyle of rock stars. Court officials were also strategic actors in social reaction against subcultural participants.

Homologically speaking, scholars and fans alike have drawn on the assumed relationship among punk and heavy metal's fast-paced rhythms, spiked and leather-clad appearance, and aggressive lyrics to make sense of the subcultural ideologies that they represent. The skepticism of punk culture toward social institutions may be the reason many punk musicians pride themselves on their *lack* of music training or skill, while the violent lyrics found in heavy metal can be seen to represent the focal concerns of metalheads. What is perhaps most important to draw from this is an understanding of the relation between music, style, deviant behavior, and audience reception. Rather than think in narrow terms about music or lyrics causing people to act in a certain way, we need to think about the larger role these subcultural objects may play in representing aspects of mainstream culture that subculturalists deal with. Themes of war, sexual predation, and anger could be found daily in news, sports, film, and television. Creating music around these themes can logically be said to represent or reflect aspects of mainstream culture rather than to be the autonomously created, sinister message of deviant musicians.

Hip-Hop Subculture and the Commodification of Deviance

Hip-hop culture, a multibillion dollar global icon in the 21st century, emerged out of the African-American ghettos of New York in the

1970s and has since morphed into a multivalent and multiracial phenomenon with a variety of popular cultural and subcultural forms. (In Chapter 7, we will read about the positive use of hip-hop culture and rap for youth enhancement and solutions to social problems.) Rap music stands as the primary creative force within hip-hop culture, while rappers themselves come with diverse biographies and desires. Some rappers are quite political, while others seem to unwittingly promote racialized, group-based violence that propels only the luckiest few out of their marginal position in society. African-American rap artists in the 1970s and early 1980s focused enormous energy on highlighting the black, lower-class experience in modern urban society (and as such it functions as a modern version of blues music as previously discussed). As such, rap songs, like those of the other genres we've discussed, "are cultural, ideological inscriptions of meanings conceived, created and constructed, and then projected by performances which suggest that certain ways of being, thinking, looking, and styling are normative, preferable, and validated" (Banfield 2010: 9).

Rap has been approached in terms of the kinds of knowledge and practice that structure its existence and development, with scholars often attempting to decipher it through analyses of lyrical content. A noted scholar on the culture of hip-hop, Tricia Rose has written about the significance of rap music. Her book *Black Noise* (Rose 1994) began with a discussion of a single word shouted by Flavor Flav, the flamboyant second man in Public Enemy. That word, "Confusion!" from the song "Can't Truss It," complements front man Chuck D's story about the legacy of slavery and the cultural confusion that contemporary African-American society has experienced as a result. Rose's overarching question concerns what rap tells us about black Americans' experiences. Her answer is that, in part, rap signifies a "forbidden narrative [and] a symbol of rebellion" (Rose 1994: 5) for millions of fans and consumers around the globe. Rap is part of a broader, "disguised criticism of the powerful [. . .that] produce[s] communal bases of knowledge about social conditions, communal interpretations of them, and quite often serve[s] as the cultural glue that fosters communal resistance" (Rose 1994: 99–100). In short, rap music is seen to collect, mediate, and represent black people's experiences of racial and classed oppressions.

Since hip-hop became truly global in the 1990s, it is necessary to study the extent to which the symbols visible/audible in rap today represent the focal concerns of hip-hop subcultural members versus satisfying the voyeuristic demands of consumer society. Multinational corporations pay millions upon millions of dollars annually to guide the creative process of rap music, while apparel, food, technological, and other types of companies have invested heavily into attracting the fans of hip-hop to their brands, resulting in rap music now being a globally recognized commercial market with its own logics. One of hip-hop's most salient features in popular culture today has to do with the masculine, competitive bias expressed in the style of rap's best-known figures. This bias is often expressed by male artists whose lyrics and style are apparently critical of some of society's most basic cultural norms, including a good education, a full-time job, and a loving, cohesive nuclear family for emotional support—cultural norms with a distinctly Anglo-European history. The masculine and racial biases can be seen in rappers' violent resistance to dominant definitions of the role of authority (e.g., N.W.A.'s "Fuck the Police" or Ice T's "Cop Killer"), as well as in their objectification of women through an embracement of the "hustler" lifestyle that endorses the forceful treatment of "bitches and hoes" (Copes et al. 2008).

Black artists in particular sought to control access to hip-hop though a rhetorical grounding of hip-hop authenticity. One needed to be black, to be from "the street," to have an "underground" sensibility, and to rap from the heart rather than for the money (McLeod 1999). With skill and the proper credentials comes recognition and status. Yet, some rappers are seen to "sell out" of the subculture by accepting record deals from major labels and moving into middle-class comfort while continuing to rap about the lower-class, urban street culture they've left behind. Since rap's emergence, some of its most popular artists have traveled far: Flavor Flav's "Confusion!" seems less about the legacy of slavery and more about his love life (VH1's reality shows, *Strange Love*, and *Flavor of Love*); Ice-T is better known today as a cop than as a "Cop Killer" (NBC's drama series, *Law & Order: Special Victims Unit*); and despite his claim with Dr. Dre that "Bitches Ain't Shit," Snoop Dogg spends much of his time on reality TV pampering his wife and daughter (E!'s *Snoop Dogg's Father Hood*).

As rap has been transformed into a global commodity, hip-hop artists and fans alike have struggled to negotiate the meaning(s) of rap. Today rap and hip-hop are commodities eagerly consumed by the middle-class. Whether in New York, Munich, or Hong Kong, middle-class urban youth preen themselves in the latest "street fashion," throw around mock gang signs, and memorize lyrics to songs that are banned on many airwaves. And no matter how true to life rappers' lyrics may be, the vast portion of record sales are derived from consumers who are totally removed from a life of poverty, drug-dealing, and pervasive interpersonal violence. To what extent is the genre today a mode of resistance against "the system," and to what extent has it come to signify a vacuous relationship with pop-cultural economics rooted in middle-class consumption of the cultural "other"? In Chapter 7, we will read about a more contemporary movement to use hip-hop culture to empower young people in a very constructive way.

Music, The Internet, and Deviant Subcultures

Part of the global commodification of hip-hop and other music genres, popular and unpopular alike, has come through the development of social media technologies, which have given industries and consumers unprecedented access to socially driven information about music and music cultures. Throughout history, media technologies, from the earliest recording processes to contemporary digitalization, have shaped and reshaped how individuals and groups experience music cultures. Let us now look at how new media like the Internet has affected the intersections of music, subculture, and deviant identity. To do this, we turn to an Internet forum dedicated to the straight-edge subculture. Straight edge emerged as an offshoot of the hardcore punk subculture in the early 1980s in the United States and now claims worldwide adherents. The term "straight edge" can be traced to a 1981 song entitled "Straight Edge" by the Washington, D.C. band Minor Threat. Its lyrics state:

> I'm a person just like you, but I've got better things to do than . . . snort white shit up my nose, pass out at shows . . . than sit around

> and smoke dope because I know that I can cope. Always want to be in touch, never want to use a crutch. I've got the straight edge!
> (Minor Threat 1981)

Such lyrics were based on "a deep hatred for [the] lifestyle" of mainstream youth as experienced by lead singer Ian MacKaye in the early 1980s (Small and Stuart 1982). Straight edge emerged as a conservative reaction to punk's anarchic orientation; it called on punks to renounce drug use and promiscuity and thereby maintain a "straight edge" over their mainstream peers. The term was taken up by an emerging youth subculture whose members resisted what they saw as consumer-driven and self-indulgent youth cultures, including the nihilism and apathy of many punks. Straight-edge songs, like most hardcore music, are fast-paced, with simple and repetitive power-driven chords. The lyrics, as seen above, stand in stark contrast to mainstream ideologies purveyed in popular radio hits. Straight-edge and other hardcore American punk bands combined the speed and energy of punk music with a mixture of critical and upbeat lyrics. In the 1980s and still today, straight-edge kids consider themselves deviant and define their values and actions in contrary terms to mainstream culture (Copes and Williams 2007).

Since the late 1990s, the straight-edge subculture has been diffused around the globe through the Internet. This diffusion has taken many forms: personal and official band websites, which may include personal stories of becoming/being straight edge, band biographies, song lyrics, and tattoo galleries; FAQs, listservs, and discussion forums; the trading of straight-edge music via peer-to-peer networks; and online stores where fans can buy straight-edge music, shirts, stickers, and so on. As a result of this subcultural diffusion, many individuals discover straight edge in a dislocated form, fractured from its musical roots. Many kids have learned about straight edge online and decided to claim a straight-edge identity. Many of them subsequently join face-to-face straight-edge music scenes, but many others do not (see Williams 2006). Those who join face-to-face straight-edge scenes usually come to agree that music is a tie that binds and that participation in a scene is an essential component of being straight edge. Many of these straight edgers argue that the diffusion of straight edge through the Internet has led to a "defusion" of the subculture, a stripping away of its resistant and counter-cultural heritage as Internet-surfing youths who happen to disapprove of drug use or sexual promiscuity (or who simply have no access to sex and drugs and want to feel good about that) locate and then appropriate the straight-edge identity.

But there are others who identify as straight edge and who rely on the Internet as their sole subcultural resource and means of subcultural interaction. This latter group tends to express the belief that anyone who lives a straight-edge lifestyle—following subcultural "rules" against drug use and promiscuous sex, for example—can be straight edge if they want to be. Such individuals tend to focus on their subcultural affiliation in terms of a personal commitment to a lifestyle rather than to membership in a local music scene. In fact, some straight edgers go so far as to re-imagine local music scenes as problems for the subculture. One vocal member of a straight-edge Internet forum argued that people too concerned with music scenes were

> blinded because you are doing what is "cool," not what you want. You are expressing your views as being, "you can only be straight-edge if you are in the cool crowd." Well I guess you're cool and I'm not. But I am straightedge because of what I want.
>
> (Williams 2006: 190).

However important music might be for the study of oppositional subcultures, there are changes occurring in contemporary societies that require us to reassess music's central status in facilitating subcultural participation and identification. Such considerations are important for at least two reasons. First, they suggest that, even when studying music, we can benefit from looking to other media forms to better understand music's relative impact in social life. Second, we can see how important music remains for many young people, especially those who rely on music culture for defining themselves. At stake are young people's subcultural identities and their social-psychological functions, including self-esteem, self-efficacy, and belonging in global subcultural networks.

Conclusion

Traditional societies have had folk music traditions that were by default popular music. In modern societies, however, many different music genres exist alongside one another. Some vie for everyone's attention, while others are happy to remain out of the limelight. Some are produced and marketed by multinational conglomerates and can be found on radio stations around the world, while others are more like time-honored folk traditions—relatively small genres that receive comparatively little public attention unless they are deemed to deviate in some important way from mainstream norms or standards of taste. Along with the many changes in norms and tastes over the last century, there have been continual contestations over definitions of what is popular and unpopular music.

These definitions are not natural, but rather are the result of definitions imposed and/or negotiated by social actors. As we have seen in this chapter, music genres that come to be structured alongside behaviors such as drug use or political opposition are most likely to be defined as deviant. And yet they need not be intentionally deviant to be defined by others as a problem. Agents of social control, both institutional and informal, actively engage in the process of defining music as popular or not. We will continue some of these ideas in Chapter 5, where we will see how the definitions of (un)popular music are guided in different ways—through thinking or ideology, through formal social institutions, and through the relatively informal process of maintaining community.

Activities

(1) What do you see as "deviant" music today? Has rap become mainstream? If so, how?

(2) Thinking back to high school, were there styles of music that the majority of students felt were bad, unchristian, immoral, etc.? How did students, faculty, and administrators deal with this music and its fans?

5

Religion, Politics, and Popular Music

Joseph A. Kotarba

We will deal with these two topics together because they share some important features. Both are based upon *belief systems*, collections of values, assumptions and ideas upon which activities and interactions are based. Belief systems are not empirical (i.e., data) based. Followers just "know" them to be true. Both tend to elicit strong emotional responses from followers, as witnessed by the recent presidential election. We'll begin our discussion with religion.

Religion

Religion has long been one of the most important topics for sociological thinking, research and writing. All of the major theorists who contributed to the emergence of sociology in the 19th century felt two ways about religion. First, religion is one of the most important institutions in society. Religion serves as a major source of meaning for people, and it reflects many of society's core attributes and values. Second, understanding religion helps us understand society in general, including its history, conflicts, and goals.

A common sociological definition of religion is "a social institution involving beliefs and practices based on a conception of the sacred (Macionis 2003: 491). The key word here is *sacred*. The sacred, or sacred things, are not ordinarily visible or observable in everyday life. The French sociologist Emile Durkheim (1953: 62), often referred to as the father of consensus or structural-functionalist thinking in sociology, made the conceptual distinction between *profane* and *sacred* objects. Profane things are ordinary things, whereas sacred things are extraordinary and worthy of attention, respect, and awe. Religion serves to teach people what is the distinction between the sacred and profane, and the proper ways to deal with both.

The four major paradigms in sociology each approach the study of religion in tune with their major assumptions of how society operates. Consensus theory focuses on the *integrative function* of society. Religion provides a basis for cooperation, a mechanism for controlling members, and a source of meaning for members to use in addressing problems in everyday life. Durkheim extended these ideas through his concept of the *totem*, which is a regular item in the world that is attributed special characteristics—even power—by the community. Following the writings of Karl Marx (1964: 27), conflict theory sees religion as all too often a powerful tool used by capitalists to control the subservient classes by controlling the values used by all (e.g., the "work ethic" that says that we should feel good simply working hard and being productive in society, regardless of whether we are paid a worthwhile wage). Everyday life sociology argues that religion is like any other social institution in that people assemble religious traditions, liturgies, theologies, and practices to create "the semblance of ultimate security and permanence" (Berger 1967: 36). And, of course, the postmodernist perspective is very interested in the way our evolving culture and the power of the mass media are blurring the distinction between the sacred and the profane. One of the best examples of this, as we will shortly see, is the way popular music can sometimes be equated with, and be used as, a form of sacred music.

One may not automatically think of religion and popular music as a topic of interest. Of course, musicologists and historians describe the intricacies of church music, and anthropologists study the ways different cultures generate different styles of religious music. Sociologists of everyday life focus on religion and popular music as two related, sometimes conflicting, but increasingly compatible, sources of meaning. In this chapter, we will explore five different ways popular music and religion relate in everyday life.

Popular Music Sometimes Critiques Religion

In 1995, "If God was one of us" was a very popular song that received much radio play. Joan Osbourne composed and performed the song. It is a very pleasant, singer-songwriter pop song. Although many critics consider it a "one hit wonder" (http://www.lyricsondemand.com/onehitwonders.html), the song elicited considerable discussion and even argument over whether it was sacrilegious (e.g., disrespectful to God) or merely a meaningless/vacuous pop song with the word God in it. Radio and television talk shows pitted religious folks against atheists.

If you listen to the song or read the lyrics, you will see that the song does not appear to say anything derogatory about God or organized religion. What it does, however, is violate Durkheim's notion of the *sacred.* Joan Osbourne's sin—pun intended—was to sing about God profanely as if he were ordinary person, and—well—not God. Many people took this as an insult to their faith. The profane portrayals of Jesus on musical productions such as *Jesus Christ, Superstar*, Madonna's "Like a Prayer," and R.E.M.'s "Losing My Religion" received the same strong reaction from Christian critics.

Popular Music Sometimes Appears to Threaten Religion

As mentioned in Chapter 2, conservative interest groups such as the Parents' Music Resource Center (PMRC) took their concerns over heavy metal music all the way to the U.S. Congress. Although the parents' concerns included a wide range of issues, their action strategy was to categorize all of them under the rubric of health. Although others may not share the parents' primarily conservatively Christian moral concerns, who could not support concerns for the health and well-being of our youth? The list of heavy metal groups, song performances, and album cover art perceived as posing threats to religion is very long. The attacks against Christianity specifically can be very explicit. One of the best catalogs of this work is a music video produced by youth minister, Eric Holmberg, "Rock'n'Roll: A Search for God."

Popular Music Sometimes Supports Religion

Everyone has heard Irving Berlin's "God Bless America" performed at baseball games, Fourth of July celebrations, and other civic events. This song may be the ultimate pop song that supports religion. These songs are predictably linked with patriotism, and this format can be traced at least as far back as Kay Kyser's World War II anthem, "Praise The Lord And Pass The Ammunition." In the realm of country music, we have a number of songs like Lee Greenwood's "God Bless the U.S.A."

We clearly see fewer and fewer popular songs that explicitly support religion. One of the main reasons for this is the increasing secularization of popular culture in general. In turn, there is even a movement within conservative Christian denominations, such as the Southern Baptist Convention, to remove patriotic songs from Church services. The separation of Church and State that the Founding Fathers of the U.S.A. hoped for is still in process.

Popular Music Can Be Spiritual Music

Nevertheless, the sacred has not been, and probably cannot be, totally removed from popular music. Beginning during the counter-cultural days of the late 1960s, we witnessed the emergence of popular music with sometimes distinctive and sometimes implicit spiritual content or effect. As a survivor of that period of our history, I can attest to the fact that a number of hippies, space cowboys, earth mothers, freaks, draft dodgers, and erstwhile baby boomers—yes, dear students, I'm talking about your parents and in some cases grandparents!—rejected their parents' religious affiliations and embarked upon spiritual journeys to find meaningful truth about life and reality. The general feeling was that organized religion was not relevant to young people's lives and moral concerns. Furthermore, young people sometimes blamed organized religion for being co-conspirators in the oppression, discrimination, and hatred being discovered in Western societies.

Spiritual music in the 1960s and onward took many forms. Following the dictates of everyday life sociology, young people found spirituality in a wide range of musical styles, whether intended or not. An acid (i.e., LSD) trip in the desert could well be perceived as a spiritual experience. Carlos Castaneda, an anthropologist at UCLA, wrote a series of incredibly popular books in the late 1960s and early 1970s that described in very elegant and mystical ways his apprenticeship with a Yaqui sorcerer in the Sonoran Desert—far out! Need we add that natural hallucinogenic substances, such as peyote, served as the medium for these psychedelic experiences? Spiritual experimentation was rampant, and few belief systems were out of bounds. Scientology, animism, Eastern meditation, Gnosticism and philosophy were each fashionable at different times for the baby boomer generation.

The popular music performers who provided the soundtrack for these spiritual voyages included the Grateful Dead, Pink Floyd, and Cream. Millions of young people discovered spiritual truth in the music of Bob Dylan, The Beatles, The Byrds and Leonard Cohen. One of the major rock artists of the 1960s who has continued to provide spiritual experiences for his fans is Van Morrison (Marcus 2010). Van began a very successful career as lead singer for Them in Northern Ireland. He embarked on a solo career in 1968 with *Astral Weeks*, an album often listed as one of the best of all time (e.g., *Rolling Stone* 2010). This album, like much of Morrison's work, borrows from Celtic mysticism to create an aural, meditative experience. The songs are sufficiently suggestive, yet open-ended in interpretation, to provide an accessible vault of meanings and feelings for baby boomers in search of meanings and feeling.

I had the opportunity to attend a Van Morrison concert at the elegant Slieve Donard Resort in Newcastle, Northern Ireland in 2015. The concert was set in the grand ballroom, following a fabulous meal and cocktails. There were approximately 300 fans in attendance, many of whom were Americans, as one might guess. The fans were generally middle-aged or older, very well dressed, totally Anglo, and extremely excited. There were eight people at our table, six of whom were from the States. Although it was a joyful scene, there was an aura that "something special was going to happen." Being the ethnographic tourist that I am, I made the rounds before the concert going table to table, to chat with as many fans as I could. In general, they were expecting someone bigger than life to appear on stage. There were fans who literally travel around the world to see Van perform. Fans were more than willing and able to link particular Van songs to special events in their life, such as the birth of a child, their wedding, or graduation from law school. They maintained play lists, much like the lists religiously—pun intended—kept by Deadheads, Grateful Dead fans. Perhaps most interesting, fans were able to interpret many of Van's songs which, on the surface, appear very open-ended in meaning, wispy, poetic, and, well, just like scripture. Have you ever been a fan like this?

Popular Music Can Be Religious Music

Some religious songs can easily be classified as popular music. One of the best examples is the "Ave Maria," one of the most cherished songs in the Catholic tradition. There are several versions of this song, but it is essentially based upon the 15th-century prayer to Mary, the mother of Jesus ("Hail Mary"). As mentioned in my Introduction to this book, Franz Shubert's classical version of this song is a staple at weddings where a Catholic presence is desired. The Ave Maria continues to be "covered" by pop music performers. The most common covers can be found on albums dedicated to Christmas music. Barbra Streisand, Joan Baez, Josh Groban, Michael Bublé, Aaron Neville, Celine Dion, Stevie Wonder, and Luciano Pavarotti have all recorded the song for Christmas albums, while international opera singer Mark Vincent and pop diva Beyoncé both included the song on their debut albums.

An interesting contemporary trend is the composition of religious music specifically designed according to popular music styles. A case in point is "contemporary Christian music" (CCM). This style of pop music began in the 1960s with the advent of "Jesus Music" among hippies and others seeking an alternative to traditional Christian music. The movement eventually included just about all styles of popular music, ranging from heavy metal and alternative rock, to hip-hop and folk/singer-songwriter (Romanowski 2001). Major artists include Amy Grant, Jars of Clay, dc Talk, Steven Curtis Chapman, and Michael W. Smith. The controversy among Christian observers is whether CCM is liturgical music or entertainment. This debate extends to perhaps the most popular style of CCM, "Praise and Worship" music. Praise and worship music is a very lush, orchestrated, choral, soothing style of music that has gained popularity across Christian denominations, including many Catholic parishes in North America. The music can be quite meditative if not hypnotic.

A Postmodern Case Study in Authenticity: John Michael Talbot

Much of our discussion of the melding of pop music and religion can be summarized in and illustrated by the life and career of John Michael

Talbot. Talbot is an American Roman Catholic singer-songwriter who is also the founder of a monastic community: the Brothers and Sisters of Charity (Talbot 1999). He is the largest selling Catholic musical artist ever, with over four million albums sold. He has authored or co-authored 15 books. John Michael tours through the U.S. in support of his monastic community nestled in the beautiful Ozark Mountains in Arkansas.

John Michael Talbot's work and career illustrate a major issue in CCM: *authenticity* (Kotarba 2009). The issue of authenticity is closely related to the issue raised above: is CCM liturgical music or entertainment? Both Catholic leadership and laypersons wrestle with this issue. In general, CCM artists are considered to be authentic if they perform music primarily as a ministry and as a method of worship. Potential critics are suspicious of CCM artists who appear to be ego-involved, lack humility, want to be stars and/or are too anxious to cross-over to a mainstream pop music audience. John Michael meets this test according to his followers—fans?—however, because he leads a simple lifestyle and does not personally profit from his talent and dedication. In a very postmodern way, John Michael is able to integrate his Internet site, concert tours, and many followers into a pristine, humble, and monastic lifestyle that will never make the cover of *People* magazine. His persona is refreshing—and authentic—to those baby boomers who are a bit overtaken by mass culture, even of an ecclesiastic sort.

John Michael Talbot's spiritual journey fits the baby boomer model discussed above (Baur 2011). In the 1970s, he was a member of the popular country rock band, Mason Proffit, that toured with such famous performers as The Byrds, Pink Floyd, and even the Grateful Dead. After performing at the Ozark Mountain Folk Fair in Eureka Springs, Arkansas in 1973, John Michael had an epiphany. He realized that drugs, alcohol, and other lifestyle excesses on, behind, and in front of the stage, were not all they were cracked up to be:

> 'Suddenly,' he recalls, 'the rock star life seemed empty and sad. It wasn't at all what I wanted my life to stand for.' It was a prophetic experience for the youngster that caused him to question his whole

> lifestyle as he began to ask, 'Isn't there something more?'. . . . Up to that point he had rubbed shoulders with the rock stars he admired and emulated. He shared stages and dressing rooms with them, which gave him an insider's view of the rock scene. After meeting some of his heroes and seeing how they really lived their lives, Talbot came to an inescapable conclusion. 'There were some real tragic scenarios being played out,' he says, 'and it caused me to stop cold and do some serious thinking.'
>
> (Baur 2011)

John Michael left the band to seek a more spiritual lifestyle. For four years, he explored Native American religions, Hinduism, Judaism, Buddhism and Fundamentalism. He joined the Jesus Movement and examined all the Christian denominations. He concluded that Catholicism was the path for him.

John Michael felt impelled to use his particular talent to experience the ascetic. He believes that sacred music is sacramental and:

> . . . from an arts perspective, both reflects and guides the faithful. That music, based on faith, can take the listener on a closer walk with God, actually taking them into the heart of the Lord. 'It brings out the mysterious and speaks the unspeakable, bringing to light that which is beyond human reason. Furthermore,' he says, 'the role of music and prayer fulfills a prophetic function. Not that musicians are prophets,' he notes, 'but they do have an obligation to lead.'
>
> (Baur 2011)

John Michael embarked on a career that, to date, has produced over 40 musical recordings and four million album sales. In 1982, he was the recipient of the prestigious Dove Award for Worship Album of the Year, *Light Eternal*, with producer and longtime friend, Phil Perkins. Four years later, he became one of only nine artists to receive the President's Merit Award from the National Academy of Recording Arts and Sciences and, in 1988 he was named the No.1 Christian Artist by *Billboard* magazine.

John Michael performs at 50 or so live concerts a year, largely at parish church venues around the country. In an interview with me, John Michael related that his audiences consisted of people who adhere to a range of religious and spiritual beliefs: Protestants, agnostics, Buddhists, Jews, and others, all with one particular need:

> They love the music. For some, it serves as a pathway to find a way. For others who have found a way for themselves, the music helps make the journey along that path pleasant, meaningful, and relevant.

John Michael Talbot is an archetypical baby boomer: postmodern, yet traditional, yet experimental. He is able to navigate through what might appear to be numerous religious and spiritual contradictions without compromising his commitment to, and acceptance by, the formal Roman Catholic Church. For example, his music is very eclectic by integrating rock, folk, ecclesiastic, classical, chant, early church music, and the music of the Medieval and Renaissance eras. He uses the funds generated by his music to support a monastic community that include married as well as single people, The Brothers and Sisters of Charity, at Little Portion Hermitage. All commit to vows of poverty, chastity, and obedience. His ministry is open to all, but he has also shared his music with Pope John Paul II and Mother Theresa (Baur 2011). His ministry is timeless, yet the infrastructure is state-of-the art recording and Internet communications. The message is simple, the media is complex, yet the encouragement to followers is to engage in spiritual readings, vigils, fasting and manual labor.

Conclusion

Christian music is not the only religious genre incorporating pop sensibilities. Matisyahu is a Jewish hip-hop artist who combines rap with beatboxing (i.e., a vocalized style of percussion), traditional vocal-jazz scat singing, Judaism's hazzan style of songful prayer, and a reggae beat (Atzmon 2016). The explosion of interest in rap music among young people involved in the resistance movements in North Africa and the Middle East often has clear Islamic characteristics.

The fact that popular music is permeating religious music should not be surprising. The history of religious and spiritual music clearly shows that religious music has always reflected local cultural norms and styles. In a consensus theory sense, religions need people. In an everyday life theory sense, people are attracted to music that fits their aesthetic values while providing practical meanings for everyday life's very changing problems and issues.

Politics

If a man were permitted to make all the ballads, he need not care who should make the laws of a nation.

—Andrew Fletcher 1997 (1703)

Within the field of popular music studies, the notion of "politics" typically denotes either political songs or protest music. In the world of pop music too, it seems that when politics and music are explicitly mixed, a listener is in for either tunes that work as a "struggle against dominant institutions like the state and economic system" (Balliger 1999: 57) or for music that serves to support existing values, like official national anthems or patriotic hymns such as "God Bless America" or Quebec's anthem, "Gens du Pays." To limit a discussion of politics in music to these genres is, however, unwise. More insightfully instead, we can say that music (popular and otherwise) has a political *structure* and *polity-forming capacity* of its own.

In the case of the contemporary popular music industry, this structure is generally understood as a cultural and political oligarchy—an arrangement of power in which a few social agents rule a mass of many. Pop music's oligarchy manifests itself through powerful commercial alliances among music production labels. These labels control the global market by promoting unlimited consumer access to musical genres and artists, but by restricting such access in actual practice. Such restriction is achieved via control of both production and distribution through the standardization of popular music sounds. Because of pop music's close relation with the rest of pop culture (movies, fashion, lifestyle, etc.), this oligarchy has the capacity to draw and even shape like-minded audiences characterized by similarities in outlooks, values, and taste. Popular music, in its capacity to draw and form communities, may then be said to be a social and political force.

Cultural and political oligarchies are important, but not the only means of framing politics and music. Politics enters music, and music enters politics, in numerous and often subtle ways. A sociological approach to music might find political values even in songs that have nothing to do with patriotism or protest. For example, even a harmlessly apolitical hook like "Na, na, na, na, na," sung by the bubbliest of bubbly pop stars has a deep cultural and political significance. According to someone like Theodor Adorno (Adorno and Hullot-Kentor 2006), the infantilization of pop songs is both a symptom and the cause of the formation of a mass culture. A mass culture is one in which people's sense of taste has been standardized by a culture industry keen on preserving the political and economic status quo rather than in the elevation of artistic and political consciousness. If Adorno and his colleagues are right, then politics is everywhere in popular music, despite the fact that we are sometimes oblivious to the hidden political realities of musical production, distribution, or consumption. It should be interesting to uncover some of the more profound political meanings that music holds in everyday life. Following our customary approach of examining the mundane in order to appreciate the deep connection between music and society, in this chapter we examine the relationship between popular music and politics, polity, and community by taking into consideration the multiple meanings of "politics" in popular music studies. We begin by examining the practice of cardboard CD packaging as a way of posing alternatives to the political, economic, and aesthetic oligarchy of the music industry. We conclude with a consideration of the power that communities can wield against unpopular music by studying the case of the West Memphis Three. Through these examples, we want to get you thinking about the importance of three concepts—ideology, institutions, and community—in developing an understanding of how power operates in the social world.

Ideology

There exist several different sociological understandings of the concept of *ideology*, yet the most basic definition simply views ideology as a set of ideas about something. By ideas, here we mean things such as values, beliefs, and ideals about social conduct. Within sociology and related disciplines the concept of ideology is inevitably a social one, in the sense that ideologies are always systems of ideas about how society is and about how it should be. Moreover, ideologies are social in the sense that they are shared by groups of people. Of course, by suggesting that ideologies are shared, we are not implying that everyone shares them; as a matter of fact, ideologies and the groups who support them are often in conflict with one another. Yet, the point that more than one individual, somewhere, at some point in time, will share an ideology is a powerful one in and of itself, and an even more powerful one in light of its consequences.

When people share an ideology, they tend to forget that alternative ideologies exist and that these alternatives are as plausible as their preferred view. What makes ideologies so powerful is that they have a tendency to legitimize behavior and to become reified. Take, for example, the idea (loaded with beliefs, values, assumptions, and so on) that classical music is "better"—that is, more refined, sophisticated, enlightened—than pop music. Ultimately there is no way of proving this to be an unchallengeable truth, yet the idea is strong enough to become so "real" in its consequences, so much a matter of fact, so "reified" that for the most part public schools all over the world abstain from teaching popular music courses. Some even formally condemn pop music as a negative influence and focus instead on instructing children to play "classical" instruments as part of their art curriculum. Here we can see how an ideology—the idea that classical music is inherently more valuable than popular music—legitimizes certain educational practices and delegitimizes others. The more an ideology becomes legitimized, the more it tends to be experienced as an incontrovertible truth and not as mere opinions, outlooks, or ideas. Indeed, the "fact" that classical music "does good things" to children, and the "fact" that rap or metal music "do bad things" to them, becomes a belief *reified*—that is, materialized—deep enough that parents "caught" exposing their wee ones to 50 Cent or Slayer promptly need to account for their "irresponsible" behavior.

In general sociological terms, people in power have at least two means of maintaining their privileges: forceful means and symbolic means.

Music is rarely used in forceful ways—though it has been used as such in the past. As examples: the FBI used popular hits to wear down Branch Davidians during the siege in Waco, Texas in 1993; in Ontario, Canada, police once blared out "boy band" music to disperse a crowd of street protesters; and military police in Iraq and Guantanamo Bay have cycled hip-hop and death metal loudly and continuously to destroy prisoners psychologically. For the most part though, music's power rests in its symbolic force, that is, as a medium for ideology.

According to many critical theorists, the ideology that is most often present in popular music is that of *conservativism*. Conservativism is the ideology supported by the alliance of commercial groups who hold the political and economic power within a capitalist society. For obvious reasons these groups have a keen interest in maintaining the status quo. The best way to maintain such a state of affairs is to sell people something they want to buy and at the same time something they want to believe in. Italian sociologist Antonio Gramsci referred to this process as hegemony. Critical theorists explain that pop music appreciation tends to work in hegemonic fashion by resulting in the appeasement of people into accepting and even supporting the status quo—whether they do this consciously or without being aware. For example, due to its merry repetitiveness, catchy simplicity, and inoffensive superficiality, the consumption of pop music is believed to lead to the regression of the listener to a child-like mental state—a regression which serves the purpose of distracting individuals away from realizing the depth of the social conditions that oppress them and others. This hegemonic function of music—that is, its complicit role in supporting the status quo—has been traditionally condemned both in light of its political consequences and the actual means used, that is the texts, sounds, and performances that made such music so "bad."

In contrast, popular music that is "good" in itself, and good in terms of its consequences for people is autonomous music; or at least, so this critical theoretical argument goes. According to this counter-hegemonic ideology, autonomous, independent, genuine music is believed to be synonymous with authenticity—something which is highly valued (at least on the surface) by many people of character and especially, and perhaps stereotypically, by artists. Autonomy and authenticity mean many different things, but they generally entail independence from shallow values—think fame, economic success, political collusion, and so on—that "corrupt" the ideal purity of musical expression. Autonomous and authentic music is often politically resistant, working as "cultural alternatives to the lifestyles of the 'mainstream.'" This type of music often falls into one of the following categories: protest against oppression or exploitation; aspiration toward a better and more just life; satire of those in power; philosophical reflection; commemoration of popular struggles; inspiration for collective movements; tribute to martyrs; expression of working-class solidarity; and critical social commentary. Regardless of the actual category that a musical performance, recording, or genre may fall into, autonomous and authentic music intends to solicit or arouse support for a movement or cause, create solidarity and cohesion, promote awareness or evoke solutions to social problems, or simply to provide hope.

Autonomy and authenticity sound like good values, but in actuality they are hardly achievable. A sociological understanding of autonomy leads us to find that music-making is, for the most part, dependent on strategic compromises and negotiation. As Becker (1982) has demonstrated, the production of art is a complex joint act between vast numbers of people with different yet related goals. Despite the myth of the lonely genius doing music on his/her own, like all social activities music-making is a collective accomplishment. As we can see below in the case of Montreal-based production label Constellation Records, despite a strong ideology of autonomy and authenticity, certain negotiations and compromises with the system are inevitable.

Politics, Technology, and Indie Music

Any new technological medium of musical expression "changes the way in which we experience music" and poses "both constraints and opportunities in terms of the organization of production" (Shuker 2001: 51). The history of music in the Western hemisphere is marked by a series of shifts from oral and live performance to musical notation and then onward to recording and dissemination through a multitude of media. From a related perspective, music's history can be said to be one of the technological transitions from a context in which the human voice was the only technology of production to one in which the voice is accompanied by a variety of sonorous technologies. If we agree that singing is a technique of expression and that musical sound is a technique or medium of expression, we should agree that music itself is a form of technology.

Like music, politics too is a form of *technology*. To understand this claim, we ought to begin by understanding technology broadly as a general body of knowledge comprised of "how-to" specifications for action. Of course, a technology is not just a collection of tools and "how-to" specifications on how to operate those tools, but also a body of values specifying how tools should be used and for what purposes. Understood this way, the difference between politics and technology is tenuous: both politics and music are technologies of expression. Politics focuses on the expression of political value and the implementation of social ideas through political means, and music focuses on the expression of aesthetic value and orients itself to sound as the tool through which expressiveness can be achieved. Politics and technology (and therefore music) are indeed inextricable. In this section we examine how technology and specific musical techniques acquire political importance and, more precisely, how different forms of technology contribute to the formation and maintenance of political boundaries between communities.

We begin in Montreal, Canada, where a relatively obscure music production company known as Constellation Records has made an interesting choice for the material with which all the CDs in their catalog are packaged: cardboard. Cardboard is a material that, once treated and adapted for the purpose of CD-packaging can constitute an alternative to the plastic generally used for the manufacturing of CD jewel cases. But why do so, when plastic is obviously more time-efficient for labor, more durable, and cheaper? And how is this choice for cardboard sociologically significant? Constellation argues that local control of technology is critical to nurturing creativity and vitality. Constellation's technological position is political insofar as it distances itself from the mainstream view of "indie" music—a synonym for independent, that is, independent from economic, political, aesthetic, and technological pressures from the rest of the music industry and mainstream music and society. Indie music labels like Constellation attempt to build unique communities on the political (some might call it apolitical) philosophy of punk and post-punk in order to separate themselves from other musical communities and exercise resistance against pressures to conform.

This is not always easy to do. While it is true that, by choosing techniques and material like cardboard over conventional plastic, Constellation artisans and artists tend to achieve a distinct identity, it is also true that dealing with recycled cardboard packaging means involving complex networks of local artisans, craftsmen, and environmentally sensitive local business suppliers, as well as applying more intensive human labor (such as cutting, folding, trimming, and drawing). This results in increasing costs and possibly lowering consumer demand. Yet, this also results in avoiding plastic and the environmental problems it embodies, and allows "the sensibility of the music [to be] reflected in and reinforced by the tactility of the package that contains it" (Constellation Records).

Constellation's alternative approach to technology does not end with cardboard. Take, for example, its politics of distribution. Far from representing a mere technical process of getting live or recorded sound from a point of origin to a destination, the process of distribution needs to take into consideration the geographic distribution of retail stores and the clients that frequent them. After all, could you reject plastic and still feel coherent about shipping off your cardboard-packaged records to a suburban shopping mall? Rather than malls, Constellation—similarly to other indie labels—then mostly attempts to rely on a network of Mom-and-Pop stores across Canada and the United States, as well as low-budget site Internet distribution and marketing via word-of-mouth and underground zine coverage. Obviously this keeps Constellation's profits to a minimum, but it also allows its artists to remain relatively free from the pressure of making marketable music.

Take, for example, its most famous band, Godspeed! You Black Emperor (GYBE). GYBE remains keen on touring small venues, playing on pitch-dark stages to avoid emphasizing their image more than their sound, refusing interviews with most media outlets, and obstinately refusing to compromise their aesthetic and political ideologies of resistance, no matter how obscure and controversial these can get. Through their music, instrumental sounds, and lyrics, GYBE and other Constellation bands are outspokenly critical of commodified and standardized musical and political expression typical of post-industrial, neo-liberal society. For example, by privileging the production of an immediate and almost "live" (as "live" as recordings can get) sound, Constellation condemns commodified duplication and mechanical reproduction. Furthermore, Constellation's music is openly political and at times their rhetoric is inflammatory.

In other instances Constellation's random noise adds to the cacophony of their politics. Take, for example, GYBE's recording *Yanqui U.X.O.* ("Yankee Unexploded Ordinance"), a wordless condemnation of American military interventionism. The music alone, in its sheer symphonic violence of ups and downs resembling the rhythms of airplanes rising and bombs falling, does all the talking. Yet, at the periphery of the sound, on the very cardboard in which the disc is enveloped, GYBE's belligerent overtones are most audible. A folder depicting a hammer inexorably squelching the word "hope" written in relief in the midst of white flying chimeras reinforces the impression of muted silence imposed by the American bomber featured on the cover. The disc itself bears the inscription: "Rockets fall on Rocket Fans"—an obvious indictment of turn-of-the-century U.S. foreign policy. "U.X.O.," GYBE adds, "is unexploded ordinance is landmines is duster bombs. All of it mixed by god's pee." The backside of the cover art blurs music and politics even more. There a chart links Sony, AOL Time-Warner, Universal, and BMG to shared financial holdings in the military/weaponry industry: a controversial but certainly thought-provoking addition to the idea of the politico-industrial-military complex. GYBE's and Constellation's ideology is one that is deeply counter-hegemonic and built on values of autonomy and authenticity as resistance—a common yet vanishing strategy in the world of trademarked alternative rock (see Moore 2005).

Institution

The most obvious reference of the word *institution* is a mental asylum. Yet within sociology the word institution has several meanings, some of which are not readily apparent. Let us begin to explain the sociological significance of institution as if we were indeed referring to mental institutions and explore that concept from the angle of popular music. Imagine that you decide to start a new band featuring the absence of any obvious trace of melody. As if the oddness of your sound was not enough, you decide to add to your tracks extremely loud, distorted recordings of half a dozen trains asynchronously operating their rusty brakes in the midst of a windstorm. Next, you decide that the band members ought to wear chicken uniforms both on and off stage. Finally, you write lyrics featuring nothing but Simglish words (the type of English featured on the video game *The Sims*) and as the band leader you proceed to scream those through a megaphone while a back-up singer randomly barks the world "sailor" in a contrived Australian accent.

Now imagine that by sheer accident your manager books you for a Christmas show at an old folks' home. While you can probably manage to leave the stage and the scene without actually being institutionalized, chances are that most of the members would want to have you committed. But why would they? The answers to this question hold the key to a better understanding of the concept of institution. First, your audience deemed you offensive because your band does not resemble, in the terms of the style of your performance, the musical styles to which they are accustomed. People believe that customs are important because they represent long-standing ways of doing things. Likewise, institutions have a clear historical impetus. Second, your reception was poor because your audience believed you lack a social organization that supports what you do. The musical industry as a whole is an example of such a social organization. Its support of custom is manifested through sale charts, awards, multi-year contracts, etc. So, because in your audience's mind your band is not backed by such organizational support, you come across to them as lacking institutional approval and therefore you are worthy of condemnation. What we have learned here is that these two components, institution as custom and institution as recognized social organization, are both important sociologically.

The formation and upholding of custom and social organization are political matters. Institutions, in other words, have a political force that is rooted in no small part in customs. Custom is no less a concern for music artists than anyone else. In fact, no matter how innovative and even revolutionary a form of art may be, it has to deal with institutional gatekeepers (Frith 1991) who enforce existing ways of doing things and existing criteria of what is good and bad. Art institutions are known by sociologists as "Art worlds" (Becker 1982: *x*): "network[s] of people whose cooperative activity, organized via their joint knowledge of conventional means of doing things, produce[s] the kind of art world that art world is known for." While institutionalization makes life difficult for original expression—and unfortunately that is too bad for you and your chicken-uniform-donning band members—it allows for familiar and customary performances to register more easily with audiences. From all of this it follows that, despite its aura of originality, much art needs to be conventional to be successful.

Community

While the previous section considered some links between music and politics as formal institutions, politics are practiced most often via communities—those informal social organizations that govern everyday life. *Community* shares its root with *communication*, the process of exchanging information. Music is obviously a form of communication, but so is the discourse surrounding it. Any investigation of the political significance of music must therefore consider music and the culture surrounding it as communication. In this section we discuss how the formation of a polity—another word for political community—is grounded in discourse.

"Discourse" is the technical term referring to the whole of communicative exchanges taking place among people, as well as to discrete instances of communication. Discourse refers to both the content of exchange and the form in which exchange takes place. Discourse is not only made of talk and words, but more importantly for us, also symbolic vehicles like musical sounds, styles, and practices. Discourse is powerful. It has the potential to repress as much as it does to create or produce. As we have seen, music can be viewed as a discursive force that "dumbs down" social groups, exerting power over what and how they consume. But music has the power to discursively form communities as well. A common example of communities formed around music is that of subcultures. The concepts of subculture and scene refer in similar ways to networks of people loosely affiliated around shared understandings, ways of communicating, and similar lifestyles. As we saw in Chapter 4, subcultural scenes include communities formed around musical genres. These have included jazz, punk, indie rock, extreme metal, rock, rap and hip-hop, goth, and straight edge, to name a few. Music communities emerge out of communicative exchanges, whether these happen at sanctioned events in dance clubs, on the radio or official band websites, or through informal channels that can be found in teens' bedrooms, at school, or online via blogs, chat forums, and social networking sites. The nature of these communities is often political in the traditional sense, as in the case of social protest music in punk and Pussy Riot, but not always. Fans of many different genres communicate their musical interests to others by chatting on MySpace or Facebook fan pages as forms of leisure and fun, with no obvious political intent.

By their very definition, communities have social boundaries. These boundaries are shaped in part through the shared interests and lifestyles of individuals. In the more traditional sense, they are also shaped by geography, as we see when we refer to a neighborhood or small town as a community. In many modern societies, especially those that control large geographical areas, small town communities are a basic fact of life. Even if you grew up claiming to be from a large metropolis like Atlanta or Chicago, you very well may have actually grown up in a nearby suburb with a small town, community feel. In such areas, communities can have a strong normative structure, meaning that members of the community are expected to more or less act similarly and share interests. Although a bit stereotypical, rural America is generally thought to be comprised of conservative local communities where everyone is expected to dress similarly, go to football games on Friday nights, and to church on Sunday mornings. When subcultural music "infiltrates" such communities and members start to express themselves in non-traditional ways, very real problems can emerge. The example of Swing Kids in Nazi Germany in the 1930s that we discussed in Chapter 4 is a very good example of this, and you may want to return to it. Likewise, the following story of the "West Memphis Three" describes the power of discourse in shaping communities and their boundaries around musical tastes.

The West Memphis Three and the Limits of Community

On May 5th, 1993, three eight-year-old boys went missing near a children's playground in West Memphis, Arkansas. The following day, police discovered the boys' submerged bodies in a wooded drainage creek nearby. The boys had been hog-tied, stripped and beaten. Two were drowned in the creek, while the third exhibited signs of sexual mutilation. The tragedy was quickly (and rightly) defined as a threat to the community, not only because of the murders, but also because of the absence of any suspects and of any obvious motive.

The threat of unknown pedophilic killers fueled speculation into who would do such a thing, but nearly a month later no suspects had been named. A local teenager named Damien Wayne Echols, however, had been questioned several times. Echols was an enigma in the community. He dyed his long hair jet black, often wore black clothes, and had expressed dissatisfaction with the overtly Christian culture that surrounded him. Amid public demand for headway in the case, news agencies started circulating stories that linked the murders to possible satanic rituals. A report on Jonesboro Arkansas KAIT evening news in early June stated that "since the very beginning of the investigation, people all around West Memphis have come forward with stories of satanic cults" (Sinofsky 1996). Television coverage of satanic activity among young people was not unique to the West Memphis case. Rather, Satanism had appeared in the previous decade as a "catch-all category for unacceptable behavior of youth ... [while] newspapers portrayed heavy metal music as a catalyst for Satanism" (Rowe and Cavender 1991: 271). The name Damien Echols, who was known to be a fan of the then-subcultural heavy metal band Metallica, began circulating among community members as a likely perpetrator.

With only two pieces of fiber as potential physical evidence, Echols, along with Jason Baldwin and Jessie Misskelley, Jr., were charged with the crime in early June 1993 after Misskelley (whose IQ was 72) emerged from a 12-hour police interrogation. Allegations similar to those found in Rowe and Cavender's (1991) study were immediately leveled against the "West Memphis Three." Once the teens were identified as the alleged killers, public reaction was swift and presented regularly in local and regional news reports. Take the following TV news interview with Pam Hobbs, the mother of one of the murdered boys, as one example.

Reporter: Do you feel like the people who did this were worshipping, uh (interrupted)
Hobbs: (interrupting) Satan? Yes I do.
Reporter: Why?
Hobbs: Just look at the freaks. I mean just look at 'em. They look like punks.

(Sinofsky 1996)

First, note how the mother was able to finish the reporter's question for him, suggesting the extent to which the community was already abuzz with stories about Satanism. Second, notice how quickly she reduced the alleged killers' guilt to their style, a fact of which the West Memphis Three themselves were well aware. Speaking about his alleged involvement during an interview while in jail, Jason Baldwin, then 16 years old, said, "I can see where they might really think I was in a cult cuz I wear Metallica t-shirts and stuff like that. . . ." Eighteen-year-old Echols pessimistically articulated the outcome of such stereotyping in a similar interview:

> The public was getting real upset seeing the cops were incompetent . . . couldn't do their jobs, so they had to do something fast. We were really the obvious choice cuz we stood out from everybody else. So it worked out to their advantage.
>
> (Sinofsky 1996)

Prior moral panics about heavy metal and Satanism provided the cultural backdrop against which the West Memphis Three were labeled and then handled by the mass media and the public alike. Stereotypical images of subcultural behaviors floated freely within the mediasphere in the early 1990s. Music and religion in particular were key dimensions of these images. The sinister tones found in 1980s heavy metal music were repeatedly defined by many community leaders as the soundtrack to youths' moral decay. Back at the West Memphis Three's trials, the prosecution's reliance on circumstantial evidence—no physical or eyewitness evidence was ever produced that could directly or definitively link any of the young men to the murders—did little to deter what Echol's called the "New Salem" atmosphere in the community at the time. Like in Lowney's (1995) study of teenage Satanism in rural Georgia, the overtly conservative Christian community in West Memphis was quick to identify these young men as folk devils and to assume the worst from them based on their musical interests, stylistic choices, and lack of popular friends.

The music that is popular (or unpopular) among communities around the country is linked to deeply significant political processes. All three teens were convicted of murder; Echols was sentenced to death, while Baldwin and Misskelley were sentenced to life imprisonment. In the same stroke, the local community of West Memphis—and indeed the larger community across America—resignified its own cohesiveness and sameness through a discourse that labeled, marginalized, and condemned three young men for their unpopular musical interests and styles. Communal discourses such as these can be slow to change, and folk devils are not quickly forgotten in either community's memory. Through its rejection of unpopular music and its alleged links to evil, West Memphis reconstituted itself as both a polity and a community. All those who agreed with the verdict, as well as the larger community of conservative Americans who supported the PMRC's values and actions in the previous decade, were active in the maintenance of a community that sometimes shows little tolerance for difference. Only in 2011, after more than 18 years of incarceration, were the West Memphis Three released from prison following new DNA evidence. Strengthened by what it sees as continual scapegoating by outsiders, the heavy metal community has for decades now been constituted in part on a distrust of authority, whether it be in the form of law enforcement, organized religion or sports, or the education system.

Continuous public discourse against heavy metal music resulted in the formation of two dialectically related communities. The discourse against unpopular music becomes a kind of sacred ritual "that draws persons together in fellowship and commonality" (Carey 1992: 18). Forced to live among the larger wary, and even hateful, community of right-thinking people, fans of unpopular music also find themselves relying on one another for community. Among those who form a community based on shared interest and shared marginalization, listening to music can be a type of communal ritual (through acts of playing, dancing, or singing, for example) that binds people together. Publicly decrying music that goes against a community's dominant culture serves a similar function. The community's condemnation of the West Memphis Three based on little more than their music interests and style represents the discursive realization of

> [a] symbolic order that operates to provide not information but confirmation, not to alter attitudes or change minds but to represent an underlying order of things, not to perform functions but to manifest an ongoing and fragile social process.
>
> (Carey 1992: 19).

Much like the comic example of the chicken-uniformed musicians at risk of being institutionalized earlier in this chapter, the West Memphis Three provide a very real instance of the extent to which musical preference is implicated in notions of polity and community.

Conclusion

The two contexts examined here—Constellation's politicized practices and community reaction toward unpopular music—show how music works as a technology in the production of the polity. Music can be used to control, shape, form, and even oppress groups, thus working as an effective tool in social organization, socialization, and community formation. As these examples have shown, politics and music are intertwined in multiple ways, often radically removed from the traditional connotation of "political music" as simply patriotic music or protest music.

Activities

(1) Has music played any part in religious activities in your family? Church? Choir? If your family is not religious, how do you and your parents deal with religious music when it occurs, say, at Christmas?

(2) Can you associate any songs or performers with your political views? Why, when and how? Are the political messages explicit or do the songs or performers elicit certain political feelings in you?

6

Class and Gender

Joseph A. Kotarba

For many sociologists the issue of social stratification lies at the very core of their research and theoretical concerns. *Social stratification*—the ordering of society into hierarchies of people in relation to the amount of broadly defined privileges they enjoy—is so important to sociologists because it holds the key to a better understanding, and consequently to the potential rectification, of social injustices. It is common for sociologists who lean toward rectifying social injustices to refer to stratification as "inequality." The term stratification has more neutral connotations than inequality, and usage of either sometimes reveals a particular sociologist's ideological preferences. Either way, the study of social stratification (or inequality) is also important to sociologists because it deals with at least three of the most important markers of social existence: class, and gender.

For the most part sociologists tend to study class and gender as either causes or effects of social and cultural forces. Even on the basis of anecdotal data that may be easily available to you, think about how variables like musical preferences, subcultural involvement, or concert attendance seem to be often related to racial, gender, or class categories. For example, we may very well observe and conclude—more or less systematically—that opera attendance is more typical amongst upper-class whites than others. Observations such as that are easy to make and difficult to refute. Yet, they often explain less than it seems. For instance, how do we explain the fact that people from other ethnic and class backgrounds enjoy going to the opera too?

In this chapter I attempt to challenge the very ideas of class and gender as conventionally understood. More precisely, I will argue that treating class and gender as "given"—that is, as characteristics that can be easily assessed along a range of discrete variables much like one would do when answering a questionnaire for a survey—and studying them as causes and effects can only tell part of a story. Instead, class and gender should be studied as intersubjective accomplishments: meaningful things that people do together (see Garfinkel 1967; West and Zimmerman 2002). By taking this approach I obviously do not intend to deny that class and gender are "real." It is obvious that they are real as it should be apparent to anyone that visible forms of discrimination, stereotyping, and disadvantage are meted out on the basis of such characteristics. Nonetheless, I will show that these characteristics are not as immutable as most people think and that they *become* real through social processes. By exposing the social dynamics of these processes we hope to show that the realities of class and gender are contingent on social action, and thus amenable to change, to being otherwise.

Everyday life sociologists argue that reality is the emergent outcome of processes of social interaction. Social realities are dependent on such factors as language and language use, history and collective memory-making, power, the social meanings of space, as well as material social forces. In other words, we believe that meaning—such as what it means to be a "man," to be "Asian," or to be "poor"—is achieved through the process of people communicating with one another in diverse situations. Such processes yield outcomes marked by *relatively* stable and *relatively* fixed agreed-upon meanings—that is, meanings open to interpretation and to change.

This chapter begins with an extended look at the literature on doing gender. This topic is arguably the clearest for pedagogical purposes, and it constitutes much of the background for our later discussions in this chapter. Our first example consists of a look into the phenomenon of making, being, and becoming a female pop star. Through a brief analysis of media coverage of the personal life of Jessica Simpson, we show that it is in the realms of visual language and spoken discourse that the social identities of famous women in music are made. The enormous attention that stars like Beyoncé, Lady Gaga, and Rihanna (but others could be mentioned) receive—especially in relation to their non-musical (e.g., gendered and sexual) lives—are examples of what historian and social theorist Michel Foucault (1990) called "confession" and thus reveal how gender and sex are subjects of discursive production, and thus of social interaction. I conclude this chapter with a look into the music of Canadian "pop punk princess" Avril Lavigne . . . well, the expression isn't mine. Actually I wonder precisely whether "pop punk princess" is a double oxymoron: can punk, a class-based musical expression, be popular amongst all classes, like a princess would be? By examining fan reviews of her debut CD we reflect on audience reception of class performance.

Doing Class and Gender

A central concern in everyday life sociology is people's talk (Garfinkel 1967). People talk in a variety of circumstances for a variety of reasons, and in the process of talking they often accomplish things. For example socio-linguists have observed that certain forms of talk are not only representational (i.e., about things, or in reference to things) but also performative, or in other words creative, constitutive of the social realities indicated in that very same talk. Think for example of the consequences of saying "I do" at a wedding ceremony. By saying "I do," a marriage is all of a sudden created. A common type of talk is that of giving *accounts* (Mills 1941; Scott and Lyman 1975). People routinely engage in "descriptive accountings of states of affairs to one another" says Heritage (1984: 136–137). Indeed, human beings determine their own future lines of conduct knowing that their conduct is open to such commentary and criticism. In other words, before they are about to do something people wonder what they are going to say if they are asked to account for what they did and why.

A common context in which people account for their actions is that of *confession* (see Foucault 1990); during religious confessions, religious followers are asked to account for what they have done wrong, to ask for forgiveness, and to express remorse. Confession must be truthful and based on values of full disclosure and trust. Within the context of religious practice confession takes places on church grounds. Yet, within the greater context of social relations confession may take place elsewhere as well. Social theorist Michel Foucault (1990) found that confession—whether by religious followers or not—was so common that confession itself served as a model for many practices of disclosure. He further commented that certain types of actions—namely those dealing with the most private aspect of one's lives, like intimate relationships, sexual behavior and sexual preferences, etc.—are especially subject to the demand for public disclosure and to being discussed ad nauseam.

Much like sex, gender, as West and Zimmerman (2002) have argued, is subject to extensive scrutiny, public talk, and stringent criteria of accountability. Gender and sex are indeed inextricable. Think for example of the rumor campaigns over the sexual orientation of *American Idol* runner up Clay Aiken and 'N Sync's Lance Bass—followed by heated announcements and revelations to the press. As these cases would show if we examined them in detail, by accounting for one's gender and sexuality people reinforce and/or contribute to the changing of attitudes, beliefs, and behaviors. Indeed, we can say that gender is an interactional "doing," a reality subject to social definitions and negotiations, and a practice undertaken by individuals in the most routine interpersonal contexts of everyday life.

Garfinkel's (1967) classic analysis of gender is illustrative of these principles. Much of value to social constructionists emerged from his study of the life of Agnes, a male-to-female transsexual who had chosen to undergo gender reassignment at the age of 17. In his study Garfinkel explained that Agnes had to re-educate herself to the gendered world in which she lived. Having lived as a male for the first 17 years of her life, and then gradually needing to adapt to her identity as a female, meant having to learn the practical methods whose knowledge and application was necessary for passing as a fully competent "normal" woman. In other words, prior to and after her surgery, Agnes "needed to display herself as a woman" and she was "obliged to analyze and figure out how to act within socially structured circumstances and conceptions of femininity" (West and Zimmerman 2002: 43) that those who are classified as women since birth learn early in their life.

Agnes's experiences showed that gender is a form of work, a social production if you will, that highlights "a complex of socially guided perceptual, interactional, and micropolitical activities" (West and Zimmerman 2002: 42) that results in the categorization of someone as a man or a woman. Gender, therefore, is a social accomplishment, something that is transparently practiced in the presence of others, and carried out according to the social norms existent within particular social situations. Gender, in sum, is an emergent feature of the categorization of social interaction, something that comes off a situation in light of people's conceptions on what is proper and on the basis of beliefs and routine activities expected of members of a sex category. A good example of this comes from what Kessler and McKenna (1978) call the gender attribution process. These authors write about a child who, upon seeing the photograph of someone in a business suit, contends that the photographed person is "a man, because he has a pee-pee" (Kessler and McKenna 1978: 154). Obviously the child cannot see the presence of a penis, but he imputes it to the person on the basis of visual signs of known masculinity (the business attire). What this case goes to show is that gender is thus imputed, or attributed, to others on the basis of the surfaces (appearance, conduct, etc.) detectable in social interaction.

Understanding gender as something that people do allows us to conceptualize the interaction between a gendered audience and a gendered social actor as a *performance*. Because all musical expressions are based on performances, the field of popular music studies thus turns out to be a convenient one for the study of gender performance. My precise interest in the following section is in how popular female musicians do gender in mediated situations and how mediated situations structure the gender performance of said musicians. I became interested in this after repeated observations that most media outlets seem to be less interested in musical sounds than they are in the mundane lives of musical celebrities. Take for example the likes of Britney Spears, Lorde, or Gwen Stefani and try and reflect on when their names are mentioned. You will quickly conclude that their music seems to matter less and less and that, despite the limited coverage of their musical performances, everyone can promptly recognize the names of these celebrities, match names with their pictures, and even talk about these celebrities' sexual and relationship histories or their preferences when it comes to fashion, style, and travel. In these cases music, it seems, takes a backseat to incessant mediated exposure to their everyday routines. In this process we can see a clear example of doing gender in the mediated situation.

I find that in the process of doing gender in the mediated situation, female celebrities enact a unique type of femininity: the female pop star or prima donna—a construction similar to what Connell (1987) called *emphasized femininity*. In what follows I dissect some common characteristics of doing emphasized femininity in the mediated situation.

Becoming a Prima Donna

The 1980s saw the start of a unique musical and cultural revolution as MTV began to bridge sound and image through the new medium of the music video (Kaplan 1987). Today, approximately four decades later, neither MTV, nor its "grown-up" music television counterpart (VH–1), or its Canadian cousin (Much Music), hardly shows music videos any more. Instead, today's MTV or Much Music viewer is greeted every day with endless gossip and talk, "reality shows," "interactive" television, alternative sports and freak shows, award shows, soaps, "college specials," and other non-musical productions defying easy categorization.

MTV is not alone in this trend. Gossip and celebrity magazines have been around for a long time, yet what seems different about recent televised iterations of this genre is that (a) in their numerous public appearances celebrities themselves seem to care less and less about the "official" reasons (like their artistic performances) that made them celebrities in the first place; and (b) celebrities and media seem to depend more and more on one another; thus entertainment media have all but relinquished their public role as critics, and celebrities have without reservation given more and more of their private lives to the intrusive eye of the popular media. The interaction of these two trends make for an interesting social situation, which allows us to study how media and female pop music celebrities interact with one another, and how out of their interaction there emerges (amongst other things) unique gender categories.

Contemporary sociologists argue that there are innumerable ways of doing gender, and therefore rather than "masculinity" or "femininity" we should speak of multiple *masculinities* and *femininities*. Speaking of masculinities and femininities allows us to reflect on the different performances of gender enacted in everyday life, and on the different scripts available for performing gender. Instead of thinking about the sex roles of a man and a woman, therefore, we could think of gender role models available to all. Take, for example, in the context of popular music, famous women like Alanis Morissette, Bette Midler, Shania Twain, Adele, Erykah Badu, Björk, and Bikini Kill's singer Kathleen Hanna. These women embody completely different notions of what it means to be "a woman." Of course something similar could be said for men: compare, for example, the variation across the gender styles of Clay Aiken, Jon Bon Jovi, Tony Bennett, Nelly, Enrique Iglesias, Garth Brooks, and Billy Joe Armstrong. Obviously different "actors" and different ways of acting out gender scripts, right? The lesson that we learn here is that there are no feminine women and masculine men or unfeminine women and unmasculine women. There simply are different ways of being feminine and masculine, of being woman and being man, and being both, or neither, or some of both.

Despite the fact that there are multiple scripts available for performing one's gender, it seems that popular entertainment media (both in their magazine and television forms) are most intrigued with *very few* particular ways of doing femininity. We refer to one of these gender categories as *postmodern prima donna*. What is a prima donna?

During the modern era the prima donna was the "first lady" of Italian opera, the leading female singer of an opera company. Legend has it that these prima donnas were affected by the "diva complex," in that their success led them to become superficial, materialistic, vain, unpredictable, irritable, unreasonable, egotistical, obsessed with their own fame, and narcissistic. Today's (postmodern) prima donnas are seemingly a bit different, judging, of course, from the public personas they display. While they maintain some of the characteristics of their earlier and modern counterparts, they also tend to resemble what Connell (1987) has called *emphasized femininity* and to embrace some of the traits that some theorists have found to be common in our contemporary, postmodern culture. Emphasized femininity rediscovers traditional (read: conservative) ways of being a woman in a retro fashion. This way of doing femininity entails "compliance, nurturance, and empathy" (Connell 1987: 187–188) and is linked with the traditional realms of the home and the bedroom. Emphasized femininity scripts demand that a woman be at peace with accommodating the desires of men and that she draw much of her sense of worth from being popular amongst them.

Yet, contemporary emphasized femininity also draws from more contemporary scripts. A contemporary prima donna blurs diverse traits by borrowing from an earlier style and recycling it in the context of the times, marked by a culture of endless superficial appearances and mediated imagery. Today's postmodern prima donnas, then, are a unique mix of "diva" and "girl next door," of princess and pauper, of cosmopolitan jetsetter and wholesome small-town girl, of hypersexualized seductress and virgin. This formula for performing gender is often applied today by several pop music stars (e.g. Taylor Swift, Britney Spears, Hilary Duff, etc.) and by the media outlets that broadcast their performances. Being a postmodern prima donna is therefore both about celebrities acting this way to be easily recognized and about media framing their public personas in this fashion to feed audiences' expectations. Being a postmodern prima donna is a complex mediated act of gender construction.

Acting like a prima donna entails, for example, regular acts of public confession to the media. Celebrity confessions are incredibly extensive these days. Anyone with media access can easily find what Jessica Simpson likes to eat, how she likes to decorate the table, that she is in the midst of considering adoptions, and that she has had fantasies about Brad Pitt, and more. Her private life, because of her continuous confessions, is constantly public and neither she nor her publicists seem to mind.

In confessing with regularity and depth, prima donnas like Jessica Simpson blur the distance between private and public spaces. A pair of concepts often used by sociologists, that of *private and public spheres*, help us understand prima donnas' performance of gender a bit better. Traditionally, sociologists explain, men's domain has been in the public sphere—for example in the work of paid employment, politics, and so forth. Women's activities and identities, instead, have been for the most part focused around the home, where "labor of love" activities such as child-rearing, relationship maintenance, and housework are meant to take place. Of course these boundaries have become blurred over time, yet sociologists find with great regularity examples of women being pulled back (or pushing themselves back) into the private sphere. For example, when musicians become famous most mass media continuously attempt to uncover their "private" lives, thus incidentally confining them again to the private sphere of child-rearing, home-making, and relationships. Jessica Simpson's own reality shows—staged in the context of her home—functioned in this sense as a return to the private sphere. Beside the aforementioned reality show, public attention to Simpson constantly focused on her dating adventures, struggles with divorce, with her body shape, and family life. Her own presentation of self in the context of children's charity work, adoption plans, promotion of both beauty and food products also continued to accentuate her emphasized femininity. To boot, her small-town ingenuity and naïveté, traditional moral values, and emotional ups and downs marked her emphasized femininity as a particularly histrionic one, punctually combined with her image as a demure yet glamorous, successful, vain, hypersexualized diva.

Confession, according to Foucault, does not uncover a pre-existing reality, but instead makes one anew. Thus, in being a consistent player in public discourse, or in other words in constantly generating talk about their private lives, postmodern prima donnas like Jessica Simpson can never logically lament "unfair media representation." The media are hardly *re-presenting* these women, since any trace of their livelihood *outside* of the media's eye seems to exist. Rather than media representation of a pre-existing reality, then this is case of actual social construction of meaning in the mediated situation. Therefore, as West and Zimmerman (2002: 42) explain, their prima donna persona is best understood as a "situated doing, carried out in the virtual or real presence of others . . . as both an outcome and a rationale" for their actions.

Being and becoming a prima donna demands careful efforts. Agnes, whom you will recall Garfinkel studied, did everything she could to pass for a "normal woman." Prima donnas like Jessica Simpson need to do everything they can to pass for diva-like "emphasized" women: star-like women who do what some others only wish they could do, including being beautiful and glamorous, talented, popular, successful, famous, graceful, and enjoying romance, yet all of it mixed with a certain grounding in conservative ideals like selflessness, sacrifice, ingenuity, innocence, willingness to stick it out during hardship, etc. Acting like a prima donna is—to borrow again from Garfinkel's (1967: 129) analysis of Agnes—attempting to be "120 per cent female," that is, managing to conduct herself appropriately in the most mundane occasions in order to be accountable as "normal" as the girl next door (with the same wishes, hopes, fears, misfortunes, limitations, etc.) and yet as "special" as the downtown girl (with the ability to make dreams and hopes come true, fearless, famed, and free, and yet at times, nostalgically longing for a simpler lifestyle). Jessica Simpson has more recently achieved "normal" and "special" through a myriad of activities expected of a contemporary prima donna: her own line of shoes and active-wear clothing, scent, a 60-pound weight loss, plastic surgery to tie it all together, hot husband, gorgeous children and, of course, her own website (jessicasimpson.com).

In conclusion, the media—as important social agents in our post-modern times—play an obvious role in setting the parameters of what constitutes normal and expected gendered behavior, for women much more stringently than for men. Doing gender in the mediated situation is, therefore, much about "doing" gender as it is about "being done" by available gender categories and preferred media casts. The activity of doing gender in the mediated situation is thus hardly free from restrictions. It is hardly possible for someone to plan in advance what type of gender performances one will engage in for the next five or ten years and then freely execute that plan. Even trendsetters like Madonna and, more recently, Lady Gaga, who have wished to play by their own rules, have often collided with insurmountable walls of expectations. Chipping away at that wall, if one wishes to build new roles is, however, an act which shows both courage and promise.

Doing Class and Gender: Is Avril Lavigne Punk?

We conclude our reflection on gender and class with an analysis of the class-based performance of Canadian rocker Avril Lavigne, who reached stardom in the spring of 2002, when she made her debut with the incredibly successful CD entitled *Let Go*. In addition to her catchy "pop-punk" hooks, Avril caught the world of pop music by storm with what—at the time—seemed like an anti-Britney Spears formula of skateboarder looks, street attitude, and dark appeal. *Let Go*, and especially her single "Complicated," reached the top of the *Billboard* charts, gained nominations for Best Pop New Artist and Best Pop Female Artist at the 2002 *Billboard* Music Awards, received five Grammy nominations, and won the Best Song, Best CD, Best Female Artist, and Best Homework Song at the 2002 Radio Disney Music Awards, as well as the MTV Video Music Award for best new artist in a video. *Let Go* also went platinum on July 12, 2002 breaking the record for short-time increases in sales and radio spins. At the time of writing, the album had sold over 15 million copies worldwide. Media appearances, endorsements, endless play of her videos, and celebrity gossip have now made Avril Lavigne one of the more successful female singers of the last decade. Her persona, especially at the time of her debut, is our object of interest here.

In examining Avril Lavigne, we are not concerned with her self or personal identity. Instead we are interested in her public persona, in other words with her public image and with the discourses surrounding her mediated presentation of self. By studying her self-presentation through the mass media as a complex and multifaceted performance, and by focusing on how she "does" class, we are interested in questioning how she stages her front before her audiences through the management of her style, physical appearance, life story, career, her status as a celebrity, her song lyrics, and even more. So far in this chapter we have examined elements of performance of gender without giving too much consideration to how audiences interpret performances. We take it upon ourselves to observe how Avril Lavigne's fans, as well as non-fans, deconstruct the credibility of her self-presentation. Our data primarily consists of reviews of *Let Go* voluntarily submitted to various websites by Internet users. Using a socio-semiotic frame of analysis we focus on how audiences interpret the authenticity of Avril Lavigne's performance of class.

As an analytical tool we can divide audiences' readings of her CD and her persona into two broad categories: the category of *hegemonic readings* and that of *counter-hegemonic readings*. The former category includes readings *preferred* by a performer. For example, when a teacher delivers a lecture in a classroom, they will hope that their students will buy into their argument without challenging them too much. A politician will have the same attitude toward a speech, a parent toward a lesson imparted to their children, and so forth. Hegemonic readings of Avril Lavigne's performances reveal that what she intended to communicate went over well with some fans. As one of my students insisted:

> Hey, I wish people would stop saying such bad stuff about Avril! So she's a punk. So? Get over it! That's how she likes to express herself. Not everyone likes to be the same as everyone else.
>
> Yeah she's punky and I hope she puts more songs out. If you like Avril, then get the CD! I am hooked on it! Get it! You will be satisfied with your purchase. She wrote all her songs AND plays her own music. She is so good! You all really need to try this CD out. I am so glad I did!

Punk music is the soundtrack of autonomy, independence, and rebellion. As we explain elsewhere in this book, these traits are often associated with the ideal of *authenticity*. Authenticity is not only a moral and aesthetic value but also something which must be concretely performed, which must be "done." When audiences believe in the sincerity of a performer and in the originality and authenticity of musical expression, a performer—regardless of how actually sincere he or she may be—has managed to convey his or her front and preferred persona well. Avril's persona—at least at the time of her debut—revolved critically around stories told about her start in the musical world. Avril rebelliously dropped out of high school when she was 16 to follow her dream of becoming a singer. Her independence from social constraints continued to mark her biography and career: Avril was believed to be uncompromising on how her records were to be produced, what her image was, and what she wanted her lyrics to communicate. Compared to the likes of Christina Aguilera, Mandy Moore, and Britney Spears her early audiences found her to be low maintenance, unpretentious and down to earth, and unaffected by her celebrity status. Her looks seemingly embodied this. Avril (and her fans) were often seen wearing work shirts and rebelliously loose neck ties—a true punk uniform of sorts, a sign which expresses at once affiliation with working-class fashion, and condemnation of middle- and executive- or debutante-class respectability.

However, what works with some audiences does not work with others. Counter-hegemonic readings of Avril Lavigne's persona point to her insincerity and manufactured authenticity. These readings can be called *oppositional.* Particularly jarring to some audiences are her inconsistencies; definitive give-aways of what seems like an attempt to commodify authenticity. As music critic Jessica Zietz (n.d.) notes: "Let me go draw a big skull and crossbones on my arm so that I can be punk too. Please. Avril Lavigne just seems fake, plain and simple."

Punk is first and foremost a class movement and ideology (Hebdige 1979). Its roots are to be found in working-class youth and in their alienation from a political and economic system that —these youth feel—commodifies all individual expressions (Hebdige 1979). Punk is also an aesthetic ideology of sorts. Its raw sound is virtue made out of necessity: studio production, good instruments, and music lessons are expensive, unaffordable, and thus deemed undesirable. Punk is therefore rough, all but pretty, gritty, and uninterested in pretentiousness. For some audiences, therefore "to call (Avril) punk is to tarnish the images of actual punk artists and their contributions to music as a whole. Please, people, stop listening to this CD, stop wearing socks on your arms, get some real music" (Zietz n.d.).

The jury will remain out on Avril Lavigne indefinitely. She has developed a chameleon-like ability to shift musical styles, personas, and career trajectory. In 2013, she returned to her punk roots with her eponymous album and a single, "Rock N Roll," produced with Chad Kroeger (see the video on YouTube—it's fun rock'n'roll again!). On the grown-up side, she established the Avril Lavigne Foundation to fight Lyme disease—which she has, in fact, sadly contracted—and the Special Olympics.

I really like Avril Lavigne—she reminds me of the "in your face, Dad" female artists my daughter and her friends grew up with in middle school, including Alanis Morissette. By pointing out attempts at the commodification of punk, these writers resist the co-optation of class and a class-based aesthetics and ideology. What these examples go to show is that impression management does not always work. Despite how well a person may play a role certain audiences will, at times, remain skeptical and challenge the sincerity and authenticity of performances. This does not take away from the notion that class is something that is performed, however.

In fact, and interestingly enough, in publicly rejecting the sincerity and credibility of Avril Lavigne's performance, these Internet users reassert the significance of performing class in certain ways and in not in others. Furthermore, in doing so they too perform class, don't they?

Final point about punk: I recently watched the American Music Awards for 2016 on TV. Those award shows are a good way to stay in touch with the most popular artists and styles. The punk band Green Day performed, showcasing a new album as is typical for these events. As the critics noted, they are "Louder, Faster, Angrier" (*Rolling Stone* 2016). In addition to the new album and commercial presence at AMA, Green Day own their own recording studio in Oakland, California and they openly supported mainstream Democratic presidential nominee Hillary Clinton. Now, does that strike you as an on-the-edge, rebellious, sacrilegious punk band? Me neither.

Conclusion

What we have attempted to demonstrate in this chapter is that class and gender are not fixed categories. In certain situations in social interaction these important markers of individual existence may look and feel as if they are unchangeable but to think of them as unchangeable does little for a critical sociological cause keen on the eradication of social injustice based on ascribed social status and qualities. If we take class and gender as performances, that is, as something that people do, we enable ourselves to think in alternative ways and to reflect on how things could be otherwise. Conceptualizing class and gender as performatives further allows us to reflect on social interaction, rather than on biology, as the site where social realities are created, communicated, and interpreted.

Activities

(1) Think of two or three female artists popular today who portray a defiant identity—hint: remember Hannah Montana? What specific characteristics of defiance seem to work with today's audience? Why?

(2) Think of two or three male artists who come across as prima donnas. Do their careers follow the discussion above on women?

7

Hip-Hop Culture and Social Change

Raphael Travis and Scott W. Bowman

In Chapter 4, you read about hip-hop culture largely in terms of its status in society at its points of origin. The world of critics and social control agents chose to see harm in hip-hop and rap music. Put differently, they viewed hip-hop as deviance. In this chapter, we will present a contrasting take on hip-hop, seeing it as a dynamic cultural movement rather than simply a subcultural phenomenon.

Hip-hop culture began as the quintessential American subculture, immersed in a unique space and time, and among a regionally specific confluence of races and ethnicities. Over the past several decades, the growth and reach of hip-hop has been immeasurable, touching both popular cultures and producing counter-cultures. Hip-hop has shaped clothing and dress, language, hairstyles, dance, accessorizing, public space and symbolic interaction. More specifically, what once began as a sporadic scattering of inner city, New York City participants has flourished into a far-reaching phenomenon that reaches the most remote locations on the planet. While there were different elements within the earliest forms of hip-hop—including emceeing, b-boying, deejaying, and graffiti—we were simultaneously witnessing an emerging knowledge of self that reinforced beholding the proverbial forest (the broader hip-hop culture) for the trees (hip-hop's elements). More than 40 years later, all forms of the hip-hop culture are indelibly entrenched within the mainstream of larger, popular global cultures and subcultures.

Global hip-hop culture is a multi-billion dollar, *econocultural industry* that has become integrated and reinforced within a variety of larger global cultures and subcultures (Morgan 2016). Over the last two years for example, as demand for streaming music via digital platforms increased and physical and digital downloads decreased, hip-hop has remained as popular as ever. Streaming digital music services like Spotify and Rhapsody report that hip-hop and R&B occupy 25 per cent of streamed content, the largest among all genres (Hooten 2015).

Constructing an uncompromising hip-hop thread that ranges from subculture to mainstream has influenced how the various parts of the culture are created, disseminated, consumed, and analyzed. This journey has a uniquely powerful influence on popular music by creating an industry based more on products and profit than recognition and respect of hip-hop as a culture, its origins, and its pioneers (Travis 2016). Simultaneously, this journey has also resulted in transformations within the culture itself (Muhammad 2015), as well as the need for its critical assessment. More specifically, negotiating how hip-hop culture is engaged and its functional use requires a critical understanding of hip-hop's tenuous position as both *co-opted culture and flexible adaptive subculture*. The purpose of the chapter is to contemplate how the forest and trees of hip-hop culture interconnect, how the vantage point of the consumer (e.g., listeners, students, practitioners) can shape the consumer's musical interaction, and the manner in which the trees provide a different narrative of hip-hop culture than the forest.

Seeing the Forest

When we look at the hip-hop forest (i.e., Industry content), we may regrettably miss the concealed value and influence of hip-hop culture's trees expressed through its music. Using the most popular artists and songs, several researchers have looked closely at content for themes and trends. On the one hand, evidence suggests content within hip-hop has become: (a) increasingly narrow; (b) a glorification of riskier elements; (c) ahistorical; and (d) inundated with conspicuous consumption (Holody et al. 2016; Podoshen et al. 2014; Primack et al. 2012). In sum, the industry and mainstream side of the musical form has become masculine gendered (Nash and Nash 2016), and the higher-risk themes of violence, misogyny, substance abuse, materialism, and conspicuous consumption are increasingly glorified (Travis 2016).

One telling example of the prevalence of conspicuous consumption comes from a recent study of hip-hop videos created between 1995 and 2008, where researchers found that 93 per cent had brand placements; up from percentages of between 30 and 40 per cent in earlier studies (Burkhalter and Thornton 2012). Preliminary research similarly suggests that individuals who prefer hip-hop music score higher in materialism and conspicuous consumption (Podoshen et al. 2014), while correlative findings show how materialism and value of high-status items is associated with unfavorable health status for young Black youth (Sweet 2010).

At the moment, highlighting the negative and high-risk trends in hip-hop culture influences how hip-hop is used for functional purposes in education, in mental health, and in other youth programming like afterschool and summer programming. However, risky trends do not mean simple exposure to hip-hop is negative, or that a more complete range of counter-narratives and empowering voices in hip-hop culture does not exist. Ample evidence highlights how the culture exists beyond the industry of popular music (Love 2015 and 2016), and that vibrant, global subcultures exist that allows hip-hop to flourish and filter through society in unique and varied ways (Muhammad 2015).

Implications: The Need to See the Trees

The number one question we get when discussing our work with hip-hop as researchers and practitioners is "What about all of that [explicit] language?" It has a powerfully negative stigma and thus influences how decision makers facilitate opportunities for integrating hip-hop strategies. Practitioners—social workers, psychologists, counselors, and even psychiatrists—are in a difficult position because it is apparent that youth listen to, know, and engage with explicit content. Yet, youth commonly do not have the opportunity to properly critique, explore, and interrogate content with a concerned and supportive adult for educational or health and well-being purposes.

At the same time the range of empowering hip-hop content is actually larger than ever. A recent effort to help synthesize all of the literature within the hip-hop studies field resulted in over 7000 entries.

This international bibliography explores a range of topics, and also includes a regional emphasis, focusing in on 27 U.S. states and more than 100 countries (Gray 2016). Additionally, evidence continues to mount about the numerous pathways to empowering engagement of hip-hop culture even among historically marginalized groups such as women (Emdin et al. 2016; Travis et al. 2016),

Adding to the variety and volume of content is hip-hop's continued regionalization. It can be a larger region, such as the city of Chicago with both its multiple generations of nationally recognized hip-hop artists, and its episodic explosions of talent. Conversely, it can be a much smaller region such as a neighborhood, like the classic hip-hop locale of Queensbridge, New York (Chang 2005). There are also regional efforts like the "51210 Movement" that bridges hyperlocal scenes between the cities of Austin (area code 512) and San Antonio (area code 210), Texas (Banbury 2016).

Even within regions, features of hip-hop culture are extraordinarily varied. Muhammad's (2015) close look at the Chicago hip-hop scene provides a powerful insight into distinct ways fundamentalists are wedded to hip-hop's historical traditions. Industry-centric artists are focused on profit, women are resisting misogynistic and exclusionary industry norms, and pro-Black artists are providing positive counter-narratives to negative portrayals of Black history and societal contributions.

Contemporary hip-hop culture is increasingly accessible to all through everyday exposure and technological advances. This increased access has contributed to more rapid and widespread skill-building in emceeing, deejaying, beat-making, and music production (Thompson 2012). The number of laptop studios, street/lunchroom celebrities, and budding entrepreneurs with skills is numerous. Coupling these trends with four decades worth of existing content, we have more raw material than ever available for professional use beyond just entertainment. Hip-hop culture is a living archive, and an expanding library of interactive content (Travis 2016).

What Can We Learn? How Can We Grow?

Present day ambassadors of hip-hop culture, whether artists, or professionals in education, mental health, the afterschool and summer sector, and health, have taken these opportunities for growth to heart. These individuals transcend simply their personal growth to engage in the hip-hop scene dedicated to strengthening the available infrastructure for young people to learn and grow. Further, the desired outcomes are for both young people and the communities they value to be at their best (Travis 2016).

Cultural Familiarity within Learning and Growth

The tools of hip-hop culture, the sensibilities and practices of the culture, and an insistence on creating and being the best, are familiar, engaging, and powerful for many young people (Emdin et al. 2016). Further, identity-centric aspects of hip-hop, such as knowledge of self in general, and pro-Black narratives more specifically, can speak directly and positively affirm perceived marginalized social identities. Prior research has found that positive racial and cultural identities are associated with empowering engagement of hip-hop, both for the self and the community (Travis and Bowman 2012; Travis 2016; Dixon et al. 2009).

Empowering engagement specific to women is another aspect of identity supported in the literature. In these spaces, women contest misogynistic narratives and instead develop new proactive frames for themselves and other women (Travis et al. 2016; Love 2016). Hip-hop is generally deemed a male-gendered space and when this intersects with influences of an industry-dominated mainstream, care must be given to create safe spaces for counter narratives (Heath and Arroyo 2014).

Identity Across Arenas

The relationships, especially when viewed within the context of Empowerment-based Positive Youth Development, are reciprocal. Identities are nurtured and reinforced within safe communities of belonging. Identities are also the gateway to discipline specific strategies (Travis 2016). For example, when working on mental health issues, gender-specific dynamics—whether it is alternative pathways to existing stressors among women (Love 2016), or men's willingness to seek professional help (Levy and Keum 2014)—highlight the prominence of identity. Identity is also critical in relation to issues of social justice and power, when conditions are evaluated to be disparate and in need of improvements. Identity is also associated with anxiety, stress, and pain relief that have physical health manifestations because of how our social identity often plays a role in where we live, learn, work, and play (Robert Wood Johnson Foundation 2011).

Education, mental health, and other helping domains are the contexts within which learning and growth goals, or agendas, exist. The strategies and activities employed exist on a spectrum from minimal

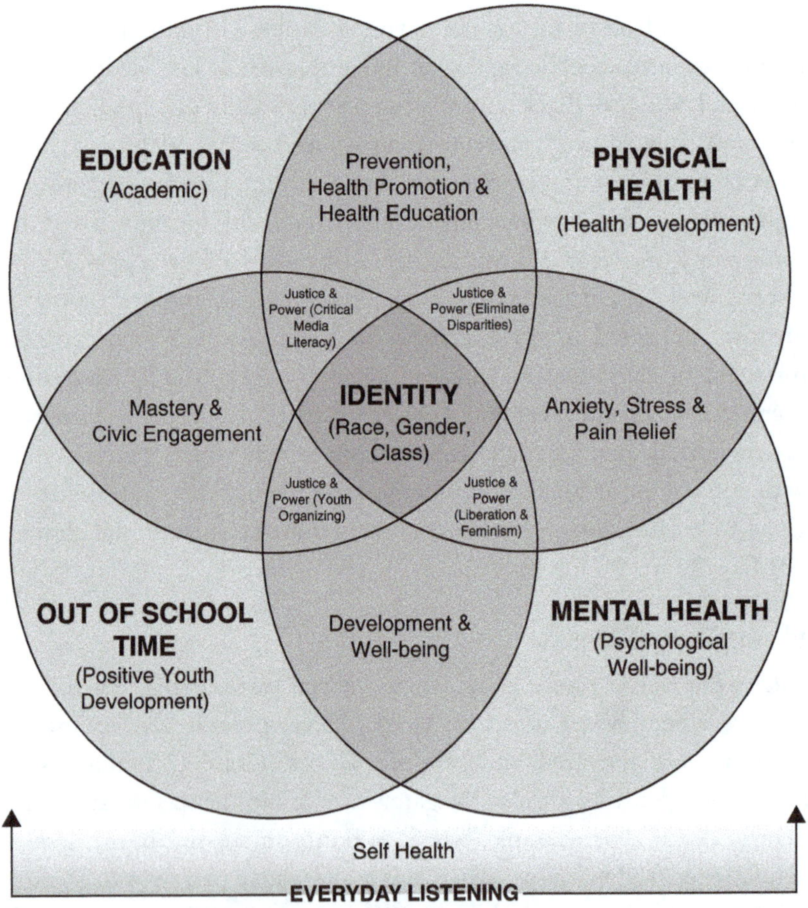

Figure 7.1 Contexts and Goals (Arenas and Agendas) for Music Experiences.
Source: Reprinted from Raphael Travis Jr. 2016. *The Healing Power of Hip Hop*. Santa Barbara, CA: ABC-CLIO.

intervention to comprehensive and advanced levels of intervention. For example, mental health strategies can simply be support and the provision of health education resources. However, mental health strategies can be advanced clinical therapy services by licensed professionals across the range of mental health providers (i.e., social workers, psychologists, music therapists). Education, afterschool and summer programming, and other interventions can similarly vary in depth, comprehensiveness, and quality. When looking at points of overlap, unique opportunities exist to build upon the interdisciplinary nature of these experiences. For example, the intersection of mental health and education has proven to be a ripe area of overlap (Emdin et al. 2016; Travis and Maston 2014).

Many afterschool and summer programs work toward standards of quality that align directly with positive development and well-being. In these spaces identity takes center with high efficacy strategies based in social-emotional learning and positive youth development. When thinking about identity within education, the first type is linked to learning in relation to *health* and the second type is linked to learning in relation to *self and community improvement*—through both personal mastery *and* civic engagement. For the latter type, the active and engaged citizen must feel a sufficient sense of belonging within a community, and assess a sufficient level of need for improvement in conditions to want to master the skills necessary to positively engage and contribute. Culturally relevant pedagogy, and more specifically, critical hip-hop pedagogy is a bridge between the two types of identity-linked education that facilitates belonging and engagement (Gosine and Tabi 2016; Hill 2009; Irby and Petchauer 2012; Ladson-Billings 1995).

In the health domain, (a) prevention; (b) the awareness and desire to make healthy choices; and (c) being open to promoting healthy attitudes and behaviors among peers, are also anchored in identity (Travis 2016). Ultimately, the most unique strategies and activities will build upon the interdisciplinary nature of these opportunities.

Hip-hop has also shown to be exceptionally interdisciplinary by academic topic (Travis 2016), while being rooted in self and social awareness (Love 2016). The result finds hip-hop abundant with opportunities for learning and growth across a variety of arenas (Travis 2016: 133). This range of topics and arenas provide many entry points and activities for present day educators, mental health professionals, and youth workers who have been immersed in the culture for decades with a keen eye to its educational and developmental value.

Innovations in Hip-Hop: Technology and Digital Music, and the DIY Generation

Advances in technology and the Internet age have added to this range of available material for hip-hop. It has greatly advanced the speed of music production, the circulation of content, and the accessibility of innovative content and ideas. In short, we are awash in music in general and hip-hop specifically. Hip-hop culture has always enjoyed its own within-culture peer-to-peer, hand-to-hand sharing through mixtapes where new and underground material circulated widely (Chang 2005; Travis 2016). Supercharge these tendencies with digital music, the web connected world, infinitely more aspiring and seasoned artists, and the global reach of hip-hop, and the result is an almost infinite range of high-quality content to skillfully use to promote learning and growth.

The DIY Generation: Unbridled Creativity

The Do-It-Yourself, or DIY generation is made possible by the advance of technology, the affordability of advanced music technology tools, and the amount of free-ware that is widely available. On top of this is a more normalized entrepreneurial cultural ethos (Sköld and Rehn 2007).

The music technology company Ableton states how their signature device, the Push (2), is "an instrument that puts everything you need to make music in one place—at your fingertips . . . hands-on control of an unlimited palette of sounds, without needing to look at a computer" (Ableton 2016). As contemporary youth can carry the entirety of musical history in their pocket through smartphones, they can also create with an unlimited palette of sound, including instruments, with just one lightweight device. Add to this the bevy of free online music production tools, and in many ways their opportunities for creative expression through music knows no bounds.

Chance The Rapper is one of the most popular and successful artists of the mid–2010s, and he demonstrates his own unique manifestation of the DIY ethos. When the Chicago emcee allowed listeners to freely download his album *Acid Rap*, and over one million downloads resulted, a bidding war developed among labels. He denied initial suitors and became the celebrated poster child for independent artists (Friedman 2016). The prize for not bowing to mainstream commercial Industry interests was believed to be creative freedom and financial autonomy. His following two projects, *Surf* and *Coloring Book*, were exclusively released (freely) through Apple music (Friedman 2016). While not a label, Apple is a major financial company. It is unclear if there are any formal label-type agreements, but Chance is still considered one of the major faces of the independent ethos.

Chance's music reflects the binary in hip-hop discussed by Love (2016) and the risk amid empowerment discussed by Travis and Bowman (2011). He leads with empowering narratives linked to self and community improvement, and often integrates spirituality. He also has tracks that embody high-risk attitudes and behaviors. The empowering elements of his catalog are what tend to shine brightest among current observers. And his attention to community building only adds to this. For example, he established his Social Works Foundation in 2016 to unite young creatives on behalf of regional community improvement goals. To this end, during election season 2016, Chance threw a free concert in the park and then led participants to a voting location under the banner of "Party to the Polls" (Roti 2016).

Chance The Rapper is the contemporary poster-child for the DIY ethos that permeates much of present day society. The value of this for hip-hop culture is that it preserves independence financially and creatively. Financial independence from major labels allows the potential for greater wealth accumulation as an entrepreneur. And, for artists that emphasize more empowering, and lower-risk attitudes and behaviors within their music, they are not pressured as much to conform to popular music trends.

Innerview and Overview

A core feature of hip-hop culture has been the ability for artists to look within *innerview* and to look outward toward society (overview) with a critical lens. Problems and solutions are contemplated and critiqued with accountability placed on the self and others (Hollander and Quinn 2016; Travis 2016). Hip-hop's attention to social issues and lack of fear to address more challenging issues like racial dynamics, equity, and justice are powerful cultural tools (Porfilio et al. 2014). Communities can be highlighted and understood, with pride and solidarity, in a way that allows mobilization for change (i.e., better community conditions). Communities are social identities that individuals ascribe to and groups with which they participate and have a sense of belonging. This may be according to gender, race/ethnicity, sexual identity, SES, or concern about issues of justice and equity—like the environment (e.g., Flint water crisis), police excessive use of force, or even global social movements (e.g., Arab Spring; see Kotarba and Lalone 2014).

Twenty Years and We the People

> All you Black folks, you must go
> All you Mexicans, you must go
> And all you poor folks, you must go
> Muslims and gays, boy, we hate your ways
> So all you bad folks, you must go.
>
> —A Tribe Called Quest

This is the hook to the song "We the People" from hip-hop legendary group A Tribe Called Quest. This track is the first single off of the album *Thank You 4 Your Service: We Got It From Here* released in 2016. It is ATCQ's first album in 18 years, and hit Billboard's #1 spot after its first week. It lands within the hip-hop diaspora in the wake of a contentious presidential election season (APA 2016; Costello 2016). ATCQ has shown maturity as a group, yet remains firmly entrenched in hip-hop's core values, a resounding demonstration that it is not only a youth culture. In fact, *Thank You 4 Your Service* is a two-generation (2-Gen) album, but it is grounded in an earlier generation of hip-hop. It is a celebratory passing of the torch, but one that has the older generation not marching off into the sunset; instead it is marching alongside the younger generation (MacInnes 2016).

Black and Blue

Another pressing issue in the present social climate is the relationship between the Black community and the criminal justice system, especially law enforcement. Between 2014 and 2016, the United States has faced a particularly challenging spate of officer-involved Black death. These events have instigated a number of important popular music tracks addressing the relationship between the Black community and law enforcement. Between the very public deaths of Michael Brown in 2014 and Philando Castile and Alton Sterling in 2016, and the emergence of the #BlackLivesMatter movement, injustice at the hands of law enforcement has crystallized as a core defining issue for the present generation.

The distress and trauma potentially resulting from widespread exposure (e.g., iPhone videos) are a concern. More distressing and potentially traumatizing is the perception that the lack of systemic justice and accountability for Black humanity is structural. It has entrenched a belief that police tactics reinforce the idea that Black and Brown lives have a limited and pre-scripted value in society.

Coupled with the perceived marginalization of other groups like the LGBTQ community, the South Asian, Muslim, and Sikh communities (Iyer and Rathod 2011; Iyer 2015), and the Latinx communities, the quest for equity and justice around law enforcement aligns strongly with social movements of the day that are very vocal about these issues. The contentiousness of the 2016 presidential election added fuel to each of these movements, before and after election day, because of stress and anxiety linked ideological conflicts and to perceptions of increased marginalization of these social identities and communities (APA 2016; Costello 2016).

Hip-hop's familiarity among popular music allows topically relevant tracks to grace the mainstream with greater ease, but also faces the scrutiny of those who do not agree ideologically. But, artists like Kendrick Lamar have such immense popularity that evidence suggests opportunities exist to walk the tightrope of entertainer and agent of change. Lamar's "Alright," the de facto national anthem of the Black Lives Matter movement, follows in the spirit of what Nina Simone's "Young, Gifted, and Black" did for Black pride and the Black Power movement of the late 1960s and early 1970s.

A renaissance of empowering hip-hop music has occurred during the last two years that spotlights disparate trends in the criminal justice system in general and in law enforcement more specifically. Mainstream industry artists like Kendrick Lamar, Jay-Z, Common, and J. Cole have songs specifically addressing these issues, alongside lesser-known but skilled emcees like Oddisee, Rapsody, AWKWORD, Add-2, and Vic Mensa. These are but a small few of the contemporary artists. Even further, the list of emcees and tracks touching on these issues extends historically over four decades, extends in breadth from mainstream (industry) to local and independent, and extends with a global reach. Hip-hop is also unique in its consistent use of a collective memory and narrative that acts as a within-group cultural dialogue. It is an ongoing discourse that reaches back to reflect on Emmett Till as much as it contemplates the tragedy of Tamir Rice (Travis 2016: 104–105).

#YouGoodMan: Hip-hop and Mental Health

> Anxiety and depression have ruled my life for as long as I can remember and I never leave the house because of it . . . I don't trust anyone because of it and I'm tired of being held back in my life. I deserve to have peace. I deserve to be happy and smiling.
>
> —Kid Cudi

These were Kid Cudi's words upon sharing with the world that he was entering a psychiatric facility due to depression and suicidal ideation (Setaro 2016). This was neither Cudi's first time discussing personal depressive symptoms, nor was it the first time issues of mental health circulated within the landscape of hip-hop culture. Kendrick Lamar, arguably hip-hop's most iconic contemporary emcee provided insight into his own bouts of depression on his track "u" from his album *To Pimp a Butterfly*. While different circumstances are at the root of their depressive symptoms, each has been transparent in their music, honest about vulnerability, and their need for help. In fact, Kaiser Permanente is using Lamar's lyrics from this album and songs "i" and "u" in video ads to encourage young people to speak about stress and anxieties (Kulp 2016).

The list of hip-hop artists integrating candid discussion about mental health are numerous, and thus the trend has been set. In a world where anxieties are high, trauma is prominent, it is great to see that exploration of mental health concerns in hip-hop is more open and accepting. Despite artist Drake's attempt to shame him, when Cudi shared his reasons for needing to check into a facility, it helped spark the #YouGoodMan campaign to help raise awareness about reaching out to others who may be in need of [mental health] support and to normalize a willingness to seek and receive help (Blaque 2016).

Moving Forward with Popular Music and Hip-Hop Culture

As authors, we are hip-hop at its most basic level and have been so long before our days as collaborative researchers. At different times in our lives, we have taped underground rap music shows on cassette tapes. We have been b-boys breakdancers, deejays, and emcees. We have worn leather medallions with an Africa image or Public Enemy's logo, and the Black Diaspora colors of red, black, and green. We have worn hi-top fades, as well as parachute pants and Raiders, Lakers, and Kings paraphernalia. We have rapped along to lyrics explaining how it's like a jungle sometimes, talking about a horse named Paul Revere, profiling our Adidas, telling Children's Stories, asking What's the Scenario?, saying it's nothing but a G Thang, and insisting we Fight the Power.

We have also been told for decades that our music and culture is a misogynistic, violence-promoting, ill-tempered, self-destructive, and non-redeeming social medium. It was explained that the lyrics were demoralizing, unhealthy, and counterproductive. We were told that *all* of the lyrics were self-hating, divisive and disrespectful. Moreover, we heard this detailed opposition to hip-hop from people of various ages, races, and agencies. Unambiguously, those who misunderstood hip-hop culture did so from the lens and birds-eye perspective of hip-hop as a forest.

During our research within the last eight years we have been able to illustrate and clarify the crucial role that the "trees" have played in the development of a more complex hip-hop culture. Specifically, we have found consistent evidence of five core empowering themes experienced by youth as they engage hip-hop culture, and rap music: (a) esteem; (b) resilience; (c) growth; (d) community; and (e) change. In these instances, hip-hop and rap are used to feel better, to do better, to be better, for a better sense of belonging, and to promote better conditions within prioritized communities (Travis and Bowman 2011; Travis and Deepak 2011; Travis, 2016).

The full range of hip-hop culture should be explored, in the present and historically. Popular music is a great way to engage young people, to connect with them, and to validate their voice and agency based on what they know and like in the moment. It is also a great foundation to explore common narratives of esteem, resilience, growth, community, and change in their favorite music that can also be found in less popular music of the present, and both popular and underground music of the past. Finally, popular music is an excellent opportunity to explore and critique risky attitudes and behaviors, and to reinforce themes of prevention and well-being with parents and professionals committed to helping youth be the best versions of themselves.

It is the culmination of these findings, as well as the findings of other hip-hop scholars, that attempt to drive home the value of hip-hop culture. The culmination of evidence suggests one direction forward, empowering engagement of hip-hop's mainstream face (the forest) and its nuanced subcultures (trees), while at the same time, investing in opportunities to mitigate risk. Ultimately, this can only occur through striving to expand the most empowering aspects of hip-hop culture, in education, mental health, afterschool and summer programs, health, and all spaces where individuals and communities can grow.

In conclusion, our research, teaching and service related to hip-hop culture resonates well with the movement in sociology towards increased engagement with the community. This engagement in our departments of Social Work and Justice Studies is a normal and traditional goal of our disciplines. We hope that, increasingly, sociologists working in applied and policy-related areas (Hanemaayer and Schneider 2014) will borrow from our experience and dedication, as we continue to borrow from insights from sociological thinking on organizations, youth, families, deviance, culture, communications, and other key social and cultural areas.

Activities

(1) Who Am I? Identify the top five groups that you feel you identify with. It can be based on race, gender, socio-economic class, or any group that you feel a part of, like: your family, a team, an interest

group, a spiritual or faith group, a neighborhood/city/state, or any collective of people you can think of. Pick one of your favorite songs that talks about one of these types of groups. What is the song saying about this group? How does it make you feel about being a member of this group? If you could pick your favorite artist to make an incredible chart-topping song about this group (think "Empire State of Mind" by Jay-Z and Alicia Keys for New Yorkers) you are a part of, who would be the artist and what specific group would it be about?

(2) Many people use music as motivation for exercise and athletics. Dr. Shauna Harrison helps people step into the best version of themselves through physical activity, often using hip-hop. What are five of your favorite songs to get you "pumped up" and motivated? Once you have identified these five songs, create a playlist of these five songs. For the next three days, play these five songs in the morning when you wake up to get your day started. If you have a roommate who will not like this exercise, use headphones. After the three days, reflect on your feelings and mood after listening to these songs. Was there any pattern or noticeable difference for you? Now reflect on your behavior and activity after listening to these songs. Was there any pattern or noticeable difference for you? What songs will you use for next week?

8

Music and Social Media

Christopher J. Schneider

We give away a lot of our music for free because *the more we give away the more we sell.* The music industry has changed in that way because of the Internet and social media.

Kevin James, bass player of indie rock band Model Stranger

When Bob Dylan famously asserted in the 1964 popular anthem song, "The Times They Are a-Changin'," he hit the nail right on the head. The lyrics to the tune can be applied in reference to numerous circumstances and events unforeseen by Dylan, such as the emergence of new music technologies, explored in this chapter. As noted by musician Gary White, one feature of the staying power of music is the timelessness of the lyrics; Dylan's anthem is just one standout example of this truism. On October 13, 2016, in recognition of the significance of Dylan's lyrics, the Swedish Academy awarded the Nobel Prize for Literature to Dylan for "having created new poetic expressions within the great American song tradition" (Kreps 2016). Although the art of music and music lyrics is timeless, I explore below how developments like Web 2.0, social media, and music streaming services have irrevocably altered the ways fans experience music, but also, how fans interact with other listeners and artists about the music they love.

According to media scholars David Altheide and Robert Snow (1979: 10), media formats influence how information like music is constituted, perceived, and then interpreted. As they explain:

> Format consists, in part, of how material is organized, the style in which it is presented, the focus or emphasis on particular characteristics of behavior, and the grammar of media communication.

Prior to the advancement of interactive media technologies and formats including social media platforms, music formats, and thus consumption practices, occurred principally in just one of three ways: (1) artist performance; (2) some form of recorded music media, mostly phonograph discs (33, 45, or 78 rpm), or; (3) through radio transmission (see Schneider 2007 for a discussion of the socio-cultural history of music and media).

The introduction of television in the 1950s prompted a shift from aural to visual consumption of music (i.e., format change) that later would crystalize with the 1981 creation of MTV (Music Television). Music has served a distinct place in the relationship between the individual and society (DeNora 2000). The individual experience both of, and in, the music scene is one example (Irwin 1977). Until the turn of the 21st century, consumption of music (both recorded and live) was limited to the physical realm such as a face-to-face in concert or with a hard copy of music media such as a vinyl record, 8-track tape, cassette, or compact disc. Now, in the 21st century, interaction and consumption of music happen largely on the Internet, where people upload, download, share, stream and purchase music on sites like iTunes, a site owned and run by Apple, Inc.

Returning briefly once more to a lyric in the "The Times They Are a-Changin'," perhaps the line "Come writers and critics who prophesize with your pen" could be amended to also include "post." As noted in one of many *Social Media Glossaries*, a post can be defined as "a Facebook status update, or an item on a blog or forum" (Fontein 2015). Facebook was launched in 2004 and is currently the world's most popular social media platform with more than one billion users. Social media, which also goes by a host of monikers such as social networking or new media, can be defined as a hybrid of media and interaction where individuals online (i.e., users) can post and interact with one another.

Posts consist of user-generated content in which one presents their version of an e-self to an e-audience (for a discussion of the e-self see

Kotarba 2013: 15–21). Hundreds of thousands of online posts are made around the world with each passing minute. Many of these posts concern music. Consider that in 2010 alone, six of the top ten most retweeted statements on the social media site Twitter were related to a music artist (Bruno 2011). How did we get to where we are in such a relatively short period of time? And, more importantly, in what ways have these changes facilitated the myriad ways that many of us now consume and experience music in our everyday lives? The story begins with digital music media.

The Rise of Digital Music Media: Napster and Web 2.0

The Internet is a global system of billions of networked devices like mobile phones, tablets, and computers. Using the Internet, any person can connect with another to exchange information. The Internet became more accessible with the widespread availability of home computers in the mid-1990s. This version of the Internet, sometimes known as Web 1.0, was available initially as a publishing platform where users could read a website but could not modify the content of the site. During the early 1990s, the MPEG 1 Audio Layer 3 (MP3) was introduced in Germany. An MP3 is a digitally compressed audio file. The size and potential for the widespread accessibly of these files coupled with Internet technology fostered the conditions for unprecedented and largely unregulated consumer access to music recordings, mostly for free. Much of this free music went undetected when MP3s were shared privately over email until Shawn Fanning unleashed Napster in 1999 at the dawn of Web 2.0.

Web 2.0 emerged in the early 2000s and distinguished much of the web as we recognize it today as a dynamic user-generated network, paving the way for music sharing sites. Napster, a controversial digital media sharing site, was software that enabled a decentralized network of connected computers where individuals could access and copy files like movies and music from other computers around the world, establishing what is usually referred to as a peer-to-peer (P2P) network.

Napster, a P2P network, enabled mass distribution of free media like music in the form of MP3s—including copyrighted music—to a global, and public audience. When individuals connect over P2P networks they can make full identical copies of another user's music, but also copies of other digital media like movies, books, and video games. For the possessor of digital music, then, an MP3 is never given up, it is not traded away or erased, rather, it is shared (copied), and therefore, indefinitely retains its *use value* as music to its possessor (i.e., an individual could keep listening to the music after another user has copied it to their computer over a P2P network). An MP3 then as a shared commodity on P2P networks provides a contemporary application of famed sociologist Karl Marx's concepts of commodities and exchange (Schneider 2011). For instance, purchasing music from a record store or even online (as a commodity that is offered for sale) loses its appeal when the very same music can easily be distributed globally on P2P networks and copied freely by anyone. This change in format has given rise to a phenomena sometimes referred to as "digital deflation," a term that explains how content like music loses its value when consumer practices move from physical to digital formats (Peoples 2016). Napster was the first P2P network of its kind and the original free site was relatively short lived. Reaction was mixed among musicians.

Free music meant that musicians were writing, recording, and producing their product (i.e., music) often for little or no compensation. Record labels were also losing money. Popular recording artists like rapper Dr. Dre and heavy metal band Metallica each filed lawsuits against Napster. Following a settlement, Dr. Dre and Metallica each agreed to make their music available on the service "once an acceptable model is in place that insures payment to artists and publishers for the use of their works" (*Billboard* 2001). Other mainstream popular artists understood why Napster was so popular. According to renowned musical innovator, Prince, "File sharing was inevitable, because ppl r tired of getting pimped at the wrecka stow [. . .] one or 2 good songs 4 eighteen dollars is CRAZY" (Schumacher-Rasmussen 2001). Singer/songwriter Dave Matthews of the Dave Matthews Band prophesized: "I don't see the sense in fighting something that is the future" (Schumacher-Rasmussen 2001). The Recording Industry Association of America (RIAA), a trade group that represents the recording industry in the U.S., sued tens of thousands of fans who downloaded copyrighted music from Napster and other P2P sites. Most individuals settled out of court for a few thousand dollars. Lawsuits against Napster and those that downloaded music from the site alienated many people. Consider the following from a fan who created a cartoon video critical of Metallica:

> 'I do own a copy of Napster, and I'm also a fan of Metallica, but this seemed absolutely ridiculous that they were doing this [i.e., waging a lawsuit],' the film's 28-year-old creator, Bob Cesca, said. 'They should have been a little more forward-thinking when it comes to technology, than rather a knee-jerk reaction, suing Napster and adversely affecting their fans.'
>
> (Simon 2000)

Napster was ultimately sued by the Recording Industry Association of America (RIAA) and shut down by legal injunction in 2001. However, the floodgates to unauthorized file-sharing had opened. There was no turning back. Many similar file-sharing sites emerged in the wake (e.g., LimeWire in 2000, Kazaa in 2001, and perhaps most notoriously, The Pirate Bay in 2003). However, it was Napster that was credited as revolutionizing music consumption in the 21st century with "Facebook, iTunes, and other towering digital giants [having] flourished using elements first teased or pioneered by Fanning's software" (Lamont 2013).

From MySpace to Music Apps

Music connects people and *social media* connects people. The two together would seem to be a perfect marriage. Although the first social networking site was developed in 1997 (boyd and Ellison 2007), it wasn't until the launch of MySpace in 2003 that music and social media would unite. MySpace was the first of the hundreds of social media sites at the time to make music and entertainment its focus. The site was one of the first to join music, blogging (an informal type of online diary), photographs and video within a single format. As characterized by one journalist at the time: "It's like a chat room crossed with a radio show" (Waugh 2005). Because of its emphasis on music, MySpace attracted tens of thousands of bands, artists and musicians from across the spectrum, ranging from mainstream bands and independent artists to unsigned acts looking to get discovered.

MySpace fundamentally changed the organization of music culture. Since recordings (i.e., digital MP3s popularized by Napster) could be added to band profiles, shared on MySpace with others, and sold directly by the artist to fans, the site very quickly became the go-to place for musicians and artists seeking to promote their products like recordings and concert tickets *and* simultaneously interact directly with fans.

By mid-2005, MySpace had in excess of two hundred thousand band profiles. Fans continued to flock en masse to MySpace to gain access to artists and celebrities. Popular music is a basic feature of youth culture (Laughey 2006). A significant percentage of users on MySpace were youth. These young music fans could gain, like never before, unprecedented access to artists by simply sending a "friend request." As Waugh (2005) notes:

> For bigger bands, accepting 'friendship invitations' from music lovers gives them an easy way to get in touch with their fans. The bands can then give previews of songs, details of gigs, and even in the case of artists such as former Smashing Pumpkin Billy Corgan regular diary entries. For unsigned groups and local artists, accepting friendship invitations is a way to get people to listen to their music.

Mainstream acts, including popular rock bands Weezer and R.E.M., streamed full albums in advance of the scheduled "street" (i.e., physical) release date. A *New York Times* report characterized MySpace as "an online teenager's bedroom" (Williams 2005). Setting songs to profile playlists on MySpace was akin to band posters on a bedroom wall—albeit with a much larger and interactive audience. These new forms of technology enabled users to manage identities through music preference in public spaces online in some ways similar to customized cell phone ringtones and text tones (Schneider 2009).

MySpace brought music and identity into the public sphere in unforeseen ways. Profile music broadcasted individually selected songs that helped define for others who a person is not only to their friends, but also, possibly to a global audience. User selection of profile music, as sociologist Erving Goffman (1959) might have suggested, acts as a form of *impression management*. In other words, the selection of a song is more than the song itself. Songs are connected to music genres, specific bands and artists, can contain lyrics, etc. Profile music then conveys various meanings by impressing upon others things like individual musical taste (e.g., hip-hop, goth, heavy metal, etc.) and maybe styles associated with particular genres (e.g., baggy clothes, dark makeup, spiked leather jackets, etc.), favorite artists, and perhaps, even an individual's mood at the time, depending on the lyrics of the profile song (love, anger, happiness, etc.). Profile music also served another important function by allowing other users of MySpace to discover music each time a page was visited, thus facilitating the growth of *much* larger online music communities. Several mainstream artists such as English rock band the Artic Monkeys and Jamaican-American rapper Sean Kingston caught their initial break on MySpace.

In 2005, MySpace was purchased by major media conglomerate News Corporation for $580 million. As the site grew astronomically in popularity, MySpace with its new corporate backing, sponsored live events, featured music videos, and streamed full live concerts by mainstream artists such as rock bands like Linkin Park. As young users continued to sign up on MySpace, the social media site was subject to increased scrutiny by law enforcement, parents, and authority figures centered initially around a moral panic associated with sexual predators' alleged use of the site (Schneider 2016a). As Magid and Collier (2007: 9) predicted, "the bad news about this growing awareness of adult scrutiny is that young MySpace users may just move on." The door of the so-called online teenage bedroom had opened wide and authority figures were peering inside bringing an end to the dominant era of MySpace (even while MySpace continues to exist). Many users fled to then rival site Facebook.

Facebook, as noted above, is presently the world's most popular social media site with more than one billion users. Facebook launched in 2004 but only gained a strong foothold in the popular culture landscape in 2007. This was the same year that Facebook introduced its "Fan Page" feature. The "Fan Page" allowed artists, public figures, brands, and businesses to connect with interested people, i.e., fans. However, the feature was generally not well received among indie acts since the feature included paid advertisement rate options for musicians. Facebook's News Feed algorithm delivers personalized content like posts; however, "most users see only a sliver of potential posts in their network each day" (Luckerson 2015). Paid advertisements allow musicians and brands to extend their reach on Facebook to provide a better chance that the intended audience will see their posts. In other words, unlike MySpace, it cost money on Facebook to connect with fans. Personal access had been monetized.

The importance of MySpace in terms of facilitating music communities cannot be overstated. Much of how people now discover music is online. In 2015, Facebook was the second-most-popular website on Earth (Luckerson 2015). The platform has gained considerable control over online interaction and limits access for musicians and fans through mechanisms like paid advertisement rate options. Principally for this reason, and unlike MySpace, no band has yet caught a break on Facebook (Herstand 2014). Perhaps musicians not getting discovered on the site is not surprising given the level of control Facebook has, but also, that the focus of the site was never music per se, but rather, on established friendship connections. Additionally, Facebook did not secure licenses to distribute music as MySpace had. Instead, in 2011 Facebook elected to upgrade its platform to allow music services, notably Spotify, a streaming service, to integrate with the social network only to keep users listening to music on the site *without having to leave Facebook*. The concern was to keep users connected to Facebook, and much less so with promoting bands and artists and sharing music as was the case with MySpace.

Music today is most commonly consumed on mobile devices (such as phones and tablet computers) that are connected to various forms of online media. In 2015, worldwide digital music sales from downloading and streaming surpassed physical albums for the first time. According to the worldwide organization International Federation of the Phonographic Industry (IFPI), "an estimated 68 million people paid for music subscription services in 2015, more than eight times the level of eight million people in 2010" (IFPI 2016a). Once powerful social media sites, most notably MySpace, have lost much of their contemporary relevance and appeal in today's evolving media landscape, in part, because of the proliferation of alternatives like streaming services and YouTube, discussed below. In terms of consumption, music has never been more popular and is now consumed at record-breaking levels (IFPI 2016b). According to the IFPI (2016a):

> Helped by the spread of smartphones, increased availability of high-quality subscription services and connected fans migrating onto licensed music services, streaming has grown to represent 19 per cent of global industry revenues, up from 14 per cent in 2014. Streaming now accounts for 43 per cent of digital revenues and is close to overtaking downloads (45 per cent) to become the industry's primary digital revenue stream.

As noted by Los Angeles singer/songwriter Ari Herstand (2014), "there will never be another MySpace." Herstand continues: "the social networking behemoths are over. They're bulky and clunky. Last decade." Apps, Herstand suggests, are the most recent shift in the evolving music-media landscape.

App is short for application. An app is software designated to perform specific tasks for individual users. Apps are designed to run on mobile devices. There are a plethora of music apps. One of the most popular is SoundCloud, an audio platform that allows users to share, record and promote content making the site a leader, until recently, in free music distribution. SoundCloud has outpaced its rivals as, for instance, in 2014, it was reported that the site had four times the global audience as competitor app Spotify. Founded in 2007, a basic feature of SoundCloud that makes it a strong rival to competitor music destination MySpace is that SoundCloud users can share content on popular social media sites like Facebook and Twitter (Van Buskirk 2009):

> Unlike MySpace songs, SoundCloud's can be embedded anywhere, have no file-size limit, let fans comment on specific parts of a recording, and allow bands to share songs publicly or only with certain contacts—the sort of flexibility we've become accustomed to on sharing and social sites like Flickr and Facebook.

Musicians like DJ Moby now use SoundCloud to debut music (Van Buskirk 2009). According to Fred Wilson, an investor in SoundCloud, the site "was about music in the YouTube sort of way, where anybody could participate. It was a bottom-up approach" (Sisario 2014). Following the launch of SoundCloud in 2008, the site attracted negative attention similar to Napster due to concerns over copyright infringement for streaming unlicensed content. Streaming is the process by which media content such as music can be played immediately over the Internet and does not have to be downloaded and stored like MP3s, as was the case with Napster. Deals were struck with major labels to keep SoundCloud from running afoul of the law. SoundCloud remains popular. In 2016, micro-blogging site Twitter reportedly invested nearly $70 million into the service, allowing users to both listen to and discover music on Twitter.

Twitter is a more recent destination for artists and fans. Artists have taken to Twitter to interact on a personal level and directly with fans as they once did largely on MySpace. On August 23, 2016, for example, rapper Kanye West tweeted a series of statements as an appeal to his 25.4 million followers (at the time of this writing 15.1 million more than the President of the United States!) to listen to his friend, singer Frank Ocean's new album. West also tweeted that radio stations should play the album. "Every station across the globe. I Heart. Clear Channel local stations. Satellite. Every station. This will make the world better." This statement was retweeted 7,366 times and "liked" 24,859 times. A retweet is reposting of another tweet and a "like" constitutes an endorsement of a tweet.

Dozens of people interacted with the tweet. Some offered support for the statement, while others observed that West seemed a bit out of touch with the times, even while being heralded by many as an innovator in the music business. According to one Twitter user: "I see your vision West, but we are in 2016 where the consumer of music doesn't listen to the radio as often." In other circumstances, artists like Kanye West have used Twitter to tell their side of the story during times of controversy, as was the case when he interrupted country music superstar Taylor Swift at the 2009 MTV Video Music awards to announce that his friend, R&B singer Beyoncé, had "the best video of all time."

Using Twitter to apologize to Swift, West then provided this Twitter missive:

> Man I love Twitter. . . . I've always been at the mercy of the press but no more . . . The media tried to demonize me. . . . They wanted yall to believe I was a monster in real life so you guys wouldn't listen or buy my music anymore. . . . I feel like they were waiting for the opportunity to go in all the way on me and when it came they beat me to a pulp. . . . Even now a lot of articles start there [*sic*] first 2 paragraphs about how much of an asshole I am.

YouTube and Participatory Culture on Social Media

The Internet, Web 2.0, social media, streaming services, and apps—all forms of new media—have each contributed to significant changes in how music is consumed and experienced in the digital era. YouTube, however, is a standout in that the site has largely dominated the music streaming industry. To illustrate a few points, I draw below from some published research in this area (see Schneider 2016b). YouTube is a video-sharing social media platform. The site is an important space of online *participatory culture*, where users upload videos (many of these music videos) and various audiences engage and interact with others around these videos (Burgess and Green 2009).

YouTube debuted in December 2005. In 2015, according to Nielsen, a measurement and ratings company, online video platforms saw 172.4 billion annual streams in the United States far outpacing all other streaming services. Google purchased YouTube in 2006 during an uproar over copyright-infringement concerns. Industry insiders suggested that the site would share a similar fate as Napster. These concerns were in response to many of the early videos uploaded by users to the site that featured copyrighted music. "YouTube's most viewed content is music videos, and many clips, though they're not quite music videos, function similarly" (Vernallis 2013: 12).

The concept of *music video* has been altered due to the participatory environment afforded by YouTube. Videos span from major label big budget productions such as professionally produced multi-million-dollar music videos once featured on MTV to user-generated clips that include videos of daily life set to a musical soundtrack and users performing amateur cover versions of their favorite songs. Numerous amateur users have broken on YouTube and developed into huge industry superstars. Consider singer Justin Bieber as a standout example. A 12-year-old Bieber uploaded a few videos of himself at a singing competition in order to share them with absent family members. Bieber's videos caught the attention of American talent manager Scooter Braun. According to Vernallis (2013: 9):

> . . . part of what separates YouTube from other media are the clips' brevity and the ways that they're often encountered through exchange with other people: a clip's interest derives from its associations with colleagues, family, friends, and contexts within communities.

Bieber has sold tens of millions of albums worldwide. He was not the first and will certainly not be the last to be discovered on YouTube. The very first user-generated "music video" uploaded to YouTube was a video entitled "tow [*sic*] chinese boys: i want it that way" (Schneider 2016b). The music video is of two Chinese college students lip-synching in their dorm room to the Backstreet Boys song "I Want It That Way." The video has been viewed millions of times and thousands of comments have been posted in response to the video. "I Want It That Way" was released in 1999 as the lead single from the Backstreet Boys multi-platinum album *Millennium*.

In "Music Videos on YouTube: Exploring Participatory Culture on Social Media" (Schneider 2016b), I provide insights on audience engagement with music videos on YouTube in response to "tow [*sic*] chinese boys: i want it that way." User engagement on YouTube focused largely on the visual elements of the "tow [*sic*] chinese boys: i want it that way" video, i.e., the lip-synching. One user noted: "good lip-synching and facial expressions oh and nice movement of the body too." A dominant theme of the comments in response to the video related to user nostalgia. Much of this had to do directly with the expressed user knowledge that the video was one of the first videos uploaded to YouTube. For some, this was the first video that they had seen on

YouTube. As one user noted: "It's like getting in a time machine watching these videos." Such statements suggest the importance of the music video as an aesthetic vehicle connecting users to the past (DeNora 2000). Meanwhile, others discussed their experiences watching the video with friends and family. These types of comments indicate that participatory music culture online extends offline:

> I remember watching this 8 years ago when I was 11. My sister showed me to cheer me up since I lost one of my friends in a freak accident. Laugh all you want, this video is probably what saved me from depression.

Given that the video had been on YouTube for the entire existence of the site, other users noted how time had passed between views. As DeNora (1999) indicates, music, and more recently music videos online, produces autobiographical memories that help assist in how users discover themselves and share these experiences with others. Another viewer says:

> I watched this video at the beginning of sixth grade with my best friend like 100 times, and we both thought it was the funniest thing EVER. little did we know what the internet had in store for us . . . I am about to graduate from high school now.

Various users recalled the first time that they had seen the video. "This was my first YouTube video! I was 5 ½ :D I'm 12 now." Other users added: "I was six when this video came out . . . im 13 now this shows how fast life goes by [*sic*]"; "I feel as old as dust. I was fifteen when this was uploaded [. . .] It was one of the first main videos I watched and I'm twenty-two now. It's amazing how much time flies by." These posts reveal some of the contemporary ways that music videos contribute meaning to individual users *and* to groups on YouTube. Participatory culture on social media, and YouTube in particular, involves a broad range of activities each related to how users accomplish mediated music, such as creating music, various performance practices that include activities like lip-synching, individual and group evaluation, and consumption.

A Case Study of an Indie Band: Model Stranger

The cultural space is crowded and saturated by media. The ever-evolving media landscape is changing not only how people consume and experience music but also how musicians gain fan support. Many major label acts have entire teams of brand managers that handle and manage the band's online presence and persona. This includes social media accounts of individual band members. The point is to attract more fans, facilitate a personal connection on an individual basis, and monetize these connections.

In many ways, today's struggling independent musicians must work much harder to get noticed and stay relevant than musicians did in the last century. Much of this *DIY* (Do It Yourself) "extra work" means maintaining an active online presence in order to attract followers. As one example, we will consider Chicago-based indie rock band Model Stranger.

Model Stranger formed in Chicago in December 2009. The band released their debut album *Dreams & Bones* the following year. Model Stranger is comprised of Stephen Francis (vocals/guitar), Kevin James (bass), and Vincent Joseph (drums). The band regularly tours the United States on its DIY ethos and has opened for international major label acts that include American rock band Candlebox and Canadian rock band Our Lady Peace. Model Stranger is on various social media such as Facebook, Twitter, YouTube, MySpace, Instagram and band sites ReverbNation and Bandcamp. Kevin James explains, "for any band on an independent level it is about direct to fan interaction," in an effort to "try and drive traffic to our webpage, our home base" (http://modelstranger.com) (Kevin James, personal communication, September 16, 2016). The band's online presence is geared toward directing traffic to their webpage because: "today's social media will not exist in twenty or thirty years, there will be something different. Look what happened to MySpace and Facebook." The band also uses Hootsuite, a social media management platform. Hootsuite allows the band to "send out tweets while we are performing on stage" as well as "program a whole month of Facebook posts in about an hour."

The band engages their fans in various ways on social media such as through music other than their own. As one example, an August 27, 2016 post on Facebook included a picture of rock band Pearl Jam's debut album *Ten* and the text "25 years ago today [*Ten* was released]. What's your favorite song?" Several people replied. Eric wrote: "It's hard to pick a favorite decade or album with these guys, much less a favorite song!" Model Stranger replied, in part, "Eric—we couldn't agree more. This record holds such a special place in our generation." Every six months the band will reassess best strategies for fan engagement online because social media is an "ever evolving process." Kevin James continues:

> The majority of everything that we do is based off of metrics and analysis. Data is gold. Given the information age that we are in we have an endless amount of data to analyze and to refine the process regarding our market, our band brand, and what types of releases and merchandise we should be doing, you know, did hoodies or t-shirts sell better on our last tour? What kinds of vinyl records should we be releasing, etc.?

As one example of a marketing strategy, Model Stranger collaborated with Austin, Texas-based rock band Midwest State of Mind on a "7-inch split" (a single release vinyl record that has one song on each side) because "vinyl is trendy." Side A includes Model Stranger's song "Stare" and side B has Midwest State of Mind's song "Fork in the Road." This partnership helps the reach of each band in two different markets (Chicago, Illinois and Austin, Texas, respectively).

The pressing included 1,000 vinyl records and each band received 500 copies for distribution. Each partnered with local record stores for Record Store Day (discussed below) where the 7-inch split vinyl was given away for free to Record Store Day customers. Why give merchandise away for free? Because "vinyl nerds [Kevin James admits that he is one of them] will play it," he continues, "I have gotten free records on Record Store Day. I always listen to them. Our ROI [return on investment] on free vinyl like this is very good." Regarding the ROI, Kevin James explains:

> The 7-inch split drives traffic to our website. We give away a lot of our music for free because *the more we give away the more we sell.*

> The music industry has changed in that way because of the Internet and social media. If someone likes us they will come to our show. They might buy a t-shirt, another vinyl; they may spend twenty or thirty bucks. We always sell more by giving music away for free (*emphasis original*).

360 Degrees: The Return to Vinyl Records

A curious trend in music production and consumption is the resurgence of vinyl records. [Full disclosure: I have myself been fully swept up in this trend]. As a matter of fact, as I write this chapter, I am listening to ZZ Top's *Eliminator* on vinyl. I picked up the record at a vinyl swap just down the street from my house in the fall last year.

Just a few years ago the future of music pointed to a digital based industry. In other words, music would be consumed largely by downloading MP3s and online streaming. Physical formats like vinyl records and CDs would eventually become obsolete. By most accounts, vinyl was nearly extinct. Retail stores that sold physical copies of albums—such as CDs, vinyl, and cassettes—closed down across the country en masse. In 2006, the once mighty behemoth music chain Tower Records filed for bankruptcy and went out of business. Then a strange and unexpected thing happened. Vinyl sales *increased* the next year. Record Store Day—a day of specially marketed vinyl records and CDs at independent music retailers—started the following year in 2008. According to the Recording Industry Association of America (RIAA) vinyl sales in 2015 matched sales figures last seen in 1988 (RIAA 2016). Industry insiders are not able to say with certainty what is behind this recent trend. What we can observe is a vibrant culture of vinyl enthusiasts online. Let us return briefly to Record Store Day. According to www.recordstoreday.com:

> This is a day for the people who make up the world of the record store—the staff, the customers, and the artists—to come together and celebrate the unique culture of a record store and the special role these independently owned stores play in their communities.

They further define a qualifying store as a stand-alone, brick-and-mortar establishment where the majority of retail is music, and stipulate that it must be privately owned by parties who are at least 70 per cent native to the state. Special vinyl (e.g., music made only available on vinyl or limited copies, etc.) and other physical releases like CDs are made exclusively for Record Store Day, which is held the third Saturday of April. The day has expanded to include the year-long "Vinyl Tuesday" an effort to encourage the release of physical music all year. Vinyl Tuesday releases are promoted on various social media where a large community of fans interact, discuss, purchase, and trade vinyl with others.

In one thread on the Record Store Day Facebook page, users discussed purchasing records. One user post read: "Vinyl is great, amazing analog sound, great artwork plus owning a piece of history." Another user noted that he does not buy records "on Record Store Day! I get them from Anazon [*sic*] & Ebay." Purchasing music online and waiting to have physical copies of vinyl (at an increased price to the buyer) sent in the mail rather than download the album digitally is a testament to the belief that the experience that vinyl affords is qualitatively better. This sentiment is echoed on Twitter and elsewhere. In response to the following @recordstoreday June 2016 tweet: "I still buy records because," one Twitter user replied: "records are art, both audibly and pictorially, cannot beat the buzz of buying vinyl #addiction," and in response to this tweet, another user replied: "couldn't agree more. Experiencing all they offer is such a complete musical experience."

We might ask the question: what exactly is so special about owning music on vinyl and other physical formats? Physical copies, it can be suggested, provide the listener with a more fully encompassing aesthetic experience. Consider vinyl. Unless you order online, one must first locate and then peruse a record store alongside other music enthusiasts. Thumb through stacks of records. You may serendipitously "discover" a record. You take it home with you. You open the record jacket to expose the artwork and lyrics and the smell of dusty or fresh cardboard that wafts under your nose (depending on if the record is new or used). You slide the vinyl out and place it on the turntable and gently set the stylus into the groove. You hear the "pop" and "crackle" before the music begins. You know that records have a finite quality and the vinyl will wear with play. You sit and take a few moments to listen to the music.

You disconnect from your connected life, if just for a brief time. You are present.

Conclusion

Some of the myriad ways that music is now experienced in an era of new media have been briefly outlined in this chapter. The ever-evolving media landscape is changing how people consume, perform, and experience music. New media has also enabled spaces for online music communities. Music is a form of mediation and has connected people since the dawn of time. As noted at the outset of this chapter such connections have occurred principally in one of three ways (including through vinyl) much throughout the last century. As this chapter has shown, music and new media are intertwined in numerous ways.

Activities

(1) Reflect upon your own favorite music videos on YouTube. Provide at least two examples that evoke past memories like those explored in the chapter and discuss what this says about you. Then briefly discuss how these musical experiences have been shared with others. Do you engage with others about YouTube music videos online? Offline? Both? Do you recognize more similarities or differences between your reflections and those in the chapter? Why or why not?

(2) Discuss how you experience music and what this might look like without new media. How different would your life be if you could only listen to music in a fixed location without the ability to travel anywhere with your entire music collection in your pocket? How would you experience music? What would be different? Can you understand the return to vinyl records? Why or why not?

9

Business in the Music Community

Rachel Skaggs and Jonathan R. Wynn

Music can be the glue that connects individuals and groups across communities. In this chapter, we seek to describe how contemporary music communities form and persist, how more macro-level structures like geography and market conditions affect these communities of music makers, and even how lyrics provide a window into this world of songwriters, refracting issues of class, gender, and place.

Formally, a *community* is: "an aggregate of social units, some of which are organizations, co-located in geographic space" (Freeman and Audia 2006). Less formally: a community is a group of individuals and organizations often located in the same place. Communities can exist for a variety of purposes, but in general, they assign value to certain traits, behaviors, skills, or resources and reward members who adopt community standards and conventions (Lin 2001). In our increasingly digital age, the Internet makes connections between people less dependent on geographic location (Stewart 2005). Online and off, communities are organized around shared interests, experiences, or values.

A group of music fans can certainly be seen as a kind of community. Die-hard followers of particular artists form fan clubs, give themselves names to brandish their allegiance (e.g., Lady Gaga's Little Monsters or Justin Bieber's Beliebers), and unite in online and offline communities to share everything from interpretations of lyrics to memorabilia. Perhaps more obscured from the public's eye are the communities of musicians and music makers who also form groups. While fans organize around the consumption of the music, there are also communities of people who work together, share interests, friendships, geographic location, and even family ties.

Sociologists think about music in many ways. Music could be seen as a micro-level phenomenon, that is, something that is organized around interactions between individuals from the deep emotions an opera fan feels when listening to a particular aria to the interactions in an indie band audience between two strangers who realize they share a favorite song. Likewise, music can also be seen as a macro-level phenomenon that is organized by the formal organizations and institutions that comprise the contemporary music industry. By thinking about music in terms of the communities that it creates, and the community that creates it, we are able to link these micro- and macro-understandings of music.

Howard Becker came up with the concept of *art world* to explain how works of art are the joint product of collective labors, not some solitary and tortured "Artist" (with a capital "A!"). He defines an art world as: "all of the people whose activities are necessary to the production of the characteristic works which that world, and perhaps others as well, define as art" (1982: 34). When it comes to music, this approach allows us to think about how songs are the product of a musical community. Songwriters write music and lyrics, studio musicians (often separate from a touring band) play the music, record engineers and sound mixers work to create a physical recording, producers serve as project managers of sorts who "make it all come together," record labels fund musical projects, distribution companies package and sell the physical and digital products, and then roadies, sound engineers and touring musicians all perform the music live on the road. Even though a musical work might be credited to a performing artist there are layers of specialized and hidden occupations held by people who do things like market the music, design the album artwork, arrange live tours, and deal with the legal framework of copyright and licensing. Becker calls the sum of these efforts—the set of associations and practices that allow for the reproduction of a cultural good—*patterned cooperation*.

Nashville as an Exemplary Case

The television show *Nashville* dramatically portrays the lives and careers of various (fictional) Nashville musicians and songwriters to millions of viewers. If you have not seen the show, imagine a soap opera-style drama that follows beautiful people through many romantic, dangerous, and contentious scenarios while they also write and perform country music to match the situations in which they find themselves.

The fictional show relies on the city of Nashville's real life reputation as "Music City" and as a place with a strong community of music makers. Nashville can, indeed, make such claims: almost 8 out of every 1,000 Nashvillians work in the music business, creating the highest density of music professionals of any city in the U.S. (Peoples 2013). Most associate Nashville's music community with the country genre, a style of commercial music that emerged in the 1920s that now includes sub-genres like, "old-time, honky-tonk, western swing, Cajun, bluegrass, rockabilly, country-pop, country-rock, folk-country, new traditionalism, hot country, and even insurgent or alternative country" (Kingsbury 1998). Country artists include older favorites like Patsy Cline and Hank Williams, so-called "Outlaws" like Willie Nelson and Charlie Daniels, and more recent superstars like Garth Brooks, Carrie Underwood, Keith Urban, and Blake Shelton. In addition to Nashville's country music industry, the city is home to the Christian and gospel music industries as well.

Because of this musical reputation and the urban development that has occurred over the past few decades, many famous songwriters and musicians previously unrelated to the Nashville country music scene move to the city to retire or for a change in pace from living in New York or Los Angeles. Artists and songwriters such as Ben Folds and Sheryl Crow now call Nashville home. Jack White of Detroit-based band The White Stripes, for example, moved to Nashville because of the: "warm embrace of those who aim to 'write hits'" (Florida 2010). White owns his own record label, studio and performance space, Third Man Records, in downtown Nashville that is known, among other things, for producing live music recordings directly on vinyl records, a process that is uncommon in the digital age.

Nashville's music industry is worth $6.38 billion annually, but as reporter David Ross laments: "Sales are down, margins crunched, marketing costs up, labels continue to buy their way up the radio charts and retail shelf space evaporates while most players do the same ole, same ole shuffle" (Ross 2009). While the 1990s country music industry benefitted from record high sales figures based around artists like Garth Brooks, Tim McGraw, Faith Hill, and Shania Twain who could sell more than a million copies of every record they released, overall declining record sales and the broader transition to a digital music market hit Nashville hard. Music piracy websites like Napster and Kazaa cut into record sales in every genre of music in the early 2000s, the shift from album-based sales to people buying singles on iTunes drastically lowered profits, and from the late 2000s until now, the popularity of digital music streaming websites like YouTube, Spotify, and Pandora have further chipped away at music industry profits. In response, record labels have developed various strategies to remain viable by consolidating, merging with other labels, and changing the ways they invest in new artists.

More than just a problem of corporate financial health, the peaks and valleys in the music industry are visible and present in the lives of the people who make up Nashville's music community and, in fact, across the city at large. For example, the decline and contraction of the music industry led to a 90 per cent decrease in the number of songwriters in Nashville who work as a staff writer for a publishing group. These changes leave both individuals and businesses in the position of trying to innovate and expand their revenue streams. In response, there has been an increase in the indie and DIY ethos among individual artists, musicians, and songwriters given the democratization of the means of producing music (e.g., software programs like GarageBand and electronic drum kits) and distributing music to mass audiences (e.g., YouTube, iTunes, Spotify) (Cornfield 2015). There also has been an increase in artist-owned and label-owned publishing groups' attempts to profit from songs' copyright value. Labels are also trying to cut costs and recoup capital investments by shifting away from contracts that require artists to make a certain number of albums with a certain number of songs and tours. New contract models include "360 deals" in which the record label owns a piece of all of the artist's revenue streams, from album to ticket sales, and single-song contracts that allow record labels to test an artist for marketability and commercial popularity before deciding to release a full record. Although it is not apparent at first glance, declining industry profits directly affect the individual and collective well-being of Nashville's music community.

Sometimes broader trends need to be illustrated in a particular event, a tangible setting. For that, we can look to a more visible, physical level where changes in the music industry appear. Music Row, the two-street-wide area of Nashville that traditionally housed the physical infrastructure of the music industry (record labels, publishing houses, recording studios, and performance rights organizations) has transformed into a place where a new business venture is more likely to be a yoga studio than a recording studio. Nashville's recent real estate boom has contributed to many of Music Row's buildings being demolished to make way for apartments and condominiums. This issue came to a head in 2014 when the historic RCA Victor Studio A, a recording studio where Elvis Presley, Dolly Parton, The Beach Boys, Willie Nelson, and hundreds of other artists recorded hit songs, was purchased by a developer who intended to replace it with condos. Newcomer Ben Folds was a tenant of the studio and, perhaps emboldened because he had just moved to the city for its rich musical legacy, was able to rally enough support over subsequent months to block the demolition and find a philanthropic group to purchase the studio and keep it as a working studio space. Studio A was a success of the Nashville music community mobilizing to save its own history, but the continual development threat to Music Row is an indication that the value of Nashville's land and cultural cachet as Music City may be higher than the current financial prospects of the music industry to produce and sell music.

Making a Music City: Informal and Formal Community Development

What makes a city with a strong music community into a "Music City?" The process of matching a cultural product like country music and place-based urban economic development requires a combination of the activities of the more formal and informal sectors of the music industry.

On the one hand, music trade organizations and record labels collaborate in myriad ways to strengthen the communities they are emplaced within while, on the other hand, there are lots of activities generated by the independent and informal aspects of the music business that stoke entrepreneurship and small businesses. It is possible, and even likely, that the more informal thread of music—its subcultural and countercultural elements—might impact our local communities to a greater extent in this era of a more globalized economy.

To further explore this phenomenon, we can first turn to the more formal facets of urban culture. To do so we can look to a theory of urban development proposed by John Logan and Harvey Molotch (1987). Logan and Molotch see an extreme commodification of space that then trickles into every aspect of urban life (e.g., cultural, social, political). These scholars make the case for looking at the strategies of city stakeholders at the local level. Logan and Molotch call this set of key actors the *Growth Machine*. They note that "growth" is a consensus held among these elites—a common vision—that aims to bring jobs, expand the tax base, attract business, and contribute to public services.

Although this constellation of groups might look different in different locations, the Growth Machine can include: a) Politicians; b) Local Media; c) Utilities (i.e., "independent" public or quasi-public agencies that are tied to a single locale, and advocate for a certain type of growth); d) Universities (e.g., Columbia, Johns Hopkins, UCLA, University of Illinois' Chicago branch, Texas; research parks tied to universities like North Carolina's Research Triangle, Boston's Route 128 and Silicon Valley); e) Museums, Theaters, Expositions, Professional Sports; f) Organized Labor (i.e., Union leaders see the benefits of bringing jobs into the community); g) Self-employed professionals and small retailers (i.e., professionals may play a part, but they also can be effective citizen opponents of Growth Machines); and h) Corporate capitalists (i.e., investment bankers and wealthy patrons).

How does the Growth Machine work? Well, a central point to remember is that places are not "discovered," but are constructed through individual and collective efforts, often through formal associations and institutions of government and the economy (Logan and Molotch 1987: 43–44). The Growth Machine's form of *placemaking*, then, is a process of some combination of six explicit goals: a) Fiscal Health; b) Employment; c) Job and Income Mobility; d) Eliminating Social Problems; e) Improving the Environment; and f) Satisfying Public Taste. Logan and Molotch posit that placemaking and urban development do not necessarily generate benefits for the collective good, but rather redistributes wealth—from collectively held goods to privately held ones—favoring the same wealthy minority that champions the idea of growth for growth's sake (1987: 98).

Why does the Growth Machine matter when we're talking about music? Well, Richard Lloyd and Terry Nichols Clark develop this approach by highlighting how culture is used in particular areas of cities to develop not growth machines, but *entertainment machines*. These sociologists note that networks of actors and groups are less interested in growth per se but that entertainment and spectacle are key strategies for making places more attractive (Lloyd and Clark 2001).

And so, the ideas of the growth and entertainment machines help us think about how music works with communities in the form of how they generate financial benefits to their economies. Economic impact reports seek to measure just how a music industry can affect its communities in fiscal terms. This perspective details the *direct economic impact* (i.e., the money brought into the city economy via the music industry in the form of jobs created and sales of merchandise), *indirect economic impact* (i.e., the local goods and services purchased by the music industry), and *induced economic impact* (i.e., how income is spent by music industry workers in the local economy) of the industry. And so, music communities from Nashville to Melbourne to Barcelona use these measures to determine how their activities benefit their communities.

Take, for example, a music festival like Austin's South by Southwest. An economic impact study would analyze how the monies generated by their own operational activities and attendees all generated a sizable economic impact of $317.2 million in 2015. Their own research indicates that those monies then flowed into the local economy: $211 million as direct impact (e.g., corporate sponsor renting a venue space or hiring a catering company), $55.5 million as indirect impact (e.g., jobs in that venue and catering company), and $50.7 million as induced impact (e.g., the groceries, rent, and services paid for by those venue- and catering-company workers). By understanding economic impact, we can begin to see the "big picture" of how music and entertainment matter to communities.

At the same time, the intersection of music and communities happens at the much more informal level as well. The players that comprise a city's Growth Machine are not always the major force in all places. And while the economic impact at this street-level might be harder to see, there are other forces at work as well. There are the smaller, more organic, subcultural or "underground" groups and venues that can give a city some prestige or cultural prominence. As compared to the Growth Machine, these more informal groupings make what is called a *scene*.

Scenes have increasingly been recognized as crucial components of thriving urban communities and have, as a result, grown into a worthy topic for sociological research (Irwin 1977; Kotarba et al. 2009; Silver et al. 2010; Krause 2003). (See also Chapter 1 in this text.) The Growth Machine might have important city stakeholders and entities playing their parts, scenes also have their key components: constellations of venues, independent labels, college radio stations, and alternative media. While noting that they might be located locally, globally or virtually, Peterson and Bennett describe a music scene as "the contexts in which clusters of producers, musicians, and fans collectively share their common musical tastes and collectively distinguish themselves from others" (2004: 1). Scenes certainly have economic components to them (e.g., music scenes need venues, art scenes need galleries, both create some jobs), but they also generate more intangible qualities, a kind of cultural effervescence. Scenes, in other words, can make an area cool.

We can now see how the formal and informal music communities work in conjunction in order to benefit themselves and our exemplary case, the city of Nashville. With the idea of the growth machine working with the entertainment machine, we can see how Nashville's formal music industry—a close web of downtown music-based institutions (e.g., Country Music Hall of Fame and Museum, Ryman Auditorium, Schermerhorn Symphony Center, a grouping of traditional honkytonks on Lower Broadway) and organizations (e.g., Music labels, the Country Music Association, Gaylord Entertainment)—are neatly emplaced in a central, identifiable area in downtown Nashville. But then there is the more informal scene, developing across the Cumberland River and away from Music Row, in East Nashville, and scattered throughout the city. The more bohemian East Nashville area is quite different from Nashville's glossy downtown, although its effects do impact housing and smaller-scale commercial ventures. After studying Chicago's Neo-Bohemia of Wicker Park, it is no surprise that sociologist Richard Lloyd is focusing on the hip music scene in Nashville's East side (Lloyd 2006, 2011).

Few cities could claim the same kind of music community that Nashville has. Seattle, as a rather famous example, had a slow-burning music scene—a wider set of live music venues and small "indie" labels across the Pacific Northwest—nurturing a set of bands that exploded into international view with the success of Nirvana in 1991. The Pacific Northwest, however, did not have a more formal music community. Austin is another example of a famous music scene, with a plethora of live music settings, but a very modest recording component, unlike Nashville. There are, in fact, dozens and dozens of underground music scenes—from the burgeoning underground Latino punk scene in Los Angeles to a hardcore metal scene in suburban New Jersey—that do not get as much attention, and might never be vaulted into international acclaim. More work can be done to trace their patterns of emergence (see Kotarba et al. 2009), but some combination of a formal and informal music community, seems to play a role.

Music as Place Character

Alongside the Growth Machine, the other big urban cultural theory over the last 40 years has been Richard Florida's idea of the *Creative Class* and how it ties to the intense inter-city competition for new residents and economic development. Florida noted that areas where creative class workers (i.e., tech, culture, and knowledge workers) were located were concentrations of talent, tolerance and technology (Florida 2002). The creative class and growth machine models are, in a way, coming to the idea of urban development via culture from opposing positions: while Logan and Molotch were looking at how large organizations shaped cities, Florida sought out what factors made places more attractive to residents and businesses. Climate, diverse amenities, local cultural scenes all appear to play a part in drawing new economic activity—and music scenes became a critical component of the battery of research that has emerged from this perspective (Florida et al. 2010). People, according to this perspective, want to move to hip and interesting places.

So, in the post-industrial moment, marked by a decline in heavy industries like manufacturing, music has increasingly become a major marketing point for cities around the globe, from Beale Street to Bogata to Berlin to Brazzaville in the Congo. Nashville may have positioned itself as "Music City, U.S.A.," but other places make similar claims. Austin, for example, claims the title of "The Live Music Capital of the World" and there are other municipal branding strategies like "Cleveland Rocks" and Detroit latching on to its musical history by promoting itself as "Motown." Seattle, Chicago, Memphis, Miami, Atlanta and other places all seek to capitalize on their music even without hitching music directly in their city's motto.

Why is it that music has gained such prominence for cities and communities? In his work after writing about growth machines, Harvey Molotch focuses on the idea of *place character* (or *place attachment*). With his co-authors, he notes that place character is a "lash-up" of local cultural traditions, the built environment, and urban governance (Molotch et al. 2000; see also Wherry 2010). There are some cultural goods that are closely linked to a locale. Buffalo wings are from Buffalo and tango dancing is connected with Buenos Aires. But music, more than any other cultural good, seems to have a very close connection with place. Music contributes to a place character.

Take Chicago for example. In the late 1800s, Chicago's power elite exploited Lake Superior iron deposits for competitive advantage over Pittsburgh as a major production center. Today, Chicago attempts to leverage its cultural resources—developing areas like Millennium Park, making a play for the 2016 Olympics, and promoting its music heritage of the Chicago Blues—to attract tourists and project the image of a thriving metropolis. Local music serves as *symbolic capital*, a resource to be extracted just like the natural iron deposits were extracted in the past. Chicago has developed an urban cultural policy based upon its musical heritage. David Grazian, in his study *Blue Chicago* quotes the city's Deputy Director of the Mayor's Office of Special Events: "We have moved from a city of manufacturing to a service-based city, where catering to leisure travelers is as important to the city as big business . . . [Blues Fest] helps foster an image of Chicago as a world-class city" (Grazian 2003: 208). Molotch et al. (2000) does an excellent job of illustrating how this occurs on the micro-level.

Chicago is a big city with a rich heritage, but as an increasing number of cities and regions look to their cultural resources in a race for employers, residents and tourists, the desire to develop place character is taking hold and music has become a vital tool in those efforts. Cities like Toronto, Denver, and Des Moines host "Music City Summits" and establish Music Coalitions through monies drawn from their local growth and entertainment machines, all convening national and international figures together in attempts to find the right combination of strategies to promote themselves.

It is important to note that there are a variety of unintended effects of the marriage between music and community, of marketing a place character around music, or any other particular form. There has been a major critique of the Creative Class thesis, centered on how few benefits reach the under-served and under-represented communities, and how music-based development serves as a handmaiden to *gentrification*, the process by which cities develop to the point that it is too expensive for original—typically poor—residents to afford rent or property taxes.

Looking more closely at the music community itself, there are other reasons to temper enthusiasm over music-based development. In places like Nashville and Austin, research indicates that the wider local community bristles at the marketing of their locality around culture or a particular kind of culture (Wynn 2015). In Nashville, some local musicians are upset that tying place character to country music comes at the expense of a wider and more diverse musical community that includes pop, gospel, and folk musicians. In Austin, some locals are upset that the place marketing of their city has led to unimaginable growth of "transplanted hipsters" at the expense of a wider and more diverse ethnic and cultural population (see Orum 2002 and Stimeling 2011). The success of music as a part of a city's place character can, paradoxically, price out the very people that success was built upon. Increasing rents and costs can potentially price musicians out of the communities they made interesting. Some cities have tried to address this issue by building affordable housing units for musicians, as Nashville built the Ryman Lofts and Austin built Bluebonnet Studios.

The Job of Making Music

Having discussed some tools for understanding music communities and the intersections of formal, structural elements of communities along with informal, interactional relationships that build communities, we can now look into one music community in greater depth. Nashville songwriters bridge the gap between informal relationships and the larger corporate music industry in the hopes of translating songs written with friends into chart-topping hits. How does this process actually happen?

Let's say that you and your college roommate decided to become songwriters and hope to make some money from writing songs together between classes and on the weekends. One day, you and your roommate happened to write a song together that you both really like, and your friend down the hall is the friend of a friend who is a working country musician. Turns out, the musician really likes your song and decides to put it on his next album. He goes into the studio, records your song, along with a few others, and six months later, releases your song as his first single. This is your big break!

Six months after that, the song goes platinum, selling 1,000,000 copies. Woo hoo! This rarely happens anymore since fans would rather listen to music on Spotify instead of buying a single or an album. A few months later, you and your roommate finally get your checks in the mail for the earnings based on the song selling 1,000,000 copies. You eagerly open your checks and are both surprised to see that you each received about $20,000 (before taxes) for your hit song. On the one hand this might seem like a lot of money for a three-and-a-half-minute song. On the other hand, this would seem low in comparison to the "platinum" success of the single.

The good news is that more money could be coming to you and your roommate through other compensation streams. These other potential income sources will compensate you for each time your song is played on the radio, in a public place like a restaurant or club, at a concert, and for using your song on television, in movies, or in video games. Even though in this scenario, you and your roommate were lucky enough to get a big hit and make some money, songwriters cannot predict which, if any, of their songs will ever become popular or earn money at all. If you are reading this chapter and are interested in learning more about the complexities of how money moves through the music industry from fans to music creators, the Future of Music Coalition (http://money.futureofmusic.org/) is a great resource.

Now that you have a sense of how someone might make money from writing a song, let us get back to thinking about the larger community and how this process fits into the bigger picture. In the music business, communities form around making music, so the face-to-face interactions that create community are organized around *work*. Work can mean different things in different situations. You might think of "work" in occupational terms, that is, as a specific position that a person is hired to do for an agreed salary or hourly wage, but in everyday language we might also call the physical place we go to do our job "work." Or we might refer to specific tasks as the "work" we have to do. In America, the typical working week is 40 hours, and in that amount of time, individuals interact with others toward achieving an agreed upon goal (Abbott 1993; Smith 1997). Work also creates a community of individuals and organizations that come together on the basis of shared goals. A work community or occupational community can be comprised of employees, bosses, co-workers, customers, clients, or other stakeholders.

For Nashville songwriters, the way work is organized can take many different forms, but in general, it differs from our understanding of more standard employment situations. Some songs are penned by only one writer, but in the country music genre typically two to four writers work together over the course of a day to write the music and lyrics of a song. Collaborations between writers might last for just one song or for dozens of songs over the course of many years. To write the song, they will sit in a writing room, a café, or just a living room and toss around ideas until the song comes together, a more informal workplace than an office. Because of improvements in technology, contemporary songwriters are now able to create high-quality "demos" either on their phones or computers that are a kind of sketch recording of how the song is supposed to sound. These recordings could be as simple as just a vocal or could be more complex by recording instrumentals or using prerecorded instruments and loops. After the song is written and the work tape or demo is recorded, the writers struggle to get the song recorded and released on an album, a process that can be very quick or take years, if they are successful at all. Writers need to get the attention of a recording artist or record label in order to get their song on an album, so members of the music community share music with each other and attempt to get their songs and their friends' songs on as many albums as possible. While the music needs to be good, social ties are very influential in determining which songs get picked.

While the day-to-day work of songwriters is informally organized, it takes place within a larger industry that has shifted from being more highly professionalized to being driven more by independent music firms over time (Cornfield 2015). As discussed above, only 10 per cent of the staff songwriting jobs that existed in the 1990s exist now, so only a small fraction of Nashville's songwriters are currently employed in staff writer positions. A staff songwriting position typically comes with a salary advance, office space, and a support staff of people whose job it is to get the songwriter's music recorded and released on commercial albums. Today, most songwriters are self-employed and are responsible for managing the business side of their work (getting songs to artists and record labels, copyrighting songs, taxes, etc.) as well as the creative labor of writing songs.

Whether a writer is self-employed or employed as a staff songwriter, the day-to-day creative work is geared toward the same ends: to write music for commercial audiences. And yet, success in this line of work is elusive and, therefore, steady income is often a real concern for songwriters. Because songwriting is uncertain and precarious employment, most professional songwriters take side jobs in other areas of the music business, connecting them to different areas of the music community. Songwriters who play an instrument can earn additional income as a studio musician. Others pursue a career as a recording artist, produce music, become a sound mixer, or work in other areas of the business.

This type of work, while providing income—maybe even the majority of their income—does not hinder their reputation as a professional musician in the way that working in a grocery store or a bank would. A benefit of taking side jobs in the music industry is that the writer can choose which studio recording gigs, song mixing projects, or production jobs to take and which ones to pass on without diminishing their focus on songwriting.

For Susan Lee (all names in this chapter are pseudonyms), a 28-year career as a Nashville songwriter has been enhanced by her side job as host for the Bluebird Cafe's open-mic night. The Bluebird is famous for its intimate "writers in the round" concert format and is regularly portrayed in movies and television shows. This side job has helped Susan meet upcoming songwriters, which eventually led her to start her own consulting business that helps aspiring songwriters develop their career skills. The networks Susan built with people in the music industry are essential to her continued success at writing songs, but the Bluebird Cafe is also an essential part of the community that creates the space for Susan and other members of the community to meet, hang out, hear each other's music, and build friendships.

Songwriter Randy Wilson has had the same weekly side job for 16 years as a church worship leader. Though this is a salaried position that requires weekly hours, the fact that the majority of his work is done on Sunday allows him to maintain weekly songwriting appointments. In this job, Randy is able to combine his religious faith and his musical talent, a fact that many people would find admirable. Additionally, Randy has made friends through his position as worship leader that have later developed into business partnerships.

Building relationships with other writers, musicians, industry leaders, and even non-music industry professionals provide weak ties that may lead to opportunities in the future. Every music industry gig expands a songwriter's network, either within or outside of the scope of the music industry—a point that illustrates the informal ways in which communities form on the basis of individual connections. Especially for self-employed songwriters, building a good reputation among a large network of people is a key part of what drives their careers.

Status, Social Closure, and Exclusion in the Music Community

While a job in another industry might require an application, a resume, a formal interview process and a long-term employment offer, jobs in the music industry tend to be more informal and allow people to collaborate on short-term projects like albums, tours, and showcases. Most jobs in this industry do not require any specific education or credentials. Without degrees, resumes, or interviews guiding these forms of employment, how is it determined who should have the opportunity to make, distribute, and perform music? The answer, you might guess, is that it's "who you know." Sociologists would call the type of arrangement where the distribution of job opportunities replies upon social networks, a *reputational labor market* (Menger 1999). In this case, the sum of face-to-face interactions creates and reproduces the community.

Since most country music songwriters are based in Nashville, there is a large pool of local talent. Writers who have a reputation for writing good songs are likely to find many opportunities for collaboration and co-writing, and those who are known for being easy to work with and friendly will also be more successful at finding co-writers. Between songwriters, a good reputation translates into more work and greater freedom in choosing with whom they will write.

While a good reputation helps songwriters find more opportunities, a bad reputation can end a career. When a community identifies with a set of norms, behaviors, and principles, they may draw social boundaries between themselves and people who do not adhere to their practices. Sociologists call this process *social closure* (Parkin 1979): groups who want to differentiate themselves from a group that they perceive to be inferior to their own set boundaries. Among songwriters, group boundaries are most distinct at the point in which aspiring songwriters and established songwriters meet.

As a new songwriter, successfully integrating into the established group involves building a network and using social network connections correctly. Reputation is multidimensional, and though aspiring songwriters should be talented in order to build a good reputation, an individual's social reputation (e.g., Are they easy to work with? Are they nice?) can be just as important as being able to write a good song. If a new songwriter is too self-promotional and comes off as only being interested in his or her career rather than becoming part of the song-writing community, they may be accused of gherming. A *gherm* (rhymes with germ and is a term unique to the country music business) is an individual who is inappropriately intrusive about building business networks and in trying to further their career by attempting to be overly personal or forceful when they meet other music industry professionals (Chapman 2010). A gherm will repeatedly attempt self-promotion in an inauthentic way when they meet someone who has had success in the music industry and will attempt to distribute copies of their music widely to "get heard." As a group, Nashville songwriters generally are known to be open, friendly, and hospitable, but this type of behavior marks a gherm as being outside of the established group and ensures that they will not be allowed to join the group. This reminds us that while the music community may appear to be open, its boundaries are guarded and enforced by its members.

Class and Gender in Music Lyrics

Tracing out the art world behind the music is not the only way to understand a musical community. We have discussed, so far, the "backstage" dynamics. This is not, however, the way readers will have likely come to understand music. Most of us encounter music as listeners, through recommendations from friends, listening to digital or terrestrial radio, or hearing a song featured in a movie or television show, or even in a commercial.

Music lyrics offer a window into the workings of musical communities, and what they can illustrate is how music communities may have different ways of seeing similar issues that emerge in conversations—and thus in the lyrics that the community writes. It is often areas of conflict around art that reveal contentious issues within communities, especially in terms of who does or does not belong to a particular community or group (Tepper 2011). As we discuss in this section, social class and gender are two points of contention in the Nashville music community, and we can uncover evidence of that conflict in song lyrics.

Songwriters, perhaps unsurprisingly, write what they know in terms of processing and sharing their feelings about their careers, relationships, and other interests. Sociologists Melton A. McLaurin and

Richard Peterson said of country music lyrics: "[T]hey express pride in being poor, being country, being southern survivors ... There is an assertion of working-class identity in these songs, but rather than being directed towards revolutionary consciousness, it encourages pride in acknowledging one's own poverty" (Peterson 1992: 56–57). The idea of a collective identity based on earning potential or financial situation is a way of talking about socioeconomic class, an idea that sociologists typically define as a person's standing in society based on their occupation, education, and financial situation. For songwriters whose careers do not require formal education and are often self-employed, their socioeconomic position relies heavily on their ability to make money from their songs. In terms of earning potential, a songwriter might strike it rich after a string of hit songs or may never be able to make a living from their trade. Songwriters certainly reflect upon their own financial situation and uncertain future through their lyrics.

The song "Crazy Town" by Rodney Clawson and Brett Jones, made popular by country artist Jason Aldean in 2010, is a great example. The lyrics point out the financial uncertainty that comes with pursuing a career in music: "One year they repossess your truck and the next you make a couple million bucks." Nashville, as rendered by this lyric, is a "Crazy Town" because success may be given or taken away at any time, not due to talent as much as to hard work and one's luck or "destiny."

In the same way that socioeconomic class appears in song lyrics, other facets of a songwriter's identity and reaction to their communities can impact the songs they write. According to Susan Lee, the typical country songwriter of past decades was a man in his twenties or thirties who was raised in a rural area or small town, was a protestant Christian, and enjoyed fishing on the weekends. While not everyone in this music community is male, white, or Christian, sometimes specific songs, events, or people expose areas of conflict around who belongs in the community. Gender, therefore, is another way lyrics illuminate these dynamics in the music community.

On the same day in July of 2014, two separate female country acts released songs into a country music movement that was heavily dominated by male artists like Jason Aldean. Singer Maggie Rose released "Girl in Your Truck Song," and the singer-songwriter duo Maddie and

Tae released their song "Girl in a Country Song." Both songs use similar hooks and reference other famous country song lyrics to comment on women and their place in country music. Despite these striking similarities, the songs have opposite messages. The choruses of the songs are illustrative of the major differences.

Maggie Rose sings, "Tonight, tonight I wanna be the girl in your truck song, the one that makes you sing along." On the other hand, Maddie and Tae sing a song in total opposition to being the girl in a guy's pickup truck. Their chorus starts, "Bein' the girl in a country song; how in the world did it go so wrong?" Both songs go on to use lyrics and common tropes from famous "bro-country" songs, a genre that is based around songs that speak of a simple life in the country typified by a guy in his pickup truck with a pretty girl, to make their points. Maggie Rose's song celebrates women's place in country music as accessories in a traditionally masculine space while Maddie and Tae's song pokes fun at that masculine space and creates a more critical view of what it means to be an ornament riding along in a man's truck.

Maggie Rose did not write "Girl in Your Truck Song," however. Rather, it was written by three hit songwriters in Nashville who had written hit songs for artists like Carrie Underwood, Bon Jovi, Taylor Swift, Keith Urban, Miley Cyrus, Celine Dion, and Kenny Chesney. In line with a more indie working arrangement, Maddie and Tae co-wrote "Girl in a Country Song" with their producer.

What was the outcome commercially? While the more conventional "Girl in Your Truck Song" crested at number 58 on the Billboard Country Airplay Chart, the "anti-bro-country" track "Girl in a Country Song" went to number 1. The success of "Girl in a Country Song" might have been its hooks or musical arrangement, but its chart topping success was more likely due to its playful critique of the conventional portrayals of women in bro-country music.

Of course, lyrics can illuminate so much more than what can be discussed here. The valorization of a hard day's work, statements of American patriotism, the importance of family, and a sort of nostalgia for a simple, small town life, are just a few of the themes that occur frequently in country music. Lyrics can reflect how things are, but they could also be about what the songwriters hope the future will bring.

Conclusion

In this chapter, we have discussed how informal relationships between people as well as formal and structural relationships between constellations of groups, organizations, and even whole cities come together to form communities.

At the more micro-level, when thinking about the relationships between musicians, songwriters, and other members of music communities, we are also inclined to think about issues of equity, access, and inclusion. Who is allowed to be part of a music community? What barriers keep people from freely participating in creating music? Does it matter if people are able to make a living from writing, recording, or selling songs?

At the more macro-level, when thinking about music communities in a geographic space, issues like commodifying culture, preserving communities, and using music communities as tools to develop cities create a number of challenging questions: how do cities champion and highlight local cultures without exploiting them? How do local informal scenes—often carefully crafted social spaces that seek to be countercultural and authentic—balance the need for support and protection from such attention?

Activities

(1) *Discover the hidden community around your favorite songs.* As discussed in this chapter, there is a somewhat hidden community at work behind your favorite song. Using digital sources, develop a "credit sheet" that lists at least three individuals (e.g., recording artist, songwriter, producer, musician, music video choreographer, etc.) and at least three organizations (e.g., record label, distributor, publisher, etc.) in the song's Art World. What kinds of "work" did they do? After you find this information, write a 1–2 paragraph response to the following prompt: using sociological concepts and ideas, what can you say about this art world? For example, were most of the individuals men? Were all of the organizations part of a major multimedia conglomerate? Resources like iTunes, the artist's website, Performing Rights Organizations (ASCAP, BMI,

SESAC), and even Wikipedia may provide helpful information for this exercise.

(2) *Uncover music communities through song lyrics.* As discussed in this chapter, areas of conflict around art often illustrate larger issues within communities. In this chapter, we gave the example of two country songs released on the same day that had two opposing takes on women's place in their community. Also in the chapter was an example of a song that portrayed an issue of socioeconomic class by pointing out the difficulty of financially "making it" in the country music community. Using song lyrics as commentary on one's community is not limited to the country music genre. In fact, many genres of music are home to songs that have a social message. Within one music genre of your choice, select two songs, one that focuses on gender and one that focuses on socioeconomic class. In 1–2 paragraphs, identify what you believe to be the music community's perspective on gender and socioeconomic class with lyrics from your pair of songs as evidence. What do these lyrics indicate about the musical community that created them?

10

The Globalization of Popular Music

A Focus on Women in Poland

Katarzyna M. Wyrzykowska

Long before the Internet revolution and the development of new media, a Canadian media theorist Marshall McLuhan claimed that the emergence of media enabling large-scale communication regardless of time and place, will make the world that we live in a global village (McLuhan 1962; 1964). Today, we know that this assumption proved to be prophetic. Modern sociological studies on globalization cover a much wider range of phenomena than just communication or mass communication. Studies on globalization take into account a diversified range of issues: from economic systems to cultural change. Moreover, social scientists are also interested in how globalization affects and changes the functioning of local communities, and thus the everyday experience of individuals. The focus in this chapter, however, is on the relationship between globalization and popular music experiences.

I will begin with a discussion of what *globalization* actually is. Roland Robertson, one of the first social scientists working on this theme, defines globalization as "the compression of the world and the intensification of the consciousness of the world as a whole" (Robertson 1992). This process of thickening and intensifying international connections refers to almost every sphere of human life: culture, economics, politics, social relationships, and lifestyles. One of the main effects of globalization processes is the emergence of the specific types of identity and social relations that operate on supra-local and transnational levels (Sztompka 2004).

Globalization as a social and cultural phenomenon generates contradictory feelings and opinions. Skeptics point out that globalization brings with it the risk of homogenizing the world, that is, a progressive assimilation of forms of social, political and economic organization, as well as uniformity of habits, customs, consumption patterns, and lifestyles. In this sense, globalization is seen as a threat to cultural diversity. Enthusiasts of globalization point to the fact that globalization allows us to come into contact with different cultures, thereby it is strengthening diversity and shaping cultural openness.

The contradiction in the assessment of the effects of globalization influenced the appearance of several concepts trying to capture the ambiguous nature of globalization. These concepts include:

- *Creolization*—the process of global flows and interconnecting of ideas and practices from different cultures, that leads to emergence of new ideas and practices. It refers to the concept of creole languages, that is, languages created as a mixture of different languages (Hannerz 1987);
- *Hybridization* (concept fairly similar to *creolization*)—the process of formation of new social and cultural as a result of mixing of already existing structures and practices (Canclini 1995);
- *McDonaldization*—the process of gradual dissemination around the World modes of thinking and acting, typical of fast-food restaurants, that is, calculability, efficiency, standardization, and predictability (Ritzer 1993); and
- *Indigenization*—the process of adapting global trends to local context (Robertson 1992).

An interesting concept associated with globalization is *Americanization*. Since the United States of America maintains a strong position in the world (economic, political, and military), it is able to promote and distribute in mass scale its own customs, lifestyles, consumption patterns, products of the artistic culture, and even language or religious beliefs

(Sztompka 2004). Interestingly, all of these concepts seem to offer particular political, cultural or critical insights on globalization.

Popular music is a perfect phenomenon to illustrate various aspects of globalization and the social changes that it induces. This is not because changes in popular music are a result of globalization, but rather because the popular music and popular music industry (in its present form) are a part of globalization and also a kind of confirmation that this process actually occurs. My analysis will be based on a study of change in popular music in Poland. A focus on this European, post-socialist country can provide an interesting take on globalization. I will first briefly present the specifics of the development of popular music in Poland from the perspective of the transition from socialism to capitalism and introduction of free market economy. Then I will discuss selected phenomena from Polish popular music in the context of the broader social and cultural change. At the end I will look carefully at the role and importance of women in popular music in Poland in order to illustrate the paradoxes of globalization.

Music, Globalization and Social Change: The Polish Perspective

Poland is a democratic country (a member of NATO and the EU), located in the east-central part of Europe. This geopolitical position is so important due to the fact that Poland is a kind of bridge between East and West Europe. Since the end of World War II and until 1989, Poland was a communist country under the Russian sphere of influence. During that time, almost every official artistic activity was controlled by the State. The government controlled the television, radio and record companies. Consequently, producing records demanded fitting into the authorities' requirements; the music that contested political reality was blocked by censorship. However, it should be noted that communist Poland was not completely isolated from the Western world, despite the government's attempts to limit the cultural flow from the capitalist world. For example, people were generally able to smuggle in Western records, and then duplicate them in multiple ("bootleg") copies on cassette tapes. Moreover, the authorities occasionally allowed concerts by selected Western artists (e.g., The Rolling Stones who performed in concert in Warsaw in 1967), in order to give the people a false sense of openness.

Musical Practices of Poles: Between Globalization and Local Trends

The year 1989 was a breakthrough not only for the Polish political scene. This date is also a symbol of a new opening for the cultural sector with the fall of communism. The Polish market was opened for foreign investment and private property rights were restored. The first sign of a new opening was the access of Western music companies (the so-called "majors") to the Polish market, as well as the emergence of private Polish music labels. Another clear indicator of change in the cultural sector was the introduction to the Polish audience of such music channels as MTV (at the beginning it was the American version, the Polish one appeared in 2000), and youth music magazines based on Western, mostly German, styles and tastes.

The opening to the Western world is visible mostly in the musical preferences of Poles. According to research carried out in recent years (OBOP 2002; TNS OBOP 2008; GUS 2012), the Poles, for the most part, prefer pop, disco polo, rock, and movie soundtracks. Pop has a particularly high popularity among people aged 15–39 years, and rock among teenagers from cities. It is not difficult to notice that which distinguishes Poles from people in other countries: the great popularity of a native music genre *disco polo* (this phenomenon is explored below in more breadth). According to the above studies, disco polo is a music genre mainly popular among the inhabitants of villages and small towns, people with primary education, and people aged more than 50 years. Put differently, disco polo is very popular among the peasantry, in traditional Polish terms, to the disdain of the urban intelligentsia (Kotarba 2002c).

In the 1960s and 1970s, foreign artists rarely appeared in the rankings of the most popular singers and bands (OBOPSP 1975); if they appeared they usually came from the other communist bloc countries. And how is it today? I conducted research in 2011–2012 for my Ph.D. thesis on this topic. I conducted in-depth, qualitative interviews with 60 secondary school students; focus groups with 28 respondents, and participatory observations of music classes in community centers, in schools, during concerts and music festivals, etc. (Wyrzykowska 2017). I asked adolescents in Warsaw about their favorite singers and music bands. They named 180 different artists, of whom approximately 65 per cent were foreign. At the top of the ranking was Australian band AC/DC, followed closely by Guns N' Roses, Iron Maiden, Metallica and two Polish bands: Dżem and Myslovitz. (It is interesting that research conducted in the 1980s among the youth provide data that AC/DC was highly regarded among young Poles (Janik 1983). This may at least partly confirm the thesis of the incomplete cultural isolation of Poland during the communist era.)

Do these findings suggest that foreign music is appreciated more than Polish music? Opinions are divided—a large number of the respondents liked both the Polish and foreign music, or even declared that they do not pay attention to the artist's country of origin. Those who firmly declared that they prefer foreign music generally justified their preferences by some critical remarks on Polish music. They pointed out that Polish artists compose songs without meaning, by ignoring crucial values and over-simplifying the world. They sing in English, thus attempting to copy the Western music model, and fail to conquer the international music market. Magda described the last two phenomena in terms of the example of Myslovitz (a pop-rock band):

> Polish musicians just really aspire to be like the West, even Myslovitz, which at the beginning had its own style, and then began to play more like a British rock band. And they tried to sell records in England, but it did not work out, because you do not go to the US with a hamburger, right? Fans are used to such a kind of music and another band playing in the same manner is not making any difference. The Poles are pathetic in being original.

Magda's statement draws attention to the problem of copying the music style of other artists. Such actions are clearly visible and inadequate when a band is trying to enter the foreign music market in which the copied music style has already been well developed.

Attempts to make a career in the foreign market are associated with the phenomenon of *Anglicization* of Polish popular music that intensified after the year 1989. This problem relates primarily to pop, rock, metal and electronic music. On one hand, some artists use English-language nicknames (e.g., "Margaret" instead of "Małgorzata," and "Honey" instead of "Honorata") and band names (e.g., Happysad, Cool Kids of Death). On the other, an increasing number of artists record their songs in English. Although in the communist era some musicians also performed songs in English, mainly to outsmart the censors. This was not a common phenomenon. It is difficult to clearly determine why artists decided to do this. One reason is the belief that the use of English communicates to the audience that they are dealing with a mature and modern band (English as an index for Western culture). It should be noted that, ironically, many of the Polish bands that have been successful worldwide (e.g., Vader, Behemoth) perform loud and fast heavy-metal music for which the quality of lyrics and pronunciation is irrelevant.

I will now return to the already mentioned Polish music genre of disco polo. It serves as a good example to illustrate the transformation of a music genre influenced by the social, cultural and technological changes occurring on a global scale. Disco polo, by itself, is a music genre quite similar to such musical styles as Italian disco and the so-called festive songs played during wedding receptions and other secular parties. Disco polo is simple dance music, performed mainly on keyboard, based on a simple rhythm and simple melodies (in some songs rhythm dominates the melody). On the textual level, it refers primarily to love and male–female relationships, and the lyrics can be often dirty and sometimes even vulgar (e.g., direct references to sexual contact). Disco polo is a relatively young music genre, first appearing in the early 1990s after the collapse of the communist system. It is difficult to say for sure what was the impulse for its creation. It appeared here and there at first and, thanks to the initial lack of copyright regulation of the music industry, quickly flourished. Cassettes with disco polo were seen everywhere in the early 1990s, from newsagents' stalls to food markets. At that time it was called "sidewalk music" as "bootlegged" cassettes were distributed on stalls or tables set up wherever there was a free spot. Despite the growing popularity of disco polo, professional critics as well as the urban intelligentsia considered it a primitive music, and a preference for this kind of music was treated as a sign of bad taste. Therefore, the public media and journalists stigmatized the genre, and the major record companies refused to produce their records, although there were some exceptions. The head of one of the major record companies in 2013 described his one-time marriage with disco polo as follows:

> We do not record disco polo. In the 90s, we recorded one album with the former star of the genre and even today I am still ashamed of this. Despite the huge audience for this genre, we do not want to be associated with disco polo.

However, people involved in the disco polo business did not care; they had their own TV program on a private channel. They set up their own record companies. They successfully toured small towns and villages across Poland, and the number of records sold was constantly increasing. The turning point came in the early 2000s. The Polish market and radio stations became filled more and more with foreign music, Polish music stations (including Polish MTV) began to appear, and the Internet brought to Poles the cultural content from almost all over the world. The first serious competitor for the disco polo market was techno music, which in the late 1990s was omnipresent in Poland (television, music magazines, concerts of numerous international techno stars, popular thematic festivals; techno dominated music repertoire in discotheques in villages and small towns, see Szlendak 1998). Rap music turned out to be the second, less obvious competitor. Hip-hop culture in Poland emerged in the mid-1990s, but its impact was noticeable only a few years later. For example, social researchers certified that rap was a musical preference among young people mainly in the cities (see Kamińska 1999). Over time, rap spread in popularity to villages and the countryside. Rap was popular mainly in the cities (hip-hop is a distinctly urban culture), but interest in this genre began to be visible over time in villages and the countryside in general.

While journalists proudly announced the ultimate demise of disco polo, the artists and the whole disco polo industry patiently survived these difficulties, mainly by maintaining contact with fans through regular concerts, and it returned with a renewed force. The second golden era of disco polo took place after 2007. The artists and disco polo producers closely observed what had been happening in popular music worldwide—especially in the field of music production, music videos and music PR and marketing. This second wave of disco polo on the visual level was nothing like the primitive productions of the 1990s. Although both the music soundtrack and lyrics had not changed much, albeit a bit less vulgar and obscene, they were performed at a higher quality aesthetic level. Let us take, for example, the band Boys, now regarded as a classic of the whole disco polo genre. In the video recorded in 1997 for the song "Peasant from Mazury/Chłop z Mazur"—Mazury is a lake and forest region located in North-West Poland—we see the Polish countryside and the band leader, Marcin Miller, performing typical farm work activities. Both Miller and other people appearing in the video are slovenly dressed, playing their roles in a very artificial and ready-made way, and the video gives the impression of an amateur production. In contrast, the video prepared in 2015 for the song "In your eyes I see heaven/W oczach niebo," a duet with the band Extazy, the Boys takes us to a modern club full of fashionably dressed people who are mostly attractive women. Looking on the production side of this video, it is made in a professional, carefully planned manner (e.g., in terms of lighting, set design, montage, and so forth). Professionalization of production (the new aesthetic that contrasts with the first wave of disco polo), combined with the skillful use of social media, and paying greater attention to the visual image of performers all create the ideal of a "new" disco polo as a completely different music. The number of disco polo listeners is constantly increasing, and new disco polo bands appear one after another. Although they declare that they are inspired by classics of the disco polo genre (Boys, Shazza, Bayer Full, and Akcent), the new disco polo stars—Weekend, Jago Young or Andre—perform music which is, in fact, professionally produced and presented in an attractive way, so they are far removed from the semi-amateur disco polo productions of the 1990s.

Although the opinion of disco polo from critics—such as journalists, mainstream media, artists performing other genres, and fanatic fans of other types of music—is still somewhat negative, the judgments have become less severe. As a confirmation of this thesis, I will present the discovery that I have made studying music experiences of Warsaw's adolescents. As it turned out, the young respondents do not see any problems making fun and partying with disco polo, despite declaring that they do not listen to this type of music in their everyday life. For example, Paweł declares that he mostly listens to metal, rock and blues, and disclosed that:

> There is disco polo, normally I do not listen to this sort of music. But as we are out with my friends or during the party, someone turns on a disco polo song that everyone knows, it is the best music to have fun and party hard.

It needs to be underscored that the phenomenon described by Paweł is common among the young people. However, if we look more closely at the disco polo revival, the emergence of a "new" quality in disco polo is an apparent evolution of the genre, because in fact we are dealing with almost the same music "product," which is presented and sold in a new "package."

The above reference to the categories from the area of economics and marketing is not incidental. We should also mention that from a strictly business perspective, after 2007, disco polo began to be treated by music producers and record labels as a product, as a commodity for which there was a high market demand. Hence, private TV networks and radio stations (despite critical comments concerning the musical quality of this genre) have launched thematic channels dedicated strictly to this music. The extensive commodification of popular music is one of the negative manifestations of globalization. In the late 1930s, German philosopher and sociologist Theodore Adorno drew attention to the problem of the mass reproduction of musical works, that led to the treatment of music not as an art, but as a product (2002 [1938]).

A Polish band Just 5 can be presented as an example of the commodification of popular music in Poland. It was created in 1997, as an exact copy of the American boy band, Backstreet Boys. Its members were selected during casting to visually mirror the members of Backstreet Boys.

The musical and textual content created by Just 5 directly refers to the American original. The gross Americanization of Just 5 came with their videos, "Coloured Dreams/Kolorowe Sny," in which attempts were made to imitate the dance style and dynamic realization of the American clips, but at a much lower budget that did not allow them to be as aesthetically polished and powerful. Nevertheless, Just 5 proved to be a commercial success, as the debut album sold more than 100,000 copies, a very good result in terms of the Polish music market. The band fulfilled the demand for this type of product on the Polish market, and the great popularity of American boy bands at that time gave hope to their Polish counterparts. But Just 5's career did not last long and finished with the end of the boy band era. Today, their music is usually treated as a kind of historically interesting fact from an earlier era in Poland's popular music.

The intensification of the cultural flows associated with globalization can experience delays that can be illustrated with the example of the Polish punk scene. In Europe, the release of the Sex Pistols' first album in 1976 is believed to mark the birth of punk, whereas the punk scene in Poland began to develop in the 1980s. In terms of musical forms (e.g., styles and instrumentation), Polish punk did not differ significantly from its British predecessor. However, it differed in terms of the worldview expressed in its songs. Several years ago, Tomasz Lipiński—the leader and co-founder of the prominent Polish punk band Brygada Kryzys stated during an interview with Tok FM radio station that for him and the rest of the band members, the leftist tone of British punk was unbearable—especially the left-wing fascination of Joe Strummer from The Clash. Having experienced firsthand the degeneration of socialism put into practice, Polish punk bands could not accept the naïve fascination with socialism expressed by their Western counterparts. In turn, Polish punk bands (often using abstract metaphors) branded their songs with the situation in the country, describing the hardships of everyday reality and trying to give to the people a hope that better days will come (see Pekacz 1992). For instance, hope for a better future is expressed in Tilt's song "Jeszcze będzie przepięknie/It will be beautiful one day" recorded in 1990 (soon after the fall of communism), but composed in the late 1980s: "It will be beautiful one day/We will live normally one day."

In the introduction to this chapter I mentioned that globalization is often identified with Americanization. But are the United States really the main reference point for the cultural practices around the world? An interesting example that undermines the identification of globalization with Americanization is the strong influence of Jamaican *ska* on Polish popular music as far back as the 1960s. In the year 1965, a female sextet, Alibabki, recorded a mini-album entitled *The Rhythms of Jamaica Ska/ W rytmie jamaica ska*. This inconspicuous album consisted of four songs arranged in the style of Jamaican ska music. Today, the presence of Jamaican music or reggae in Poland does not surprise anyone. Whereas the common perception is that the boon in this type of music had been caused by the transformation of the political system in Poland, the surprising fact is that Jamaican music has been present in the Polish scene since the 1960s. This attitude is well captured in one of the YouTube comments placed under the Alibabki song entitled "Jamaica ska": "I would never expect ska in Poland in 1965!"

Women, Popular Music and Globalization

In 1997, a Polish pop-rock band Big Cyc recorded a song and a video called "World is Ruled by Women/Światem rządzą kobiety." The song is produced in a mixed musical convention including elements of rock, punk and march music. The lyrics are clusters of unrelated topics, in which selected Polish female singers are successively mentioned. Senior divas of popular music (Irena Santor) and experienced artists (Maryla Rodowicz) appear as well as singers from the younger generation (Katarzyna Nosowska, Edyta Górniak or Natalia Kukulska). Female artist presentations are separated by a short chorus: "*There is no help, / nowadays only women sing*." The song's video is based on the concept of fashion shows. The female singers are represented on a platform by their satirical models, while the audience greets them with enthusiasm. The entire video is produced in a sadomasochistic theme; even the figures representing various female singers are dressed in a provocative and somewhat vulgar way.

Did the Big Cyc song ring true then and does it ring true today? Over the course of the seven or more years I have been studying Polish popular music sociologically—whether in terms of youth musical practices, the

Poles' amateur music scenes, the phonographic industry or professional musical careers—women remain a distinct minority in the music industry (Gałuszka et al. 2013). For example, women were merely five out of 50 respondents in the Polish record companies' study. How can we explain the small numbers of women working in executive or managerial positions in popular music in Poland? One explanation might be the relative (un)importance of music in women's everyday life. In my study of musical practices among Warsaw's adolescents I tried to understand why the girls seemed less engaged in music than the boys. It turned out that for many of the female respondents, music is important, but they might better fulfill their artistic needs by engaging in theater or dance (Wyrzykowska 2017).

It also seems that certain dated stereotypes of women in music still have currency in Polish culture. Those gender stereotypes are primarily related to issues such as physical abilities (e.g., what instruments the women are able to play); psychological factors (e.g., cognitive limitations) and socially prescribed roles in music (e.g., what women could and should do, and what is improper for women). My teenage respondents, both boys and girls, indicated that among their peers there exists the widespread belief that if girls play an instrument, it should be the violin or piano. Drums or the electric guitar are exclusively reserved for boys. "Have you ever seen a girl playing drums?" Kacper asked incredulously, yet rhetorically. Consequently, when it comes to playing music together, girls usually play on the aforementioned instruments, or serve as vocalists. Are these ideas only social beliefs, or can they be observed in action? At this point it is worth recalling what Szymon (one of the male respondents) said:

> Sz: People mainly think that girls are vocalists. I often watch videos on YouTube showing how amateurs play instruments. And when a girl plays guitar, bass or even drums—everybody is shocked. And also there are comments like: I want you to be my wife! . . . (People are shocked because) maybe the majority have adopted the stereotype that women are weak and incapable of such thing. Personally, I do not accept this point of view. Maybe girls have other interests than music, but there are also some girls who like to express emotions through music.

The continued existence of these stereotypes among some youth is important for understanding the character of women's musical engagements. These stereotypes can block them from engaging in any significant musical activity.

The stereotypical ideas about women in music described above lead to contrary expectations. On one hand, the women in music are expected to make modern songs, to be creative, not to copy solutions from Western artists, but to propose to the audience something new and original. On the other hand, the public opinion seems much less forgiving for women. If you analyze the media discourse on popular music it is not hard to see that far more attention is paid to female rather than male artists. Interestingly, their artistic achievements are not the main topic, but rather a discussion about their private life (e.g., difficult childhood and turbulent divorce), controversial appearance (e.g., too deep a neckline and too short a skirt, etc.), and the unfortunate statements on social media (e.g., engaging in political quarrels with other artists). For example, for a few days in September 2016, the Polish media discussed pop singer Natalia Kukulska's appearance on the talent show "The Voice of Poland." She was standing next to a waitress who was holding glasses with champagne on a tray. She was pregnant at the time. The issue that a pregnant woman—a mother of two children—allowed herself to be filmed next to alcohol was raised. Only a few commentators pointed out that the singer did not drink the alcohol and she had no influence on which shots would be selected for the final version of the program.

Analyzing Polish popular music in the context of the presence of women and globalization, we should also deal with how women are represented in popular music. Disco polo provides an excellent example, as women, femininity and love are some of the main topics of songs in this genre. A woman is an object of desire, an object of dreams, as Akcent earnestly sings:

> Your eyes, those green eyes make me crazy/Stars probably gave you all the shine/And I gave you my heart/You fall in love, you fall in love like this only once.

In turn, the band Andre sings:

> Such a modest girls/Such a sexy bomb/Suddenly in my life appeared/Beautiful girl, it's not a dream/Little, mischievous like a miracle.

While Playboys sings:

> And you're my lady/I want you babe/You provoke me, I know how you feel/You are my love/Heart passion/My senses, my drugs.

All these songs are accompanied by very graphic and telling videos, showing the same pattern: the camera is focused on the band/singer and on the girl/girls, who are always dressed fashionably, with their hair combed and full makeup. However, the female representation in these videos can be confusing for the audience. For instance, in the cited song by Andre we concurrently hear about a modest girl and, yet, see scantily dressed woman with full makeup. I should stress that these videos are very popular on the Internet. Andre's video currently has over 50 million hits on YouTube. Although contemporary disco polo songs and music videos are not as frivolous as those of the 1990s, they still present aesthetics that continue to perpetuate the stereotypical ways of (re) presenting women (i.e., sexualization and a focus on the woman's body).

Will Poland Be Like the Rest of Us?

Of course, the above discussion of the presence and representation of women in music is not a solely Polish phenomenon. These features of gender are quite noticeable in other Western countries and cultures (see O'Neill 1997). In the U.S.A. and Great Britain, men still dominate rock, pop, and country bands whereas women dominate the solo and group vocalists' category. However, what distinguishes the Polish case is the way music reflects significant and dramatic socio-political changes in Polish society. Although the political transformation from socialism to democracy occurred almost 30 years ago, Polish culture is a platform for two opposing normative orders: traditional and postmodern. This tension is not simply between cassette tapes and YouTube, but between very conservative Catholic values and the market-driven mass media. Contradictory expectations of women in popular music are a manifestation of this process. Moreover, these different dimensions of women's presence in Polish popular music show paradoxes of globalization. The political transition in Poland carried with it the promise of cultural change and hope for rapid societal development. Material objects and technology diffused rapidly, but social and cultural change is a long process, especially when you consider the contrasts in values and worldviews. Full adoption of such values connected to globalization as openness, and a positive attitude towards diversity requires more time, and sometimes their full acceptance (due to the specific historical conditions) can be impossible. Whether differences by gender are a manifestation of societal value differences or a function of the music industry internationally is a topic to be explored, with great policy implications.

Conclusion

In this chapter, I illustrated the complexity of globalization through the example of Polish popular music. It is difficult to agree with the statement that globalization brings only homogenization and standardization of culture. Societies are living organisms that dynamically respond to emerging changes. British sociologist Anthony Giddens emphasizes that people do not accept indiscriminately everything presented to them, but rather try to reflexively shape their own identity (1991). Therefore, the globalization processes are subject to constant (re)interpretation and clashing with local trends all the time. At this point we must make a distinction between the two phenomena appearing in the area of popular music that are closely linked to globalization: *cultural imitation* and *cultural inspiration*. The former refers to a fully conscious and exact copying of cultural patterns. This action is often accompanied by a desire to reach a commercial success, and little attention is paid to the artistic value of music created during that process (e.g., the Polish boy band Just 5). In contrast, cultural inspiration lies in making a creative use of the cultural content available in the global world. This strategy was adopted by the Polish punk movement, or the band Alibabki, who referred to the works of other artists, and in doing so were able to offer their own original compositions. In this case, you cannot talk about the exact copying of other people's ideas, but rather about making creative references to someone else's artistic work.

Therefore, the homogenization or standardization are not the only possible scenarios for development of contemporary popular music.

Activities

(1) As discussed, globalization leads to constant cultural flows, interpenetration and mixing of music genres. This phenomenon is easy to analyze through the example of rap music. Examine the list of twelve Polish rap music songs below. Find online video clips for the songs and answer the following questions:
   (a) What are the main similarities and differences between Polish and American rap? (Videos 1–6) Make at least 5 observations.
   (b) How are women and femininity presented in Polish rap music videos? (Videos 7–12)
   List of Polish rap songs:
   1. Kaliber 44—Plus i minus
   2. Paktofonika—Jestem Bogiem
   3. Molesta—Wiedziałem, że tak będzie
   4. Peja/Slums Attack—Głucha Noc (feat. Medi Top & Mientha)
   5. Numer Raz & DJ Zero—Ławka, chłopaki z bloków
   6. Vienio—Nowe Bloki (feat. Hades)
   7. Ascetoholix—Suczki
   8. Sokół feat. Pono & Franek Kimono—W aucie
   9. Mezo—Aniele (feat Liber)
   10. Wdowa—Zapomniałam (feat. Czesław Śpiewa)
   11. Sokół i Marysia Starosta—Wyblakłe myśli
   12. Remo feat. Doniu, Amila—Without You (Pozdro z piekła)

(2) Globalization critics usually point to the fact that it brings unification of cultures and the disappearance of local cultural diversity. Your task is to prepare a short (max. 8 minutes) presentation in which you introduce arguments (at least 3) in defense of globalization. In your presentation, use some examples from the area of popular music, in terms of an example of one artist, or in terms of an example of various artists or songs.

BIBLIOGRAPHY

Abbott, Andrew. 1993. "The Sociology of Work and Occupations." *Annual Review of Sociology*, 19: 187–209.

Ableton. 2016. *Push 2: Music At Your Fingertips.* Retrieved from https://www.ableton.com/en/push/.

Adorno, Theodor. 1949. *The Philosophy of Modern Music.* New York: Seabury Press.

Adorno, Theodor W. 1976. *Introduction to the Sociology of Music.* Trans. E.B. Ashton. New York: Continuum.

Adorno, Theodor W. 2002 [1938]. "On the Fetish-Character in Music and the Regression of Listening." In R. Leppert (ed.), *Essays on Music.* Berkeley: University of California Press.

Adorno, Theodor and Robert Hullot-Kentor. 2006. *Philosophy of New Music.* Minneapolis: University of Minnesota Press.

Altheide, David L. and Robert P. Snow. 1979. *Media Logic.* Thousand Oaks, CA: Sage.

American Psychological Association [APA]. 2016. "Stress in America: U.S. Presidential Election." Retrieved from http://hiphop.apa.org/news/press/releases/stress/2016/presidential-election.pdf.

Atzmon, Thaddeus. 2016. "Musical Pastiche." In Christopher J. Schneider and Joseph A. Kotarba (eds.), *Symbolic Interactionist Takes on Music*, pp. 185–195. Bingley, UK: Emerald Group Publishing Limited.

Baker, Houston A., Jr. 1993. *Black Studies, Rap, and the Academy.* Chicago: University of Chicago Press.

Balliger, Robin. 1999. "Politics." In Bruce Horner and Thomas Swiss (eds.), *Key Terms in Popular Music and Culture*, pp. 54–63. New York: Blackwell.

Banbury, Jonafa. 2016. "The Church and the Streets: An Ethnographic Study of the Christian Hip Hop Music Scene in Central Texas." In Christopher J. Schneider and Joseph A. Kotarba (eds.), *Symbolic Interactionist Takes on Music*, pp. 151–168. Bingley, UK: Emerald Group Publishing Limited.

Banfield, William C. 2010. *Cultural Codes: Makings of a Black Music Philosophy.* Lanham, MD: Scarecrow Press.

Barnes, Ken. 1988. "Top 40 Radio: A Fragment of the Imagination." In Simon Frith (ed.), *Facing the Music*, pp. 8–50. New York: Pantheon.

Baudrillard, Jean. 1983. *Simulations.* New York: Semiotexte.

Baudrillard, Jean. 1994. *Simulacra and Simulation.* Ann Arbor, MI: University of Michigan Press.

Baur, Bernard. 2011. "John Michael Talbot: Biography." http://www.johnmichaeltalbot.com/biography.php.

Becker, Howard. 1963. *Outsiders.* New York: Free Press.

Becker, Howard. 1982. *Art Worlds.* Berkeley: University of California Press.

Becker, Howard. 1986. *Doing Things Together: Selected Papers.* Evanston, IL: Northwestern University Press.

Bendix, Reinhard. 1978. *Max Weber: An Intellectual Portrait.* Berkeley: University of California Press.

Benjamin, Walter. 1969. *Illuminations.* New York: Schocken.

Bennett, Andy. 2001. *Cultures of Popular Music.* Buckingham, UK: Open University Press.

Bennett, Andy and Richard A. Peterson. 2004. *Music Scenes.* Nashville, TN: Vanderbilt University Press.

Berendt, Joachim E. 1982. *The Jazz Book: From Ragtime to Fusion and Beyond*, trans., H. Bredigkeit and B. Bredigkeit with Dan Morgenstern). Brooklyn, NY: Lawrence Hill Books.

Berger, Peter. 1967. *The Sacred Canopy: Elements of a Sociological Theory of Religion.* Garden City, NY: Doubleday.

Billboard. 2001. "Metallica, Dr. Dre Settle Napster Lawsuits," July 12. Retrieved September, 2016 from www.billboard.com/articles/news/79142/metallica-dr-dre-settle-napster-lawsuits.

Blaque, Marcus. 2016. "You Good Bro? Elaborating on My Years of Depression + Mental Health." Retrieved from https://medium.com/@marcusblaque/you-good-bro-elaborating-on-my-years-of-depression-mental-health–4108391415d3#.9pqtpt5hv.

Bloom, Allan. 1987. *The Closing of the American Mind.* New York: Simon and Schuster.

Blumer, Herbert. 1969. *Symbolic Interactionism: Perspective and Method.* Englewood Cliffs, NJ: Prentice-Hall.

Bourdieu, Pierre. 1984. *Distinction: A Social Critique of the Judgment of Taste.* Cambridge, MA: Harvard University Press.

boyd, danah m. and Nicole B. Ellison. 2007. "Social Network Sites: Definition, History, and Scholarship." *Journal of Computer-Mediated Communication*, 13(1): 210–230.

Braunstein, Peter. 1999. "Disco." *American Heritage Magazine*, 50(7). Available online at http://www.americanheritage.com/content/november-1999.

Broome, Paul J. and Clay Tucker. 1990. *The Other Music City: The Dance Bands and Jazz Musicians of Nashville 1920 to 1970.* Nashville, TN: American Press Print, Co.

Bruno, Anthony. 2011. "Twitter, Music, and Monetization," March 26. *Billboard Magazine.*

Buckland, Fiona. 2002. *Impossible Dance.* Middletown, CT: Wesleyan University Press.

Burgess, Ernest W. 1926. "The Family as a Unit of Interacting Personalities." *The Family*, 7: 3–9.

Burgess, Jean and Joshua Green. 2009. *YouTube: Online Video and Participatory Culture.* Cambridge: Polity Press.

Burkhalter, Janée and Corliss Thornton. 2012. "Advertising to the Beat: An Analysis of Brand Placements in Hip-Hop Music Videos." *Journal of Marketing Communications*, 20(5): 1–17. doi:10.1080/13527266.2012.710643.

Burr, Ramiro. 2000. *Billboard Guide to Tejano and Regional Mexican Music.* New York: Billboard Books.

Cagle, Van M. 1995. *Reconstructing Pop Subculture.* Thousand Oaks, CA: Sage.

Campbell, Michael. 2007. *Rock and Roll: An Introduction.* 2nd Edition. Andover, UK: Cengage Learning.

Canclini, Nestor Garcia. 1995. *Hybrid Cultures: Strategies for Entering and Leaving Modernity.* Minneapolis: University of Minnesota Press.

Cante, Richard C. 2008. *Gay Men and the Forms of Contemporary US Culture*. Farnham, UK: Ashgate.

Carey, James W. 1992. *Communication as Culture*. New York: Routledge.

Chang, J. 2005. *Can't Stop Won't Stop: A History of the Hip-Hop Generation*. New York: Picador

Chapman, Marshall. 2010. *They Came to Nashville*. Nashville, TN: The Country Music Foundation Press; Vanderbilt University Press.

Charmaz, Kathy. 2000. "Grounded Theory: Objectivist and Constructivist Methods." In Norman K. Denzin and Yvonna S. Lincoln (eds.), *Handbook of Qualitative Research*, pp. 509–535. Thousand Oaks, CA: Sage.

Clair, Jeffrey, David Karp, and William Yoels. 1993. *Experiencing the Life Cycle*. Springfield, IL: Charles Thomas.

Clark, Terry Nichols. 2003. "Introduction: Taking Entertainment Seriously." In Terry Nichols Clark (ed.), *The City as an Entertainment Machine*, pp. 1–17. Research in Urban Policy series, vol. 9. Bingley, UK: Emerald Group Publishing Limited.

Clarke, David. 2003. *The Consumption Reader*. New York: Routledge.

Clarke, John, Stuart Hall, Tony Jefferson, and Brian Roberts. 1976. "Subcultures, Cultures, and Class." In Stuart Hall and Tony Jefferson (eds.), *Resistance through Rituals*, pp. 9–74. London: Routledge.

Cohen, Sara. 1995. "Sounding Out the City: Music and the Sensuous Production of Place." *Transactions of the Institute of British Geographers*, 20(4): 434–446.

Cohen, Stanley. 2002 [1972]. *Folk Devils and Moral Panics* (3rd ed.). London: Routledge.

Coleman, James S. 1961. *The Adolescent Society*. Glencoe, IL: The Free Press.

Collin, Matthew. 1997. *Altered State: The Story of Ecstasy Culture and Acid House*. London: Serpent's Tail.

Condry, Ian. 1999. "The Social Production of Difference: Imitation and Authenticity in Japanese Rap Music." In Heide Fehrenbach and Uta G. Poiger (eds.), *Transactions, Transgressions, Transformations: American Culture in Western Europe and Japan*, pp. 166–184. Providence, RI: Berghahn.

Connell, R.W. 1987. *Masculinities*. Berkeley: University of California Press.

Constellation Records. Retrieved from cstrecords.com.

Copes, Heith and J. Patrick Williams. 2007. "Techniques of Affirmation: Deviant Behavior, Moral Commitment, and Subcultural Identity." *Deviant Behavior*, 28(3): 247–272.

Copes, Heith, Andy Hochstetler, and J. Patrick Williams. 2008. "'We Weren't Like No Regular Dope Fiends': Negotiating Hustler and Crackhead Identities." *Social Problems*, 55(2): 254–270.

Cornfield, Daniel B. 2015. *Beyond the Beat: Musicians Building Community in Nashville*. Princeton, NJ: Princeton University Press.

Costello, M. 2016. "The Trump Effect: The Impact of the Presidential Campaign on Our Nation's Schools." Montgomery, AL: Southern Poverty Law Center. Retrieved from https://www.splcenter.org/sites/default/files/splc_the_trump_effect.pdf.

Crawford, George. 2004. *Consuming Sport: Fans, Sport, and Culture*. London: Routledge.

Croom, Adam M. 2015. "Music Practice and Participation for Psychological Well-being: A Review of How Music Influences Positive Emotion, Engagement, Relationships, Meaning and Accomplishment." *Musicae Scientiae*, 19(1): 44–64. doi:10.1177/1029864914561709.

Crosby, David and Carl Gottlieb. 1988. *Long Time Gone*. New York: Doubleday.

Cummings, Sue. 1994. "'Welcome to the Machine:' The Techno Music Revolution Comes to Your Town." *Rolling Stone*, April 7: 15–16.

D'Andrea, Anthony. 2007. *Global Nomads: Techno and New Age as Transnational Countercultures in Ibiza and Goa*. London: Routledge.

Davis, Joanna. 2006. "Growing Up Punk: Negotiating Ageing Identity in a Local Music Scene." *Symbolic Interaction*, 29: 63–69.

DeNora, Tia. 1999. "Music as Technology of the Self." *Poetics*, 27: 31–56.

DeNora, Tia. 2000. *Music in Everyday Life*. Cambridge: Cambridge University Press.

DeNora, Tia. 2003. *After Adorno: Rethinking Music Sociology*. Cambridge: Cambridge University Press.

Denzin, Norman K. 1992. *Symbolic Interactionism and Cultural Studies*. Cambridge: Blackwell.

Denzin, Norman K. 1997. *Interpretive Ethnography*. Thousand Oaks, CA: Sage.

Dewey, John. 1916. *Democracy and Education*. New York: Macmillan.

DiMaggio, Paul (ed.). 2010. *Art in the Lives of Immigrant Communities in the United States*, with introduction by Paul DiMaggio and Patricia Fernández-Kelly. New Brunswick, NJ: Rutgers University Press.

Dixon, Travis, Yuanyuan Zhang, and Kate Conrad. 2009. "Self-Esteem, Misogyny and Afrocentricity: An Examination of the Relationship between Rap Music Consumption and African American Perceptions." *Group Processes & Intergroup Relations*, 12(3): 345–360.

Douglas, Jack D. 1976. *Investigative Social Research: Individual and Team Field Research*. Beverly Hills, CA: Sage.

Douglas, Jack D. 1984. "The Emergence, Security, and Growth of the Sense of Self." In Joseph A. Kotarba and Andrea Fontana (eds.), *The Existential Self and Society*, pp. 69–99. Chicago: University of Chicago Press.

Durkheim, Emile. 1953. *Sociology and Philosophy*. New York: Free Press.

Emdin, Christopher, Edmund Adjapong, and Ian Levy. 2016. "Hip-Hop Based Interventions as Pedagogy/Therapy in STEM: A Model from Urban Science Education." *Journal for Multicultural Education*, 10(3): 307–321.

Erlmann, Veit. 1996. "The Aesthetics of the Global Imagination: Reflections on World Music in the 1990s." *Public Culture*, 8: 467–487.

Featherstone, Mike. 1991. "The Body in Consumer Culture." In Mike Featherstone, Mike Hepworth, and Bryan S. Turner (eds.), *The Body: Social Process and Cultural Theory*, pp. 170–196. Thousand Oaks, CA: Sage.

Ferris, Kerry and Jill Stein. 2011. *The Real World: An Introduction to Sociology*, 3rd Edition. New York: W.W. Norton.

Fine, Gary A. 1979. "Small Groups and Culture Creation: The Idioculture of Little League Baseball Teams." *American Sociological Review*, 44(5): 733–745.

Finn, Gerry P.T. and Richard Giulianotti. 2000. "Prologue: Local Contests and Sporting Difference and International Change." In Gerry P.T. Finn and Richard Giulianotti, *Football Culture: Local Contests, Global Visions*. London: Frank Cass.

Florida, Richard. 2002. "The Economic Geography of Talent." *Annals of the Association of American Geographers*, 92(4): 743–755.

Florida, Richard. 2010. "Jack White and the 'Pro-Real Experience' Economy," July 16. *The Atlantic*. Retrieved September 13, 2012 from www.theatlantic.com/entertainment/archive/2010/07/jack-white-and-the-pro-real-experience-economy/59896/.

Florida, Richard, Charlotta Mellander, and Kevin Stolarick. 2010. "Music Scenes to Music Clusters: The Economic Geography of Music in the US, 1970–2000." *Environment and Planning A*, 42: 785–804.

Flynn, Mark A., Clay M. Craig, Christina N. Anderson, and Kyle J. Holody. 2016. "Objectification in Popular Music Lyrics: An Examination of Gender and Genre Differences." *Sex Roles*, 75(3–4): 164–176. doi:10.1007/s11199-016-0592-3.

Fontein, Dara. 2015. "The Social Media Glossary: 207 Essential Definitions." *Hootsuite*, October 13. Retrieved September 9, 2016 from https://blog.hootsuite.com/the-2015-social-media-glossary-207-essential-definitions/.

Foucault, Michel. 1990. *The History of Sexuality: An Introduction.* New York: Vintage.
Frank, Thomas and Matt Weiland. 1997. *Commodify Your Dissent: Salvos from the Baffler.* New York: Norton.
Freeman, John H. and Pino G. Audia. 2006. "Community Ecology and the Sociology of Organizations." *Annual Review of Sociology*, 32: 145–169.
Friedlander, Paul. 1996. *Rock and Roll.* Boulder, CO: Westview.
Friedman, Andrew. 2016. "Why Chance The Rapper is Not a Truly Independent Artist." Retrieved from http://hip hop.factmag.com/2016/05/20/chance-the-rapper-independent/.
Frith, Simon. 1981. *Sound Effects.* New York: Pantheon.
Frith, Simon. 1991. "Anglo-America and Its Discontents." *Cultural Studies*, 5: 261–273.
Frith, Simon. 2000. "The Discourse of World Music." In Georgina Born and David Hesmondhalgh (eds.), *Western Music and Its Others*, pp. 305–322. Berkeley: University of California Press.
Frith, Simon. 2002. "Music and Everyday Life." *Critical Quarterly*, 44: 35–48. doi:10.10.1111/1467–8705.00399.
Frith, Simon. 2007. *Taking Popular Music Seriously.* Aldershot, UK: Ashgate.
Fuller, Richard and Richard Myers. 1940. "The Natural History of a Social Problem." *American Sociological Review*, 6: 320–329.
Furstenberg, Frank. 1991. *Divided Families.* Cambridge, MA: Harvard University Press.
Gałuszka, Patryk, Katarzyna Korzeniewska, Katarzyna M. Wyrzykowska, and Aleksandra Jagiełło-Skupińska. 2013. *Rynek fonograficzny w Polsce 2011/2012.* Warsaw: IMiT & POLMiC/ZKP.
Gans, Herbert. 1968. *Popular Culture and High Culture.* New York: Basic Books.
Garfinkel, Harold. 1967. *Studies in Ethnomethodology.* Englewood Cliffs, NJ: Prentice-Hall.
Garofolo, Reebee. 2013. *Rockin' Out.* 6th Edition. Upper Saddle River, NJ: Pearson.
Gecas, Viktor. 1981. "Contexts of Socialization." In Morris Rosenberg and Ralph H. Turner (eds.), *Social Psychology: Sociological Perspectives*, pp. 165–199. New York: Basic Books.
Geertz, Clifford. 1996. "Afterword." In Keith H. Basso and Steven Feld (eds.), *Senses of Place*, pp. 259–262. Santa Fe, NM: SAR Press.
George, Nelson. 1998. *Hip Hop America.* New York: Penguin.
Giddens, Anthony. 1991. *Modernity and Self-Identity: Self and Society in the Late Modern Age.* Cambridge: Polity Press.
Giddens, Anthony. 2000. *Runaway World.* New York: Routledge.
Gilroy, Paul. 1993. *The Black Atlantic: Modernity and Double Consciousness.* Cambridge, MA: Harvard University Press.
Główny Urząd Statystyczny (GUS). 2012. "Uczestnictwo ludności w kulturze w 2009 roku." Warsaw. Retrieved September 13, 2016 from http://stat.gov.pl/cps/rde/xbcr/gus/kts_uczestnictwo_ludnosci_w_kulturze_w_2009.pdf.
Goffman, Erving. 1959. *The Presentation of Self in Everyday Life.* Garden City, NY: Doubleday.
Gosine, Kevin and Emmanuel Tabi. 2016. "Disrupting Neoliberalism and Bridging the Multiple Worlds of Marginalized Youth via Hip-Hop Pedagogy: Contemplating Possibilities." *Review of Education, Pedagogy & Cultural Studies*, 38(5): 445–467. doi:10.1080/10714413.2016.1221712.
Gray, John. 2016. *Hip-Hop Studies: An International Bibliography and Resource Guide.* Nyack, NY: African Diaspora Press.
Grazian, David. 2003. *Blue Chicago: The Search for Authenticity in Urban Blues Clubs.* Chicago: University of Chicago Press.
Green, Andy. 2012. "Carly Rae Jepsen: 'I Want to Do Justin Bieber Proud.'" *Rolling Stone*, June 1.

Grossberg, Lawrence. 1992a. *We Gotta Get Out of This Place*. New York: Routledge.

Grossberg, Lawrence. 1992b. "Rock'n'roll in Search of an Audience." In James Lull (ed.), *Popular Music and Communication*, pp. 152–175. Newbury Park, CA: Sage.

Gruenewald, David A. 2003. "Foundations of Place: A Multidisciplinary Framework for Place-Conscious Education." *American Educational Research Journal*, 40(3): 619–654.

Guzman, Betsy. 2001. "Census 2000 Paints Statistical Portrait of the Nation's Hispanic Population." Retrieved April 3, 2008 from www.census.gov/Press-Release/www/2001/cb01-81.html.

Halbert, Shawn and Joseph A. Kotarba. 2007. "Using Popular Music to Interpret the Drug Experience." In Edward Murguia, Melissa Tackett-Gibson and Ann Lessem (eds.), *Real Drugs in a Virtual World: Drug Discourse and Community Online*, pp. 197–213. Lanham, MD: Lexington Press.

Halkitis, Perry N., Joseph J. Palamar, and Preetika Pandey Mukherjee. 2007. "Poly-Club-Drug Use among Gay and Bisexual Men: A Longitudinal Analysis." *Drug and Alcohol Dependence*, 89: 2–3.

Hall, Stuart. 1968. *The Hippies: An American "Moment."* Birmingham: Center for Contemporary Cultural Studies, University of Birmingham.

Hanemaayer, Ariane and Christopher J. Schneider (eds.). 2014. *The Public Sociology Debate: Ethics and Engagement*. Vancouver, BC: University of British Columbia Press.

Hannerz, Ulf. 1987. "The World in Creolization." *Africa*, 57: 546–559.

Harkness, Geoff. 2012. "True School: Situational Authenticity in Chicago's Hip-Hop Underground." *Cultural Sociology*, 6(3): 283–298. doi:10.1177/1749975511401276.

Heath, Travis and Paulo Arroyo. 2014. "'I Gracefully Grab a Pen and Embrace It': Hip-Hop Lyrics as a Means for Re-authoring and Therapeutic Change." *International Journal of Narrative Therapy and Community Work*, 3: 31–38. Retrieved from http://libproxy.txstate.edu/login?url=http://search.ebscohost.com.libproxy.txstate.edu/login.aspx?direct=true&db=sih&AN=99811613&login.asp&site=ehost-live.

Hebdige, Dick. 1979. *Subculture: The Meaning of Style*. New York: Methuen.

Hemphill, Paul. 1970. *The Nashville Sound: Bright Lights and Country Music*. New York: Simon and Schuster.

Herd, Denise. 2009. "Changing Images of Violence in Rap Music Lyrics: 1979–1997." *Journal of Public Health Policy*, 30(4): 395–406. doi:10.1057/jphp.2009.36.

Heritage, John. 1984. *Garfinkel and Ethnomethodology*. Cambridge: Polity Press.

Herman, Andrew, John Sloop, and Thomas Swiss. 1997. *Mapping the Beat: Popular Music and Contemporary Theory*. New York: Blackwell.

Herstand, Ari. 2014. "There Will Never Be Another Myspace." *Digital Music News*, March 17. Retrieved September 9, 2016 from www.digitalmusicnews.com/2014/03/17/there-will-never-be-another-myspace/.

Hesmondhalgh, David and Keith Negus. 2002. *Popular Music Studies*. London: Arnold.

Hill, Marc Lamont. 2009. *Beats, Rhymes, and Classroom Life: Hip-hop Pedagogy and the Politics of Identity*. New York: Teachers College Press.

Hill, Trent. 1992. "The Enemy Within: Censorship in Rock Music in the 1950s." In Anthony DeCurtis (ed.), *Present Tense: Rock & Roll and Culture*, pp. 39–71. Durham, NC: Duke University Press.

Hitzler, Ronald. "Pill Kick: The Pursuit of 'Ecstasy' at Techno-Events." *Journal of Drug Issues*, 32: 459–465.

Hochschild, Arlie. 1983. *The Managed Heart*. Berkeley: University of California Press.

Hollander, Justin and Jennifer Quinn. 2016. "More than Noise: Employing Hip-Hop Music to Inform Community Development Practice." *Community Development*, 47(5): 652–669. doi:10.1080/15575330.2016.1210662.

Holody, Kyle J., Christina Anderson, Clay Craig, and Mark Flynn. 2016. "'Drunk in Love': The Portrayal of Risk Behavior in Music Lyrics." *Journal of Health Communication*, 21(10): 1098–1106. doi:10.1080/10810730.2016.1222032.

Holstein, James and Jaber Gubrium. 2003. "The Life Course." In Larry Reynolds and Nancy Herman-Kinney (eds.), *Handbook of Symbolic Interactionism*, pp. 835–856. Walnut Creek, CA: AltaMira Press.

Hooton, Christopher. 2015. "Hip-Hop is the Most Listened To Genre in the World, According to Spotify Analysis of 20 Billion Tracks." *The Independent*. Retrieved February 16, 2016 from http://hip hop.independent.co.uk/arts-entertainment/music/news/hip-hop-is-the-most-listened-to-genre-in-the-world-according-to-spotify-analysis-of-20-billion-10388091.html.

Horsfall, Sara, Jan-Martijn Meij, and Meghan Probstfield. 2013. *Music Sociology*. Boulder, CO: Paradigm Publishers.

Illouz, Eva. 1997. *Consuming the Romantic Utopia*. Berkeley: University of California Press.

International Federation of the Phonographic Industry (IFPI). 2016a. "An Explosion in Global Music Consumption Supported by Multiple Forms." *Facts and Stats*. Retrieved September 17, 2016 from www.ifpi.org/facts-and-stats.php.

International Federation of the Phonographic Industry (IFPI). 2016b. "IFPI Global Music Report." *News*. Retrieved September 17, 2016 from www.ifpi.org/news/IFPI-GLOBAL-MUSIC-REPORT-2016.

Irby, Decoteau J., and Emery Petchauer. 2012. "Hustlin' Consciousness: Critical Education Using Hip-Hop Modes of Distribution." In Brad J. Porfilio, and Michael J. Viola (eds.), *Hip Hop(e): The Cultural Practice and Critical Pedagogy of International Hip-Hop*, pp. 302–322. New York: Peter Lang.

Irwin, John. 1977. *Scenes*. Beverly Hills, CA: Sage.

Iyer, Deepa. 2015. *We Too Sing America: South Asian, Arab, Muslim, and Sikh Immigrants Shape Our Multiracial Future*. New York: The New Press.

Iyer, Deepa and Jayesh M. Rathod. 2011. "9/11 and the Transformation of U.S. Immigration Law and Policy." *Human Rights*, 38(1): 12–14.

Jacobsen, Michael Hviid and Soren Kristiansen. 2015. *The Social Thought of Erving Goffman*. London: Sage.

Jakubowski, Kelly, Sebastian Finkel, Lauren Stewart, and Daniel Müllensiefen. 2016. "Dissecting an Earworm: Melodic Features and Song Popularity Predict Involuntary Musical Imagery." *Psychology of Aesthetics, Creativity, and the Arts*. http://dx.doi.org/10.1037/aca0000090.

Jameson, Frederic. 1991. *Postmodernism: Or, the Cultural Logic of Late Capitalism*. Durham, NC: Duke University Press.

Janik, Leszek. 1983. "Rock jako przedmiot zainteresowań młodziey." *Kultura i Społeczeństwo*, 3: 127–139.

@JayZClassicBars, 2011. Retrieved September 12, 2016 from twitter.com/jayzclassicbars.

Jenkins, Henry. 2006. *Convergence Culture: Where Old and New Media Collide*. New York: New York University Press.

Jones, LeRoi. 1963. *Blues People*. New York: Morrow.

Kamińska, Barbara. 1999. "Miejsce muzyki w życiu młodzieży." In M. Manturzewska (ed.), *Psychologiczne podstawy kształcenia muzycznego*. Warsaw: Akademia Muzyczna im. Fryderyka Chopina.

Kaplan, E. Ann. 1987. *Rocking Around the Clock*. New York: Routledge.

Kerouac, Jack. 1957. *On The Road*. New York: Viking Press.

Kessler, Suzanne and Wendy McKenna. 1978. *Gender: An Ethnomethodological Approach*. New York: Wiley.

Kingsbury, Paul. 1998. *The Encyclopedia of Country Music*. Oxford: Oxford University Press.

Klineberg, Stephen L. 2009. *Houston's Economic and Demographic Transformations: Findings from the Expanded 2009 Survey of Houston's Ethnic Communities.* Houston, TX: Rice University Publication.

Klitzman, Robert. 2006. "From 'Male Bonding Rituals' to 'Suicide Tuesday': A Qualitative Study of Issues Faced by Gay Male Ecstasy (MDMA) Users." *Journal of Homosexuality*, 51(3): 7–32.

Klönne, Arno. 1995. *Youth in the Third Reich: Hitler-Youth and their Enemies* (in German). Munich: Piper.

Kotarba, Joseph A. 1984. "A Synthesis: The Existential Self in Society." In Joseph A. Kotarba and Andrea Fontana (eds.), *The Existential Self in Society*, pp. 222–231. Chicago: University of Chicago Press.

Kotarba, Joseph A. 1987. "Adolescents and Rock'n'Roll." *Youth and Society*, 18: 323–325.

Kotarba, Joseph A. 1991. "Postmodernism, Ethnography and Culture." *Studies in Symbolic Interaction*, 12: 45–52.

Kotarba, Joseph A. 1992. "Conceptualizing Rock Music as a Feature of Children's Culture." Presented at the annual meeting of the Society for the Study of Symbolic Interaction, Pittsburgh, Pennsylvania (August).

Kotarba, Joseph A. 1993a. "The Rave." A report submitted to the Texas Commission on Alcohol and Drug Abuse, Austin.

Kotarba, Joseph A. 1993b. "The Rave Scene in Houston, Texas: An Ethnographic Analysis." Presented at the annual meeting of the American Sociological Association, Miami, Florida (August).

Kotarba, Joseph A. 1994a. "The Postmodernization of Rock and Roll Music: The Case of Metallica." In Jonathon S. Epstein (ed.), *Adolescents and Their Music*, pp. 141–164. New York: Garland.

Kotarba, Joseph A. 1994b. "The Positive Functions of Rock'n'Roll Music." In Joel Best (ed.), *Troubling Children*, pp. 155–170. New York: Aldine.

Kotarba, Joseph A. 1997. "Reading the Male Experience of Rock Music: Four Songs About Women." *Cultural Studies*, 2: 265–277.

Kotarba, Joseph A. 1998. "The Commodification and Decommodification of Rock Music: Rock en Español and Rock Music in Poland." Paper presented at the annual meeting of the SSSI Couch-Stone Symposium, February 21, Houston.

Kotarba, Joseph A. 2002a. "Rock'n'Roll Music as a Timepiece." *Symbolic Interaction*, 25: 397–404.

Kotarba, Joseph A. 2002b. "Baby Boomer Rock'n'Roll Fans and the Becoming of Self." In Joseph A. Kotarba and John M. Johnson (eds.), *Postmodern Existential Sociology*, pp. 103–126. Walnut Creek, CA: AltaMira Press.

Kotarba, Joseph A. 2002c. "Popular Music and Teenagers in Post-Communist Poland." *Studies in Symbolic Interaction*, 25: 231–244.

Kotarba, Joseph A. 2006. "Introduction: Conceptualizing Popular Music." *Symbolic Interaction*, 29: 12–3.

Kotarba, Joseph A. 2007. "Music as a Feature of the Online Discussion of Illegal Drugs." In Edward Murguia, Melissa Tackett-Gibson and Ann Lessem (eds.), *Real Drugs in a Virtual World: Drug Discourse and Community Online*, pp. 161–179. Lanham, MD: Lexington Press.

Kotarba, Joseph A. 2009. "'I'm just a Rock'n'Roll Fan:' Popular Music as a Meaning Resource for Aging." *Civitas*, 9 (1): 118–132.

Kotarba, Joseph A. 2013. *Baby Boomer Rock'n'Roll Fans: The Music Never Ends.* Lanham, MD: Roman & Littlefield.

Kotarba, Joseph A. 2018. "The Theoretical Intersection of Science and Music." *Qualitative Sociological Review*, 14, 1.

Kotarba, Joseph A. and John M. Johnson (eds.). 2002. *Postmodern Existential Sociology*. Walnut Hills, CA: Alta Mira.

Kotarba, Joseph A. and Nicolas J. Lalone. 2014. "The *Scene*: A Conceptual Template for an Interactionist Approach to Contemporary Music." *Studies in Symbolic Interaction*, 42: 53–68.

Kotarba, Joseph A. and Phillip Vannini (eds.). 2006. Special issue of *Symbolic Interaction*, 26 (1, Winter) on "Popular Music and Everyday Life."

Kotarba, Joseph A., Jennifer L. Fackler, and Kathryn M. Nowotny. 2009. "An Ethnography of Emerging Latino Music Scenes." *Symbolic Interaction*, 32(4): 310–333.

Krause, Holly. 2003. *Site and Sound: Understanding Independent Music Scenes*. New York: Lang.

Kreps, Daniel. 2016. "Dylan's Silence 'Impolite and Arrogant.'" *Rolling Stone*, October 22. Retrieved October 24, 2016 from www.rollingstone.com/music/news/nobel-prize-member-calls-bob-dylans-silence-arrogant-w446283.

Kruse, A. 2016. "'They Wasn't Makin' My Kinda Music': A Hip-Hop Musician's Perspective on School, Schooling, and School Music." *Music Education Research*, 18(3): 240–253. doi:10.1080/14613808.2015.1060954.

Kulp, Patrick. 2016. "Kaiser is Using Kendrick Lamar Lyrics to Spark a Conversation About Depression." *MashableUK*. Retrieved from http://mashable.com/2016/10/15/kaiser-kendrick-depression-ad/#.yrIQA6.KkqG.

Ladson-Billings, Gloria. 1995. "Toward a Theory of Culturally Relevant Pedagogy." *American Educational Research Journal*, 32(3): 465–491.

Lamont, Tom. 2013. "Napster: The Day the Music was Set Free." *The Guardian*, February 24. Retrieved September 9, 2016 from www.theguardian.com/music/2013/feb/24/napster-music-free-file-sharing.

Laughey, Dan. 2006. *Music and Youth Culture*. Edinburgh: Edinburgh University Press.

Leary, Timothy. 1983. *Flashbacks: A Personal and Cultural History of an Era*. New York: Putnam.

Lenning, Emily. 2012. "Discovering the Theorist in Tupac: How to Engage Your Students with Popular Music." *International Journal of Teaching & Learning in Higher Education*, 24(2): 257–263. Retrieved from http://libproxy.txstate.edu/login?url=http://search.ebscohost.com.libproxy.txstate.edu/login.aspx?direct=true&db=eue&AN=89252209&login.asp&site=ehost-live.

Levine, David. 1991. "Good Business, Bad Messages." *American Health*, May 10: 16.

Levy, Ian and Brian TaeHyuk Keum. 2014. "Hip-Hop Emotional Exploration in Men." *Journal of Poetry Therapy*, 27(4): 217–223. doi:10.1080/08893675.2014.949528.

Lewis, George. 1983. "The Meaning's In the Music and the Music's In Me: Popular Music As Symbolic Communication." *Theory, Culture and Society*, 1 (January): 133–141.

Light, Alan. 1992. "About a Salary or Reality: Rap's Recurrent Conflict." In Anthony DeCurtis (ed.), *Present Tense: Rock & Roll and Culture*, pp. 219–234. Durham, NC: Duke University Press.

Lin, Nan. 2001. *Social Capital: A Theory of Social Structure and Action*. Cambridge: Cambridge University Press.

Lloyd, Richard. 2006. *Neo-Bohemia: Art and Commerce in the Postindustrial City*. New York: Routledge.

Lloyd, Richard. 2011. "East Nashville Skyline." *Ethnography*, 12(1): 114–145.

Lloyd, Richard and Terry Nichols Clark. 2001. "The City as an Entertainment Machine." In Kevin Fox Gotham (ed.), *Critical Perspectives on Urban Redevelopment*, pp. 357–378. Research in Urban Sociology, vol. 6. Bingley, UK: Emerald Group Publishing Limited.

Logan, John R. and Harvey L. Molotch. 1987. *Urban Fortunes: The Political Economy of Place*. Berkeley: University of California Press.

Love, Bettina L. 2015. "What is Hip-Hop-Based Education Doing in Nice Fields Such as Early Childhood and Elementary Education?" *Urban Education*, 50(1): 106–131. doi:10.1177/0042085914563182.

Love, Bettina L. 2016. "Complex Personhood of Hip Hop & the Sensibilities of the Culture that Fosters Knowledge of Self & Self-Determination." *Equity & Excellence in Education*, 49(4): 414–427. doi:10.1080/10665684.2016.1227223.

Lowney, Kathleen S. 1995. "Teenage Satanism as Oppositional Youth Subculture." *Journal of Contemporary Ethnography*, 23 (4, January): 453–484.

Luckerson, Victor. 2015. "Here's How Facebook's News Feed Actually Works." *Time*. Retrieved September 17, 2016 from: http://time.com/3950525/facebook-news-feed-algorithm/.

Lull, James. 1992. *Popular Music and Communication*. Newbury Park, CA: Sage.

Lyman, Stanford and Marvin Scott. 1970. *A Sociology of the Absurd.* New York: Goodyear.

MacInnes, Paul. 2016. "A Tribe Called Quest: We Got It from Here . . . Thank You 4 Your Service Review—A Passing of the Torch." *The Guardian*. Retrieved from https://hiphop.theguardian.com/music/2016/nov/17/a-tribe-called-quest-we-got-it-from-here-thank-you-4-your-service-review-a-passing-of-the-torch.

Macionis, John J. 2003. *Society: The Basics*. New York: Pearson.

Magid, Larry and Anne Collier. 2007. *MySpace Unraveled: What It Is and How to Use It Safely*. Berkeley, CA: Peachpit Press.

Marcus, Greil. 2010. *When That Rough God Goes Riding: Listening to Van Morrison*. San Francisco: PublicAffairs.

Market, John. 2001. "Sing a Song of Drug Abuse: Four Decades of Drug Lyrics in Popular Music—From the Sixties Through the Nineties." *Sociological Inquiry*, 71: 194–220.

Martin, Linda and Kerry Segrave. 1993. *Anti-Rock: The Opposition to Rock'n'Roll.* Hamden, CT: Da Capo.

Marx, Karl. 1964. *Economic and Philosophic Manuscripts of 1844*. New York: International Publishers.

Matza, David and Gresham Sykes. 1964. *Delinquency and Drift.* New York: Wiley.

Maxwell, Morgan L., Jasmine A. Abrams, and Faye Z. Belgrave. 2016. Redbones and Earth Mothers: The Influence of Rap Music on African American Girls' Perceptions of Skin Color. *Psychology of Music*, 44(6): 1488–1499. doi:10.1177/0305735616643175.

McLeod, Kembrew. 1999. "Authenticity Within Hip-Hop and Other Cultures Threatened with Assimilation." *Journal of Communication*, 49(4): 134–150.

McLuhan, Marshall. 1962. *The Gutenberg Galaxy: The Making of Typographic Man*. Toronto: University of Toronto Press.

McLuhan, Marshall. 1964. *Understanding Media: The Extensions of Man*. New York: McGraw Hill.

McRobbie, Angela. 1978. "Working Class Girls and the Culture of Femininity." In CCCS Women's Study Group (eds.), *Women Take Issue*, pp. 34–54. London: Women's Study Group.

Mead, George Herbert. 1934. *Mind, Self, and Society.* Chicago: University of Chicago Press.

Menger, Pierre. 1999. "Artistic Labor Markets and Careers." *Annual Review of Sociology*, 25: 541–574.

Merleau-Ponty, Maurice. 1962. *Phenomenology of Perception*. London: Routledge & Kegan Paul.

Middleton, Richard. 1990. *Studying Popular Music.* Philadelphia: Open University Press.

Mills, C. Wright. 1941. "Situated Actions and Vocabularies of Motive." *American Sociological Review*, 5: 904–913.

Mills, C. Wright. 1959. *The Sociological Imagination.* New York: Oxford University Press.

Minor Threat. 1981. "Straight Edge." *Minor Threat* [EP]. Washington, DC: Dischord Records.

Mogelonsky, Marcia. 1996. "The Rocky Road to Adulthood." *American Demographics*, 18 (May): 26–29.

Molotch, Harvey, William Freudenburg, and Krista E. Paulsen. 2000. "History Repeats Itself, But How? City Character, Urban Tradition, and the Accomplishment of Place." *American Sociological Review*, 65(6): 791–823.
Moore, Ryan. 2005. "Alternative to What? Subcultural Capital and the Commercialization of a Music Scene." *Deviant Behavior*, 26: 229–252.
Morgan, Marcyliena. 2016. "'The World is Yours': The Globalization of Hip-Hop Language." *Social Identities: Journal for the Study of Race, Nation and Culture*, 22(2): 133–149. doi:10.1080/13504630.2015.1121569.
Muggleton, David. 2002. *Inside Subculture: The Postmodern Meaning of Style*. London: Berg.
Muhammad, Kareem R. 2015. "Everyday People: Public Identities in Contemporary Hip-Hop Culture." *Social Identities: Journal for the Study of Race, Nation and Culture*, 21(5): 425–443. doi:10.1080/13504630.2015.1093467.
Murguia, Edward, Melissa Tackett-Gibson, and Ann Lessem (eds.). 2007. *Real Drugs in a Virtual World: Drug Discourse and Community Online*. Lanham, MD: Lexington Press.
Nash, Jeffrey E. and Dina C. Nash. 2016. "Feminizing a Musical Form: Women's Participation as Barbershop Singers." In Christopher J. Schneider and Joseph A. Kotarba (eds.), *Symbolic Interactionist Takes on Music*, pp. 45–59. Bingley, UK: Emerald Group Publishing Limited.
Natella, Arthur A. 2008. *Latin American Popular Culture*. Jefferson, NC: McFarland.
Nidel, Richard. 2004. *World Music: The Basics*. London: Routledge.
Nissenbaum, Stephen. 1997. *The Battle for Christmas*. New York: Vintage.
Nowotny, Kathryn M., Jennifer L. Fackler, Gianncarlo Muschi, Carol Vargas, Lindsey Wilson, and Joseph A. Kotarba. 2010. "Established Latino Music Scenes: Sense of Place and the Challenge of Authenticity." *Studies in Symbolic Interaction*, 35: 29–50.
O'Neill, Susan A. 1997. "Gender and Music." In David J. Hargreaves and Adrian C. North (eds.), *The Social Psychology of Music*. Oxford and New York: Oxford University Press.
Orum, Anthony M. 2002. *Power, Money & the People: The Making of Modern Austin*. Eugene, OR: Wipf and Stock Publishers.
Ośrodek Badania Opinii Publicznej (OBOP). 2002. "Preferencje muzyczne Polaków." Warsaw. Retrieved September 13, 2016 from www.tnsglobal.pl/archiwumraportow/2002/01/01/preferencje-muzyczne-polakow/#more-1233.
Ośrodek Badania Opinii Publicznej i Studiów Programowych (OBOPSP). 1975. "Zainteresowania muzyczne Polaków." Warsaw. Retrieved September 13, 2016 from www.tnsglobal.pl/archiwumraportow/1975/10/30/zainteresowania-muzyczne-polakow/#more-3915.
Pacini-Hernandez, Deborah. 1993. "Spanish Caribbean Perspectives on World Beat." *The World of Music* (Berlin), 35: 48–69.
Pareles, Jon. 1988. "Heavy Metal, Weighty Words." *The New York Times Magazine*, July 10: 26–27.
Parkin, Frank. 1979. *Marxism and Class Theory: A Bourgeois Critique*. New York: Columbia University Press.
Parsons, Talcott. 1949. *Essays in Sociological Theory, Pure and Applied*. Glencoe, IL: The Free Press.
Patch, Justin. 2013. "Total War, Total Anti-War: Music, Holism and Anti-War Protest." *Ethnomusicology Review*. 18 (online blog).
Paterson, Mark. 2005. *Consumption and Everyday Life*. New York: Routledge.
Pekacz, Joseph. 1992. "On Some Dilemmas of Polish Post-Communist Rock Music in Eastern Europe." *Popular Music*, 11(2): 205–208.
Peoples, Glen. 2013. "Want a Job in the Music Business? These are the Cities You Should Live In." *Billboard*, August 13, 2013.
Peoples, Glenn. 2016. "Recording Industry 2015: More Music Consumption and Less Money." *Billboard*. Retrieved September 17, 2016 from www.billboard.com/articles/

business/6835350/recorded-industry-2015-consumption-grew-revenues-digital-deflation.

Peterson, Richard A. 1992. "Class Unconsciousness in Country Music." In Melton A. McLaurin and Richard A. Peterson (eds.), *You Wrote My Life: Lyrical Themes in Country Music*, pp. 35–62. Yverdon, Switzerland: Gordon and Breach Science Publishers.

Peterson, Richard A. 1997. *Creating Country Music: Fabricating Authenticity*. Chicago: University of Chicago Press.

Peterson, Richard A. and Andy Bennett. 2004. *Music Scenes*. Nashville, TN: Vanderbilt University Press.

Peterson, Richard A. and David G. Berger. 1996. "Measuring Industry Concentration, Diversity, and Innovation in Popular Music." *American Sociological Review*, 61: 175–178.

Pilkington, Hilary. 1994. *Russia's Youth and Its Culture: A Nation's Constructors and Constructed*. London: Routledge.

Podoshen, Jeffrey, S., Susan A. Andrzejewski, and James M. Hunt. 2014. "Materialism, Conspicuous Consumption, and American Hip-Hop Subculture." *Journal of International Consumer Marketing*, 26(4): 271–283. doi:10.1080/08961530.2014.900469.

Porfilio, Brad, Debangshu Roychoudhury and Lauren M. Gardner (eds.). 2014. *See You at the Crossroads: Hip Hop Scholarship at the Intersections: Dialectical Harmony, Ethics, Aesthetics, and Panoply of Voices*. Boston, MA: Sense Publishers.

Primack, Brian A., Erin Nuzzo, Kristen R. Rice, and James D. Sargent. 2012. "Alcohol Brand Appearances in US Popular Music." *Addiction*, 107(3): 557–566.

Psathas, George. 1973. *Phenomenological Sociology: Issues and Applications*. New York: Wiley.

Record Store Day. 2016. "About Us." Retrieved September 9, 2016 from www.recordstoreday.com/CustomPage/614.

Recording Industry Association of American (RIAA). 2016. "Vinyl (Still) Rocks \m/," August 10. Retrieved September 9, 2016 from www.riaa.com/vinyl-still-rocks/.

Riesman, David. 1950. *The Lonely Crowd*. New Haven, CT: Yale University Press.

Ritzer, George. 1993. *The McDonaldization of Society*. New York: Pine Forge Press.

Ritzer, George and Jeff Stepnisky. 2014. *Sociological Theory*. 9th Edition. New York: McGraw-Hill.

Robert Wood Johnson Foundation [RWJF]. 2011. "How Does Where We Live, Work, Learn and Play Affect Our Health?" Retrieved from http://hip hop.rwjf.org/content/dam/farm/reports/issue briefs/2011/rwjf71339.

Robertson, Roland. 1992. *Globalization: Social Theory and Global Culture*. London: Sage.

Rolling Stone. 2010. "500 Greatest Albums of All Time." Retrieved July 1, 2010 from www.rollingstone.com.

Rolling Stone. 2016. "Louder, Faster, Angrier." September, retrieved on September 8, 2016.

Romanowski, William D. 2001. *Eyes Wide Open: Looking for God in Popular Culture*. Grand Rapids, MI: Brazos Press.

Rose, Tricia. 1994. *Black Noise: Rap Music and Black Culture in Contemporary America*. Middletown, CT: Wesleyan University Press.

Rosenbaum, Jill L. and Lorraine Prinsky. 1991. "The Presumption of Influence: Recent Responses to Popular Music Subcultures." *Crime and Delinquency*, 37(4): 528–535.

Ross, David M. 2009. "Country's Shrinking Middle Class." *Music Row*, July 13. Retrieved on February 2, 2017 from www.musicrow.com/2009/07/countrys-shrinking-middle-class/.

Ross, Herbert (Director). 1984. *Footloose*. Paramount Pictures.

Roti, Jessi. 2016. "Chance the Rapper Performs Concert, Leads March to Polls." *Chicago Tribune*. Retrieved from http://hip hop.chicagotribune.com/entertainment/ct-chance-the-rapper-concert-vote-rally-grant-park-ent-1107-story.html.

Rowe, Laurel and Gray Cavendar. 1991. "Caldrons Bubble, Satan's Trouble, but Witches Are Okay: Media Constructions of Satanism and Witchcraft." In James T. Richardson, Joel Best, and David G. Bromley (eds.), *The Satanism Scare*, pp. 263–275. New York: Aldine de Gruyter.

Roychoudhury, Debangshu and Lauren M. Gardner. 2012. "Taking Back Our Minds: Hip-Hop Psychology's (HHP) Call for a Renaissance, Action, and Liberatory Use of Psychology in Education." In Brad J. Porfilio and Michael J. Viola (eds.), *Hip Hop(e): The Cultural Practice and Critical Pedagogy of International Hip-Hop*, pp. 234–248. New York: Peter Lang.

Rumble, John W. 1978. "The Emergence of Nashville as a Recording Center: Logbooks from the Castle Studio, 1952–1953." *Journal of Country Music*, 8(3): 22–41.

Sandstrom, Kent, Kathryn Lively, Dan Martin, and Gary Alan Fine. 2013. *Symbols, Selves, and Social Reality*. 4th Edition. London: Oxford University Press.

San Roman, Gabriel. 2013. "Top Five Anti-War Songs Ten Years After Iraq." *The Village Voice*, March 20th (online blog).

Sartre, Jean Paul. 1945. *The Age of Reason*. Paris: Gallimard.

Schneider, Christopher J. 2007. "Music and Media." In George Ritzer (ed.), *Blackwell Encyclopedia of Sociology*, vol. 6, pp. 3129–3134. Malden, MA: Blackwell Publishing.

Schneider, Christopher J. 2009. "The Music Ringtone as an Identity Management Device." *Studies in Symbolic Interaction*, 33: 35–45.

Schneider, Christopher J. 2011. "Using the MP3 to Learn Selections of Marx's Capital." American Sociological Association *TRAILS*. Retrieved September 9, 2016 from http://trails.asanet.org/Pages/Resource.aspx?ResourceID=12502.

Schneider, Christopher J. 2016a. *Policing and Social Media: Social Control in an Era of New Media*. Lanham, MD: Lexington Books | Rowman & Littlefield.

Schneider, Christopher J. 2016b. "Music Videos on YouTube: Exploring Participatory Culture on Social Media." *Studies in Symbolic Interaction*, 47: 97–117.

Schneider, Christopher J. and Joseph A. Kotarba (eds.). 2016. *Symbolic Interactionist Takes on Music*. Bingley, UK: Emerald Group Publishing Limited.

Schumacher-Rasmussen, Eric. 2001. "Napster Dividing Artists from Prince 2 Dave Matthews." *MTV News*, March 2. Retrieved September 9, 2016 from www.mtv.com/news/1441222/napster-dividing-artists-from-prince-2-dave-matthews/.

Scott, Marvin B. and Stanford Lyman. 1975. "Accounts." In Dennis Brissett and Charles Edgley (eds.), *Life as Theater: A Dramaturgical Sourcebook*, pp. 171–191. Chicago: Aldine.

Seay, Davin and Mary Neely. 1986. *Stairway to Heaven: The Spiritual Roots of Rock'n'Roll*. New York: Ballantine.

Setaro, Shawn. 2016. "Kid Cudi Checks Into Rehab for Depression, Shares Message for Fans." Retrieved from http://hip hop.complex.com/music/2016/10/kid-cudi-rehab-depression.

Shank, Barry. 1994. *Dissonant Identities: The Rock'n'Roll Scene in Austin, Texas*. Middletown, CT: Wesleyan University Press.

Shuker, Roy. 2001. *Popular Music: The Key Concepts*. New York: Routledge.

Silver, Daniel, Terry Nichols Clark, and Clemente Jesus Navarro Yanez. 2010. "Scenes: Social Context in an Age of Contingency." *Social Forces*, 88(5): 2293–2324.

Simon, Richard B. 2000. "Metallica's Anti-Napster Crusade Inspires Backlash." *MTV News*, May 31. Retrieved September 9, 2016 from www.mtv.com/news/971500/metallicas-anti-napster-crusade-inspires-backlash/.

Sinofsky, Bruce. 1996. *Paradise Lost: The Child Murders at Robin Hood Hills*. New York: New Video Group.

Sisario, Ben. 2014. "Popular and Free, SoundCloud Is Now Ready For Ads." *The New York Times*, August 21, B, p. 3.

Sköld, David and Alf Rehn. 2007. "Makin' It, by Keeping It Real: Street Talk, Rap Music, and the Forgotten Entrepreneurship from 'the 'Hood'." *Group & Organization Management*, 32(1): 50–78. Retrieved from: http://journals.sagepub.com/doi/pdf/10.1177/1059601106294487.

Small, Adam and Peter Stuart. 1982. *Another State of Mind* [film]. Los Angeles: Better Youth Organization.

Smith, Vicki. 1997. "New Forms of Work Organization." *Annual Review of Sociology*, 23: 315–339.

Sokolowski, Robert. 2000. *Introduction to Phenomenology*. Cambridge: Cambridge University Press.

Stahl, Matthew Wheelock. 2004. "A Moment Like This: American Idol and Narratives of Meritocracy." In Christopher J. Washburne and Maiken Derno (eds.), *Bad Music: The Music We Love to Hate*, pp. 212–233. New York: Routledge.

Stewart, Daniel. 2005. "Social Status in an Open-Source Community." *American Sociological Review*, 70(5): 823–842.

Stimeling, Travis D. 2011. *Cosmic Cowboys and New Hicks: The Countercultural Sounds of Austin's Progressive Country Music Scene*. Oxford and New York: Oxford University Press.

Stuessy, Joe and Lipscomb, Scott. 1998. *Rock and Roll: Its History and Stylistic Development*. 3rd Edition. Upper Saddle River, NJ: Prentice-Hall.

Sweet, E. 2010. "'If Your Shoes are Raggedy You Get Talked About': Symbolic and Material Dimensions of Adolescent Social Status and Health." *Social Science & Medicine*, 70(12): 2029–2035. doi:10.1016/j.socscimed.2010.02.032.

Swidler, Ann. 1986. "Culture in Action: Symbols and Strategies." *American Sociological Review*, 51(2): 273–286.

Szemere, Anna. 2001. *Up From the Underground: The Culture of Rock Music in Postsocialist Hungary*. University Park, PA: Pennsylvania State University Press.

Szlendak, Tomasz. 1998. *Technomania. Cyberplemię w zwierciadle socjologii*. Toruń: Wydawnictwo Graffiti BC.

Sztompka, Piotr. 2004. *Socjologia. Analiza społeczeństwa*. Kraków: Wydawnictwo Znak.

Talbot, John Michael. 1999. *The Music of Creation*. Collegeville, MN: Liturgical Press.

Tepper, Steven. 2011. *Not Here, Not Now, Not That!: Protest Over Art and Culture in America*. Chicago: University of Chicago Press.

Thompson, Jason D. 2015. "Towards Cultural Responsiveness in Music Instruction with Black Detained Youth: An Analytic Autoethnography." *Music Education Research*, 17(4): 421–436. doi:10.1080/14613808.2014.930117.

Thompson, P.A. 2012. "An Empirical Study into the Learning Practices and Enculturation of DJs, Turntablists, Hip Hop, and Dance Music Producers." *Journal of Music, Technology & Education*, 5(1): 43–58.

TNS Ośrodek Badania Opinii Publicznej. 2008. "Muzyczny portret Polaków." Warsaw. Retrieved September 13, 2016 from http://wyrzykowska.net/wp-content/uploads/2014/10/Muzyczny-portret-Polak%C3%B3w.doc.

Travis, Raphael Jr. 2016. *The Healing Power of Hip Hop*. Santa Barbara, CA: ABC-CLIO.

Travis, Raphael Jr. and Scott W. Bowman. 2011. "Negotiating Risk and Promoting Empowerment through Rap Music: Development of a Measure to Capture Risk and Empowerment Pathways to Change." *Journal of Human Behavior in the Social Environment*, 21(6): 654–678.

Travis, Raphael Jr. and Scott W. Bowman. 2012. "Ethnic Identity, Self-Esteem and Variability in Perceptions of Rap Music's Empowering and Risky Influences." *Journal of Youth Studies*, 15(4): 455–478.

Travis, Raphael Jr. and Scott W. Bowman. 2015. "Validation of the Individual and Community Empowerment Inventory: A Measure of Rap Music Engagement among

First-Year College Students." *Journal of Human Behavior in the Social Environment*, 25(2): 90–108. doi:10.1080/10911359.2014.974433.
Travis, Raphael Jr. and Anne Deepak. 2011. "Empowerment in Context: Lessons from Hip-Hop Culture for Social Work Practice." *Journal of Ethnic & Cultural Diversity in Social Work*, 20(3): 203–222.
Travis, Raphael Jr. and Alexis Maston. 2014. "Hip-Hop and Pedagogy, More Than Meets the Eye: What Do We Expect, What Will We Measure?" In Brad Porfilio, Debangshu Roychoudhury and Lauren M. Gardner (eds.), *See You at the Crossroads: Hip Hop Scholarship at the Intersections*, pp. 3–28. Boston, MA: Sense Publishers. doi:10.1007/978-94-6209-674-5_1.
Travis, Raphael, Scott W. Bowman, Joshua Childs, and Renee Villanueva. 2016. "Musical Interactions: Girls Who Like and Use Rap Music for Empowerment." In Christopher J. Schneider and Joseph A. Kotarba (eds.), *Symbolic Interactionist Takes on Music*, pp. 119–149. Bingley, UK: Emerald Group Publishing Limited. doi:10.1108/S0163-239620160000047017.
Turner, Victor. 1975. *Dramas, Fields, and Metaphors.* New York: Cornell University Press.
Ulman, Richard and Harry Paul. 2006. *The Self Psychology of Addiction and Its Treatment.* New York: Brunner-Routledge.
Van Buskirk, Eliot. 2009. "SoundCloud Threatens MySpace as Music Destination for Twitter Era." *Wired*, July 6. Retrieved September 17, 2016 from www.wired.com/2009/07/soundcloud-threatens-myspace-as-music-destination-for-twitter-era/.
Vannini, Phillip. 2008. "Social Semiotics." In Michael H. Jacobsen (ed.), *Sociology of the Unnoticed: An Introduction to the Sociologies of Everyday Life.* London: Palgrave Macmillan.
Veblen, Thorsten. 2006. *Conspicuous Consumption.* New York: Penguin.
Vernallis, Carol. 2013. *Unruly Media: YouTube, Music Video, and the New Digital Cinema.* New York: Oxford University Press.
Vom Lehn, Dirk. 2014. *Harold Garfinkel: The Creation and Development of Ethnomethodology.* Walnut Creek, CA: Left Coast Press.
Wallace, Claire and Raimund Alt. 2001. "Youth Cultures under Authoritarian Regimes: The Case of the Swings Against the Nazis." *Youth and Society*, 32(3): 275–302.
Walser, Robert. 1993. *Running with the Devil: Power, Gender and Madness in Heavy Metal Music.* Middletown, CT: Wesleyan University Press.
Washburne, Christopher and Maiken Derno (eds.). 1999. *Bad Music: The Music We Love to Hate.* New York: Routledge.
Waugh, Rob. 2005. "The Site Where Fans Call the Tune." *The New York Times*, June 19. N&D, p. 14.
Weber, Max. 1918 (1946). "Politics as a Vocation." In Hans Gerth and C. Wright Mills (eds.), *Essays in Sociology*, pp. 118–129. Fair Lawn, NJ: Oxford University Press.
Weinstein, Deena. 1991. *Heavy Metal: A Cultural Sociology.* New York: Lexington.
West, Candace and Don Zimmerman. 2002. "Doing Gender." In Stevi Jackson and Sue Scott (eds.), *Gender: A Sociological Reader*, pp. 42–47. New York: Routledge.
Wherry, F. 2010. "Producing the Character of Place." *Journal of Urban History*, 36(4): 554–560.
Williams, Alex. 2005. "Do You MySpace?" *The New York Times*, August 28, 2005.
Williams, J. Patrick. 2006. "Authentic Identities: Straightedge Subculture, Music, and the Internet." *Journal of Contemporary Ethnography*, 35(2): 173–200.
Williams, J. Patrick. 2009. "The Multidimensionality of Resistance in Youth-Subcultural Studies." *Resistance Studies*, 2(1): 20–33.
Williams, J. Patrick. 2010. "Music, Symbolic Interaction, and Study Abroad." *Studies in Symbolic Interaction*, 35(1): 223–240.

Williams, J. Patrick. 2011. *Subcultural Theory: Traditions and Methods*. Cambridge: Polity Press.

Williams, J. Patrick and Heith Copes. 2005. "'How Edge Are You?' Constructing Authentic Identities and Subcultural Boundaries in a Straightedge Internet Forum." *Symbolic Interaction*, 28(1): 67–89.

Williams, Wendy M. 1998. "Do Parents Matter?" *Chronicle of Higher Education*, 45 (December 11): B6–B7.

Willis, Paul E. 1978. *Profane Culture*. London: Routledge and Kegan Paul.

Wilson, Stan Le Roy. 1989. *Mass Media/Mass Culture*. New York: Random House.

Wynn, J. 2015. *Music/City: American Festivals and Placemaking in Austin, Nashville, and Newport*. Chicago: University of Chicago Press.

Wyrzykowska, Katarzyna. 2017. *Muzyka, młodzież i styl życia. O uczestnictwie w kulturze muzycznej warszawskiej młodzieży*. Warsaw: Warszawskie Wydawnictwo Socjologiczne.

Yalom, Irvin. 1978. *Existential Psychotherapy*. New York: Basic Books.

Zietz, Jessica. n.d. "Avril Lavigne: Rising Star or Rising Asshole?" Retrieved September 23, 2012 from http://avrilsucks.tripod.com/al/id9.html.

Zurcher, Louis. 1977. *The Mutable Self*. Beverly Hills, CA: Sage.

CONTRIBUTORS

Scott W. Bowman, Ph.D., is an Associate Professor in the School of Criminal Justice at Texas State University. Dr. Bowman earned his Ph.D. in Justice Studies from Arizona State University with an emphasis on racial and socioeconomic inequalities. His current teaching and research interests include race and crime, socioeconomic status and crime, hip-hop and positive youth development, and juvenile justice. His recent research appears as various academic journals and books on a variety of criminological and sociological topics, including a two volume, edited book on race and prisons entitled *Color Behind Bars: Racism in the U.S. Prison System.*

Joseph A. Kotarba, Ph.D., is Professor of Sociology at Texas State University. He is also a faculty member at the Institute for Translational Sciences at the University of Texas Medical Branch, Galveston. Dr. Kotarba received his doctorate from the University of California, San Diego. His major areas of scholarly interest are culture, science, health and illness, deviance, everyday life social theory, and qualitative methods. Dr. Kotarba's most recent books are *Symbolic Interactionist Takes on Music: The Couch-Stone Papers*, co-edited with Christopher J. Schneider (Emerald Press, 2016); *The Death and Resurrection of Deviance*, co-edited with Michael Dellwing and Nathan W. Pino (Palgrave Macmillan, 2014); and *Baby Boomer Rock 'n' Roll Fans* (Rowman & Littlefield, 2013), for which he received the 2014 Charles Horton Cooley Award for Best Book from the Society for the Study of Symbolic Interaction.

He also received the Society's George Herbert Mead Award for Lifetime Achievement (2009), and the Mentor's Excellence Award (2010). He is currently conducting research on music experiences among the elderly, and the relationship of music to the scientific experience.

Christopher J. Schneider is Associate Professor of Sociology at Brandon University in Manitoba, Canada. He received his Ph.D. from the Department of Justice Studies at Arizona State University. Dr. Schneider's recent book is *Policing and Social Media: Social Control in an Era of New Media* (Lexington Books, 2016). He is the 2016 recipient of the Society for the Study of Symbolic Interaction's Early in Career Award, awarded to scholars who have made significant contributions within the first ten years since the completion of their Ph.D. His research and commentary have been featured in hundreds of news reports across North America, including the *The New York Times.*

Rachel Skaggs is a doctoral candidate in Vanderbilt University's Department of Sociology. The questions that guide her research center around how workers in post-bureaucratic employment situations (freelance, project-based, self-employed, and other forms of free agency) are able to craft careers out of a series of self-directed projects and jobs, especially in culture industries. Rachel is the Book Review Editor for the international sociological journal *Work and Occupations* and is a research fellow at Vanderbilt's Curb Center for Art, Enterprise, and Public Policy. Rachel's dissertation focuses on the career pathways of Nashville songwriters.

Raphael Travis's research, practice and consultancy work emphasize positive youth development over the life-course, resilience, and civic engagement. He also investigates music, especially hip-hop culture, as a source of growth and risk in people's lives. Dr. Travis is an Associate Professor at Texas State University in the School of Social Work. He is also Executive Director of FlowStory, PLLC, blending social work and public health expertise to guide applied research and health promotion strategies. Dr. Travis is the author of *The Healing Power of Hip Hop* and his latest research appears in a variety of peer-reviewed academic journals.

Jonathan R. Wynn, an Associate Professor of Sociology at the University of Massachusetts Amherst, is an urban sociologist focusing on interactions between individuals and institutions. In addition to articles in *City & Community*, *Qualitative Sociology*, *Media, Culture & Society*, *Sociological Forum*, *Cultural Sociology*, *Contexts*, *Ethnography*, and *Sociological Theory*, his two major publications are *The Tour Guide: Walking and Talking New York* (2011) and *Music/City: American Festivals and Placemaking in Nashville, Austin, and Newport* (2015), both with the University of Chicago Press.

Katarzyna M. Wyrzykowska received her Ph.D. in Sociology in 2012 from the Institute of Philosophy and Sociology of the Polish Academy of Sciences, where she still serves as a researcher. Dr. Wyrzykowska is a Member of the Research Committee of Polish Music Council. She is Chair of the Warsaw Department of the Polish Sociological Association, and Secretary of the Sociology of Arts Section of the Polish Sociological Association. Her research interests focus on the sociology of music, music market research and the methodology of qualitative research.

Cover Acknowledgments

Front Cover: Clockwise from top center

- Dad and daughter (on the cell phone) on the lawn at the Backstreet Boys concert at the Cynthia Woods Mitchell Pavilion in Woodlands, Texas (2014). Photo credit: Joseph A. Kotarba
- Jessica Harper reading from her book, *The First Collection of Criticism by a Living Female Rock Critic*, at the Texas Book Festival in Austin, Texas (2015). Photo credit: Joseph A. Kotarba
- Joe Kotarba and Ray Wylie Hubbard at the Tavern in the Gruene in New Braunfels, Texas (2013). Photo credit: Joseph A. Kotarba
- Maggie Colleen Cobb performing at the welcome BBQ for the Couch-Stone Symposium ("Symbolic Interactionist Takes on Music") in San Marcos, Texas (2014). Photo credit: Joseph A. Kotarba
- Three Justin Bieber fans at the Houston Livestock Show and Rodeo in Houston, Texas (2013). Photo credit: Joseph A. Kotarba
- Model Stranger (2015). Photo credit: Julia Ciaccio
- The Peterson Brothers performing at the Susanna's Kitchen Coffee House at the Wimberley United Methodist Church in Wimberley, Texas (2016). Photo credit: Joseph A. Kotarba
- Paul Stickel and Chris Kotarba performing with Def Piper at the Law Rocks! competition in San Francisco, California (2014). Photo credit: Joseph A. Kotarba
- Katy Perry and Elmo on *Sesame Street* (2010). Photo credit: Public Broadcasting System

- Van Morrison concert poster, the Slieve Donard Resort in Newcastle, Northern Ireland (2015). Photo credit: Joseph A. Kotarba
- Darrion "Chi-Clopz" Borders of the Mindz of a Different Kind group (2014). Photo credit: Raphael Travis
- Matthew Kotarba and Hanna, of Ellipser, at the Sahara Lounge in Austin, Texas (2015). Photo credit: Joseph A. Kotarba

Back Cover: Top down on the right side

- The words of jazz musician Herbie Hancock archived at the National Museum of African-American History and Culture in Washington, D.C. (2016). Photo credit: Joseph A. Kotarba
- A London underground poster for the Beatles Store on Baker Street (2015). Photo credit: Joseph A. Kotarba
- Dr. Eugene Halton, Professor of Social Theory at Notre Dame University and regular performer at blues clubs on the south side of Chicago, playing harmonica at the Society for the Study of Symbolic Interaction reception in Las Vegas, Nevada (2011). Photo credit: Joseph A. Kotarba
- The Latino Children's Choir performing at the Fifth Anniversary celebration of the Centro Cultural Hispano in San Marcos, Texas (2015). Photo credit: Joseph A. Kotarba
- A fan at the South by Southwest Music Conference and Festival in Austin, Texas (2014). Photo credit: Joseph A. Kotarba

Index: Sociological Concepts